· GRATEFUL NATION ·

GLOBAL INSECURITIES

A series edited by Catherine Besteman and Daniel M. Goldstein

· GRATEFUL NATION ·

STUDENT VETERANS AND THE RISE
OF THE MILITARY-FRIENDLY CAMPUS

Ellen Moore

Duke University Press   Durham and London   2017

© 2017 Duke University Press
All rights reserved
Printed in the United States of America on acid-free paper ∞
Text designed by Courtney Leigh Baker
Typeset in Whitman by Westchester Publishing Services

Library of Congress Cataloging-in-Publication Data
Names: Moore, Ellen, [date] author.
Title: Grateful nation : student veterans and the rise of the
"military-friendly" campus / Ellen Moore.
Description: Durham : Duke University Press, 2017. |
Series: Global insecurities | Includes bibliographical
references and index.
Identifiers: LCCN 2017018614 (print) |
LCCN 2017022676 (ebook) |
ISBN 9780822372769 (ebook)
ISBN 9780822368809 (hardcover : alk. paper)
ISBN 9780822369097 (pbk. : alk. paper)
Subjects: LCSH: Veterans—Education (Higher)—United
States. | Veterans—Education (Higher)—California.
Classification: LCC UB357 (ebook) | LCC UB357 .M65 2017
(print) | DDC 378.1/9826970973—dc23
LC record available at https://lccn.loc.gov/2017018614

THIS BOOK IS DEDICATED TO
VETERANS RETURNING FROM WARS AND
TO ALL THOSE COMMITTED TO
ENDING WAR

Contents

Preface

My interest in veteran support and higher education is rooted in my family history. I was born on a U.S. military base to an Army captain father and a pacifist mother, and have lived in communities where I was exposed to the diverse worldviews of both military members and civilians. My father grew up during the Depression in a working-class family in Fresno, California, then a small agricultural town. For my father, military service and GI Bill education benefits provided a pathway to academic opportunities that eventually enabled him to join the professional class and later provided me with a straightforward pathway into college. Within my family narratives of social mobility are inextricably tied to narratives of military service. Thus, my research on military veterans in college involves multiple layers of my identity as a student, a daughter, a university instructor, a civically engaged citizen, a writer, and an analyst.

As this book goes to press in the spring of 2017, the rhetoric of war has returned to America with renewed force. Daily life in the United States is marked by a heightened sense of vulnerability and anxiety about national security. We are warned that enemies at home and abroad threaten U.S. jobs, families, homes, and a presumed singular U.S. cultural identity. This national insecurity problem has come with an built-in solution: militarized interventions in the form of expanded and instrumental use of deadly force by police, walled-off militarized border zones, and local sheriffs deputized as deportation "force multipliers" in multiple, simultaneous wars against perceived enemies.

At this fearful and precarious time in history, this book argues that it is crucial to engage in difficult conversations about war and peace, consent and dissent, social conformity and social difference, and about what it takes for a nation to be demonstrably secure. Yet finding common ground across diverse worldviews can be difficult, especially when the country is involved in highly contested military and political conflicts. We are living in a highly polarized ideological environment that suppresses nuance, heterogeneity of thought, and comfort with ambivalence. This polarization is apparent in national discussions about the economy, national security, health care, immigration policies, education, and policing. A similar polarization is apparent in discussions about military veterans, military service, and the current wars.

News and social media stories about military veterans routinely characterize participants, institutions, or actions dichotomously as pro- or antiwar, pro- or antiveteran, and pro- or antimilitary. But what do these dichotomous terms really mean? This question surfaced time and time again as I became immersed in veteran support services. The three years I spent in and around veteran communities showed that these dichotomies cannot adequately describe diverse beliefs held by military members, veterans, and civilians about relationships with the military and the contemporary wars. These labels take a broad brush to ideological dispositions, inhibiting critical exchange.

I began this research by asking veterans about their experiences in the military and in college. With time, my findings led to new questions as I observed tensions in the making and unmaking of soldier and student identities. I was troubled by the deployment of an antiveteran label against those who voiced dissent from military policies or actions. This labeling precluded critiques of wars that caused soldiers to die on the battlefield and to take their own lives at war or at home. My experience showed that this formulation was no accident but instead emerged from a militarized common sense that conflates support for veterans with support for the institutional military and silent acquiescence to the wars, which in turn serves to rationalize and enable a permanent state of war.

My hope is that this book will provide analysis to help people differentiate between support for veterans and support for the wars in which they fought. It challenges dualistic understandings of pro- or anti-military, veteran, and war to broaden our discussion about what it means to be a soldier, veteran, or civilian in a country at war. The book looks closely at military recruits' experiences, at the transitions from civilian to combatant and back again into civilian society. By analyzing the influence of popular narratives about veterans and veterans' needs on college campuses, I find, among other things, that the simple gesture of thanking soldiers for their service can be transformed into tacit support for war. In offering this gesture, I ask that we carefully consider not only what we honor with our gratitude but also what we suppress.

Acknowledgments

The act of writing a can be a solitary effort, but many people contributed to this book and I am grateful for their inspiration, critique, advice, and technical assistance during the many stages of research and writing. First and foremost, I want to thank the veterans who spent many hours in conversation with me, and without whom this book would not exist. For reasons of confidentiality, I can't name them, but I am grateful for their generosity of spirit in trusting me with their stories and sharing their experiences, their accomplishments, and their conflicts. From these veterans I learned that service and sacrifice can and do take many forms. Many chose to speak with me because they wanted their experience to be shared for the benefit of other veterans; that is my hope as well. I have done my best to be faithful to their stories, even as my conclusions and analysis may not be universally shared by participants.

My sincere gratitude also goes to the college instructors and staff who allowed me to observe their work on behalf of student veterans. Those who perform the difficult work of designing and providing support services typically do not receive the credit they deserve, and these instructors and staff worked long hours providing behind-the-scenes support to the veterans profiled in this book. While my analysis offers a critical perspective of social forces that produce militarism on campuses, this book is in no way intended to diminish the importance of the work of these service providers. Among them I found extraordinary teachers and advisors, and their commitment to veterans' educational success was a continuing source of inspiration.

This book comes out of my dissertation research, for which I was fortunate to receive advice and mentorship from exceptional critical scholars. Their intellectual influence on this work is indelible. I am deeply indebted to Jean Lave for her ongoing and steadfast guidance, for her willingness to help me clarify arguments and confront intellectual dilemmas, and for offering me a postdoc-toral scholarly home and workspace at the Slow Science Institute. Many thanks to Gillian Hart for helping me to understand processes of articulation and for highlighting the enduring relevance of Gramsci's work. I am deeply indebted to Wendy Brown for encouraging me to push past easy formulations and to strive for analysis that reflected the complicated—and complicating—humanity of all those involved in this study.

Thanks to all of my colleagues at the Slow Science Institute for their in-tellectual support and comradeship during the preparation of this book. I'm indebted to the Slow Science Institute for providing the space to develop this book in the company of visiting scholars and fellows from across the San Fran-cisco Bay Area, the United States, and from around the world. Affiliates are too numerous to name here, but particular thanks go to Jean Lave, Cheryl Holtzmeyer, Mike Dwyer, Ashwin Jacob Mathew, Rodrigo Ribeiro, and Janaki Srinivasan for their interdisciplinary curiosity, their critical engagement with and feedback on this research, and for practicing slow science in a fast-science world.

I am deeply grateful to my teachers and colleagues at the UC Berkeley Cen-ter for Research on Social Change (CRSC) and the Institute for the Study of Societal Issues, from which I received not only financial assistance but incal-culable support and intellectual mentorship. Profound and enduring thanks go to mentors Christine Trost, Deborah Freedman Lustig, and David Minkus for their extensive feedback on early chapter drafts. Special thanks also go to CRSC fellows Margo Mahan, Ricardo Huerta Niño, Erica Mitsako Boas, and Hector Fernando Burga, who read and critiqued early versions of chapters. My argu-ments were strengthened through their critical feedback, and my spirits were buoyed by their supportive camaraderie.

Thanks to members of the Social and Cultural Studies writing group: Becky Tarlau, Chela Delgado, Nirali Jani, Cecilia Lucas, and Kimberly Vinall for read-ing and commenting on many iterations of this work.

The research and writing of this book were made possible with assistance from the Toto Fellowship at the University of California Berkeley Graduate School of Education. A dissertation fellowship from the Jack Kent Cooke Foun-dation gave me the opportunity to spend one year solely devoted to writing and analyzing my research data.

It is a pleasure and an honor that this book found a home in the Duke University Press Global Insecurities Series, and I am grateful to editors Cath-erine Besteman and Daniel Goldstein for opening that door. Thanks to the Duke University Press editorial staff, particularly to Gisela Fosado and Lydia

Rose Rappoport-Hankins, for their guidance and assistance through the production process. I am grateful to the anonymous reviewers for their helpful feedback and suggestions. Special thanks goes to David Vine for his careful reading and rereading of this manuscript. His critical insights made this a better book. I am also grateful to Jessica Cobb for her analytic acuity and stellar editorial advice. I am indebted to Catherine Lutz, both for her critical military scholarship that has informed and animated this project and for her early words of encouragement about this book.

Many friends and family have supported this project in a variety of ways. Thanks to Kirsten Irgens-Moller, Christopher Ho, Monica Moore, Sally Fairfax, Philip Moore, David Szanton, Martha Moore, Lincoln Cushing, Adrianne Aron, Bart Shulman, Becky Tarlau, Adam Kruggel, Norman Solomon, Cheryl Higgins, Jodi Levin, Aaron Hughes, Dan Cowles, and Helene Schulman Lorenz for their support, which included giving editorial feedback, technical assistance, graphic design advice, accompaniment on research trips, transcription and research assistance, and general encouragement over the course of writing this book.

Thanks to Leah Halper and Helene Schulman Lorenz for opening their homes to me on research trips for this book, and for sharing meals, ideas, contacts, and critiques.

Finally, to Charlie, Josie, and Maya: thank you for your patience with my absences and my research-related preoccupations. Thank you for reminding me every day and in countless ways that knowledge production is important, but that family is forever.

Introduction

On the sunny suburban campus of Los Olmos Community College, a palpable buzz of anticipation—made up of equal parts excitement and tension—circulated around Parking Lot B. The college had been preparing for Veterans Day for weeks. Members of the campus veterans club put finishing touches on the tables in the courtyard, setting up signs and ferrying food for invited guests, as support service providers arranged brochures and pens, keychains and water bottles advertising social services for veterans. In the parking lot, a fifty-foot Tiller hook-and-ladder fire engine was parked with its ladder extending high above campus. Attached to its rungs flew flags of the five branches of military services. Students from the school's police and firefighter public safety programs stood in parade rest position (feet shoulder-width apart, hands touching behind backs) and practiced crowd-control techniques as they formed a human perimeter around the parking lot, which on this day also served as a helicopter landing pad. The daylong event began with an aerial military salute—a flyover and landing on campus grounds of a Vietnam War–era Twenty-Fifth Infantry Division Huey helicopter. Hundreds of observers on the ground watched as the helicopter descended slowly, ceremoniously circling above campus before touching down. Upon landing, a team of officers in Army combat fatigues jumped from the aircraft to pose for pictures, as the crowd of observers applauded and whooped in appreciation.

The opening ceremony was followed by formal presentations from a local Air Force base color guard.[1] After the formal flag salute, two Los Olmos students sang the U.S. national anthem and "God Bless America," while the crowd of students, faculty, administrators, and community supporters stood solemnly facing the flags, hands placed over hearts or saluting hand-to-forehead. The atmosphere at Los Olmos that day was at once festive and solemn, both reverential and celebratory. It was clear that this occasion was meant to commemorate both veterans and the wars in which they fought, as well as the institutional military to which they had belonged.

A few days later in another part of the state, a group of student veterans sat in a classroom on the campus of Southwest University (SU) listening to a talk given by a local Veterans Affairs (VA) representative. This was a veterans' orientation class, where student veterans were welcomed and introduced to the campus. Meeting weekly, student veterans received instruction in academic norms, expectations, and customs of the university. On that day in November, there was an unmistakable feeling of affection in the room, extended to every one of the thirty (twenty-eight men, two women) student veterans. It appeared that all student veterans were welcomed and cared for in this space. Whatever tips students had picked up in the first weeks of school, they shared with the group: the importance of keeping aware of deadlines, how to avoid late fees, and how to get into classes if they missed the enrollment deadline. They shared information about special adaptive equipment available for veterans with disabilities, and advised one another on the intricacies of GI Bill benefits, with tips on how to plan the semester to ensure that they wouldn't run out of money before graduating. The student veterans offered advice about which classes to take and suggested taking harder classes during summer session, when there would be less pressure; they exchanged information about which professors were particularly friendly toward veterans, and which professors were supportive of military polices.

On this day the class listened attentively to the VA representative talk about what it was like to come to the large urban university campus in the late 1960s to recruit students to enlist in the military. The speaker, who was also a veteran of the Vietnam War, opened his presentation by saying that the university "has its own legacy, not always friendly to the military," and recounted a story about his friend, a former marine and Vietnam War veteran, who was sent to recruit students on the SU campus: "[My friend] said that as a Marine recruiter, he was more afraid coming to this campus than he was at Khe Sanh." While the reference to one of the deadliest land battles of the Vietnam War was assumed to be hyperbolic and students chuckled appreciatively at the characterization, it nonetheless positioned SU as a frighteningly hostile place—enemy territory in which marines could expect to be physically attacked or even killed. This speaker invoked a past imaginary—rather than present reality—of the contemporary university as hostile to the U.S. military. In doing so, he positioned his recruiter friend, himself, and his audience of current student veterans as beleaguered victims of a collegiate environment unsympathetic to the mission of the U.S. military and to veterans.

These two examples illustrate seemingly opposite phenomena faced by contemporary veterans on college campuses. Symbols of military valorization and patriotism are the new normal on many campuses, as college administrators, faculty, staff, and students are encouraged to express gratitude for service and sacrifice by veterans, yet there is a concurrent and abiding mythology that contemporary college campuses are unwelcoming to war veterans and hostile to their viewpoints. This book is about the tensions arising from these simultaneous and contradictory discourses, and about how these distinct narratives—of increasing military valorization and ostensible hostility toward veterans—are taking place on college campuses amid an absence of discussion about the actual wars in which the U.S. military is engaged. It is also about how this absence of discussion serves to obviate dissent and distance the U.S. civilian population from the human consequences of war. In combination, these social processes help to erase and thus naturalize a state of permanent war.

College campuses are often spaces of critique and dissent, yet over a decade into the widely unpopular contemporary wars (collectively known as the Global War on Terrorism, or GWOT), college campuses are largely silent about the wars. At the same time, these wars have militarized daily life in the United States. Some signs of the militarization of social space are new, like police-deployed surveillance drones and decommissioned armored personnel carriers patrolling city streets.[2] Other signs of militarization have become commonplace to the point of being unremarkable: civilians driving Hummer-branded vehicles, children carrying camouflage-patterned backpacks to school, and the Homeland Security apparatus marking everyday life in U.S. airports, government buildings, hospitals, electronic communications, mass media, and entertainment.

Our social world is also militarized, although in less noticeable ways. Everyday consciousness is informed by a militarized common sense, which I define as the embedded worldview that war is a natural and necessary aspect of maintaining and protecting nationhood; military priorities are more important than nonmilitary ones; and war veterans should serve as positive public symbols of U.S. military actions. Militarized common sense naturalizes the valorization of the military on college campuses. Militarized common sense is a salient social force that portrays the interests of the individual soldier as inseparable from the interests of the institutional military and military projects.

The U.S. military has been in and around the academy for a long time. Indeed, two of the oldest colleges in the nation, West Point (est. 1802) and Annapolis

Naval Academy (est. 1845), were founded by and are administered by the armed services. But today the ties between the military and higher education are both more ubiquitous and less obvious: U.S. departments of Defense and Homeland Security pour billions of research dollars into the development of weapons and cybersecurity systems, robotics and biometric identification systems used by official and unofficial military organizations around the globe.[3]

The militarization of the academy has been the subject of extensive scholarship as have military efforts to organize support from civilian academics.[4] Much of the existing scholarship documents ways that the military has guided, gathered, shaped, and suppressed knowledge to further military goals through research grants and academic partnerships; and chronicles ways in which academics are recruited for military purposes through research funding, endowed chairs, and preferential access to information.[5]

The direct financial relationship between the U.S. military and American universities dates back at least to World War II, when universities were presented with a willing and wealthy patron in the U.S. armed forces. As a result, many universities expanded the scope of their research and academic departments, especially in disciplines of physics, chemistry, biology, and technology.[6] Military funding of academic institutions continued after World War II and has increased dramatically since that time, most notably after September 11, 2001. For example, the U.S. Department of Defense (DoD) awarded 12,753 prime contracts to colleges and universities in 2000, worth a total of $4,449,065,114; by 2006, the DoD had awarded 62,488 such contracts worth $46,748,542,346.[7]

The post-9/11 increases in DoD funding of academic research have been accompanied by a comparable rise in military tuition payments to American colleges and universities. From 2002 to 2011, over 4 million education benefits claims were filed by U.S. military veterans, representing more than 30 billion dollars.[8] In an era in which higher education is defined and shaped by permanent budget crises, student veterans bring billions of dollars in guaranteed tuition to college campuses, creating strong financial incentives for colleges to project themselves as friendly toward the U.S. military in pursuit of GI Bill–funded veterans.

This book examines the effects of military training and the contemporary wars on student veterans, and it traces effects of military-valorizing discourse on the institutions of higher education in which veterans enroll. Just as civilians must learn to become soldiers and adapt to military life, veterans must learn to become college students by adapting to civilian academic norms and practices. In turn, the presence of student veterans on college campuses transforms institutional practices and discourse. Institutional initiatives designed to welcome veterans to college ultimately welcome military viewpoints and suppress debate about the current wars. Thus, the militarization of common sense on college campuses narrows and suppresses democratic debate.

Some scholars and veterans' affairs specialists assume that civilian campus cultures are hostile toward veterans and argue that this ostensible hostility causes difficulty for student veterans.[9] My analysis shows that veterans' academic challenges are caused not by collegiate hostility toward the military but by multiple factors, including disjunctions between veterans' military training and academic demands, and psychological trauma engendered by their experiences in war. My analysis also shows that student veterans are challenged by pervasive cultural expectations that they should serve as venerated representatives of the current wars, and that these cultural expectations form part of a growing militarized common sense on campuses. The assertion that college campuses are hostile to veterans is not only unwarranted but also harmful, inhibiting critical analysis of military projects and generating silent consent to war. This silencing erases veterans' lived experiences, including those that may give rise to their own critiques of war.

Veterans and Higher Education

This book is a meditation on the interplay between civilian academic and military worlds, but it didn't start out that way. It began as a research project about veterans in higher education and ended up as an exploration of social processes of militarization and education. I began the research as an attempt to understand a jarring statistic I heard quoted in 2008: 96 percent of all recruits had signed up for GI Bill educational benefits upon enlistment, but only a small fraction (8 percent according to one study) of those who signed up actually made use of their benefits.[10] Though this number changed significantly after 2008, I decided to explore the reasons for this disparity as well as the obstacles faced by war veterans in college.[11]

Narratives of the returning soldier have fueled popular and political imaginations since Homer's *Odyssey*. After every U.S. war, veterans have returned from combat to reenter noncombatant communities, where their presence is utilized for different purposes: to reaffirm national identity, to become symbols of national strength and protection, or conversely—particularly in the case of veterans returning from World War I and the war in Vietnam—as symbols of government neglect. The body and welfare of the returning soldier-cum-veteran becomes a "contested site where memory, biography and personal histories call attention to, challenge and resist unified and traditional versions of American identity and government."[12]

The esteem in which veterans historically have been held by society has been reflected in a system of pensions and bonuses, developed in response to shifting political will and military necessity.[13] From widows' pensions to ceremonial burials to college tuition, veterans' bonuses have been used in various capacities: as inducements to enlist, wages for soldiers' labor, and remediation for wounds suffered in battle. Prior to the Civil War, soldiers received military bonuses of land and money. After the Civil War, veterans received cash bonuses for fighting. World War I veterans came home to a contracted economy, no jobs, and no land grants, and they rebelled.[14]

The Servicemen's Readjustment Act of 1944—commonly known as the GI Bill of Rights, or simply the GI Bill—provided returning veterans with social supports for civic and economic engagement, including housing, education, and health care.[15] World War II veterans were not only welcomed home as heroes and hailed as the Greatest Generation, they were also the beneficiaries of one of the largest federal wealth redistribution initiatives in U.S. history.[16] Popular and scholarly accounts of the history of the GI Bill reflect a discourse of reverence for World War II soldiers who returned victorious from what was embraced by civilians as the "Good War." The original GI Bill was rooted in the idea of veteran exceptionalism, the belief that military veterans deserve benefits other citizens do not because they had sacrificed by going to war. The legislation reflected a New Deal approach to social welfare, providing special benefits to members of the armed forces who, as stated by President Franklin D. Roosevelt, make "greater economic sacrifice and every other kind of sacrifice than the rest of us, and are entitled to definite action to help take care of their special problems."[17]

The dominant narrative of the World War II era described military service as a democratizing force that prepared young recruits for educational and economic success. Military service, it was said, provided both the means and method of preparing young (male) Americans to return to participation in civilian life.[18] Military training was positioned as a transformative process. By instilling values of discipline, patriotism, heroism in combat, duty, and citizenship, military service was supposed to turn unformed young boys into college-bound men. In this narrative, war was a catalyst and crucible for men's character, regardless of background.[19]

This narrative shifted significantly alongside changes in the U.S. political economy. The end of military conscription in 1973 made the decision to join the military a vocational option rather than a civic duty, and the erosion of New

Deal policies shifted the political tide against government entitlements.[20] The clear popular support for military conflicts enjoyed by the U.S. government during World War II did not persist for other conflicts.

Many Americans believe that U.S. military service is a route to upward social mobility, an equalizer of economic opportunity, and guarantor of higher education. Historical narratives of social mobility and economic opportunity are interwoven with narratives of wartime military service, but with the end of mandatory conscription in 1973, military service became even more closely linked to the promises of educational opportunity and social mobility.[21] Today, many high school students and young adults enlist in the armed forces to access college funding. Recruiters promise that military service will pay for college and prepare young men and women to attend.[22] However, many veterans never realize this promise. The low rates of utilization of educational benefits reported in 2008 indicated that returning war veterans were not enrolling in college, or they were dropping out before graduating. To try to understand this troubling trend, I began to study the experience of veterans on contemporary college campuses.

Much of the literature on war veterans in college identifies three major obstacles to veterans' success in higher education: First, there is a claim that military enlistees tend to be academically unprepared for college because many come from working-class backgrounds and choose military enlistment as an alternative to lower-wage jobs or unemployment.[23] Second, there is a claim that combat veterans face enduring symptoms of trauma that interfere with reintegration in civilian classrooms.[24] Third, some campus student affairs literature claims that civilian college campuses are unfriendly to the U.S. military, driving military veterans away from college.[25]

By limiting its focus to these three obstacles, the current literature ignores the structural causes of veterans' difficulties in college and assumes that military recruits are marked by intellectual and psychological deficits. The first claim that veterans may not be prepared for academic rigors of college is belied by the fact that many contemporary first-generation college student veterans successfully complete and excel in higher education. Moreover, military recruiters' promise of college education as a benefit of the military contract implies that regardless of background, service members should be able to take advantage of that benefit after discharge. As to the second claim, it is true that some veterans face enduring symptoms of combat trauma that interfere with reintegration in civilian classrooms.[26] Indeed, some student veteran participants in this research suffered from posttraumatic stress reactions that negatively affected their classroom performance. However, it is unlikely that war trauma is the major factor in inhibiting postsecondary achievement, given the successes of GI Bill recipients from World War II and the Korean War.[27]

The final obstacle—unfriendly college campuses—was identified based on two unsupported assumptions: that civilian college campuses are antimilitary and that all veterans have uniformly positive associations with the institutional military. Regarding the first assumption, campuses such as Stanford, Harvard, and Columbia, having banned the ROTC (Reserve Officer Training Corps) during the heated Vietnam War protests of the 1960s and '70s have since welcomed back the ROTC and implemented robust veteran support programs, similar to many public colleges and universities across the country. As to the second assumption, many war veterans are highly ambivalent about the institutional U.S. military as well as the wars in Iraq and Afghanistan. Yet the stereotype that many college campuses are antimilitary persists, forming part of a veteran support discourse on college campuses that venerates military policies and projects and silences debate about the wars.[28]

The chapters that follow show how, through everyday practices, militarism becomes part of the hidden curriculum of college life—in the ways teachers are instructed to treat veterans deferentially in their classrooms, and in their avoidance of talking about the wars for fear of offending veterans. Through analyzing the words of individual veterans, I trace larger narratives of war, military support, and public dissent to understand how military ideology is lived and practiced in daily life.

But what do we mean when we talk about militarism? The U.S. wars in Iraq and Afghanistan have brought about renewed discussions among social scientists regarding empire, militarism, and militarization. In the United States, "militarization" is most commonly used to refer to contexts of war, but this book argues that our everyday, domestic social world is also deeply militarized.[29]

Scholarly notions of militarism and militarization are contested and multifaceted. Lesley Merryfinch observed, "Like electricity, 'militarism' can best be described by its effects. When military goals, values and apparatus increasingly dominate a state's culture, politics and economy, militarism is on the rise."[30] Michael Mann broadens the concept of militarism beyond a narrow focus on military institutions to refer to "a set of attitudes and social practices which regard war and the preparation for war as a normal and desirable social activity."[31] Thus, militarization involves embedding military priorities into the civilian sphere; this entails shifts in both public consciousness and in social practices.[32] Similarly, Edward P. Thompson warned against an overly narrow focus on concepts such as "the military-industrial complex" because this "suggests that [militarism] is confined in a known and limited place: it may threaten to push forward, but it can be restrained, contamination does not extend through the whole societal body."[33] Writing during the Cold War, Thompson observed, "the USA and the USSR do not have military-industrial complexes: they are such complexes."[34]

Cynthia Enloe describes militarization as "a step-by-step process by which a person or a thing (such as an institution) gradually becomes controlled by the military or comes to depend for its well-being on militaristic ideas. The more militarization transforms an individual or a society, the more that individual or society comes to imagine military needs and militaristic presumptions to be not only valuable but normal."[35] Peter Kraska offers straightforward, if somewhat circular, working definitions for both militarism and militarization: "Militarism is a cultural pattern of beliefs and values supporting war and militarization that comes to dominate a society. Militarization is the preparation for that activity."[36]

"War created the United States," writes Michael Sherry, and although many Americans profess antipathy toward wars and war making, U.S. history has been shaped by militarism.[37] The U.S. government has deployed troops to fight in military conflicts—as leading proponents or in background roles—for most of its relatively brief history as a nation. From 1775 to 2015, troops of the U.S. armed forces were openly deployed in 315 foreign and domestic armed conflicts.[38] These include not only U.S. wars considered by historians and the general public to be major conflicts but also wars of expansion and annexation, military occupations, and conflicts to protect U.S. business interests abroad.[39]

While U.S. military engagement domestically and worldwide has been a near-constant feature of the nation's history, the contemporary period is marked by a heightened sense of vulnerability and anxiety about U.S. national security. This has given rise to what Andrew Bacevich calls the "New American Militarism": an era of permanent, preemptive war. Bacevich writes that prior to September 11, 2001, U.S. presidents had consistently claimed that the United States declared war solely as a last resort. However, after the 2001 attacks, George W. Bush called for a new military strategy in which the United States would no longer passively allow enemies to strike. Speaking at West Point Military Academy in 2002, G. W. Bush vowed to "take the battle to the enemy, disrupt his plans, and confront the worst threats before they emerge."[40] Bacevich argues that this represents a fundamental shift in U.S. military policy in which going to war becomes a first, rather than a last, resort: "Bush's remarks indicated that he was actually referring not to preemption, but to preventive war. This became the essence of the Bush Doctrine."[41]

Wars are always destructive in terms of infrastructure and human life, to opposing combatants and to civilians caught in the crossfire. Since September 11,

2001, the wars in Iraq and Afghanistan have led to over 108,000 U.S. casualties, including 6,800 deaths (with 298 suicides), 45,889 wounded in action, and 56,874 other medical evacuations due to injury or disease.[42] U.S. soldiers died by rocket-propelled grenade fire and improvised explosive devices (IEDs)—weapons responsible for approximately half of all deaths and injuries in Iraq and Afghanistan. U.S. wartime casualties also include soldiers who died in vehicle crashes, from electrocutions, heatstroke, friendly fire, and battlefield suicides.[43]

Of course, casualties are not limited to, nor even most pronounced among, officially designated fighting troops. It is estimated that over 210,000 civilians in Afghanistan, Iraq, and Pakistan have been killed or wounded as a result of U.S.-led military actions in these countries since 2001.[44]

According to Martin Shaw, militarism develops not only when war-making ideology is strong, but also more generally as military valorization affects social relations and practices.[45] In the past, military glorification was designed to rally public support for specific geopolitical conflicts, but the contemporary period is marked by perpetual and regionally diffuse wars, like those of the Global War on Terrorism. In this context, military valorization is infused into everyday civilian life. The institutional military is taken for granted as protective, necessary, and unquestionable.

Adopting Matthew Sparke's characterization of the Global South, my research found that militarism is "everywhere but always somewhere."[46] That is, even as militarism is omnipresent, its effects are felt in multiple specific sites. In particular, this book analyzes within the field of education the mechanisms that produce militarized common sense in individual soldiers, in supporters of military veterans, and in the academic institutions in which veterans enroll as students. It explores everyday militarism as social practice in which we all consent and participate.[47] This book raises the question: what social processes enable military-valorizing cultural patterns, beliefs, and values to take hold and become dominant, particularly at a time when the country is engaged in a series of unpopular wars?

The ideas of Italian cultural theorist Antonio Gramsci are helpful to understand the question of how ideas are adopted through cultural diffusion of common sense, by which Gramsci means the "incoherent set of generally held assumptions and beliefs" of conventional thought that becomes naturalized and taken for granted in society.[48] Through daily practices and habits, military valorization becomes embedded in daily practices and social relations. Yet while processes of militarization coincide with and are amplified by a generalized conservative entrenchment on college campuses, military-valorizing assumptions and attitudes are not some kind of false consciousness imposed from above.[49] Rather, campus discourses of military valorization come from students, teachers, administrators, staff, and surrounding communities; they arise from and gratify a societal need to support and care for those sent to fight wars.

Gramsci wrote about periods of conservative entrenchment as periods when dominant logics, assumptions, and attitudes become "permanently consolidated, organized ideologically, and exalted lyrically" and that they become embedded in daily practices and relations.[50] This book traces ways in which militarist logics, assumptions, and attitudes become consolidated through college programs, organized ideologically through "best-practice" literature, and exalted lyrically in valorizing discourse that conflates those who fight wars with a unifying military mission. In doing so, this book explores the construction of unstated but operative alliances between military projects and the academy.

The production of militarized common sense creates social meaning and consent for military projects, and involves the creation of national and military identification within society. This process is facilitated by the promotion of what I call—borrowing from Michael Billig—"banal militarism," or everyday symbols and practices that conflate the interests of the nation and its people with the interests of the military.[51] Billig's notion of banal nationalism refers to manifestations of nationalist ideology in daily life. Symbols such as national flags, which are metaphors of both warfare and freedom, are used in everyday contexts, including classrooms, sporting events, children's clothing, television advertising, and department store sales. The mobilization of these symbols in everyday life creates an imagined solidarity with the national project by conflating the interests of the nation-state with those of its citizenry. This occurs in commonplace practices and rituals; for example, the phrase "Our soldiers are fighting for our freedoms" produces affiliations and unities of interest among and between the civilian subject, the military subject, and the goals of the nation-state. Ritualized expressions of gratitude such as "Thank you for your service" express gratitude for service on military projects and implicitly assume a unity with military missions. These phrases articulate military interests with the everyday ideological habits, symbols, discourse, and practice surrounding veteran support. In doing so, these phrases both produce and are produced by militarized common sense on college campuses and in the broader civil society.

Many public stories are told about contemporary war veterans, yet these stories are portrayed through a narrow range of narratives. Designated the "New Greatest Generation" by Joe Klein in *Time* magazine, veterans are depicted at times as heroes returning to a society that does not sufficiently appreciate military sacrifice; at other times they are portrayed as psychologically wounded and suicidal; at other times as violent and unstable.[52] In the midst of these public tropes about veterans, there are overlooked and untold stories about veterans' experience of war and of reincorporation into civilian society. Many veterans do experience psychological sequelae of combat trauma, but their personal stories are not reducible to that. While I did not start out to explore the effects of combat trauma in veterans, the topic surfaced in conversations because posttraumatic reactions formed part of participants' daily experience and affected their classroom performance. Veterans in this study did experience real and persistent psychological aftereffects of combat trauma, and for many of them, understanding the meaning of their suffering was intimately tied to understanding their own actions as combatants.

The cognitive, social, and emotional lives of many former soldiers are profoundly affected by combat stress. Since the American Psychiatric Association first included post-traumatic stress disorder (PTSD) in its *Diagnostic and Statistical Manual of Mental Disorders* in 1980, most research on the disorder has focused on trauma associated with threats to soldiers' lives and safety. Yet a growing body of literature acknowledges that veterans also experience psychological trauma from being perpetrators of wartime violence.[53] This research indicates that soldiers experience moral injury from "perpetrating, failing to prevent, bearing witness to, or learning about acts that transgress deeply held moral beliefs and expectations."[54] Research carried out by the VA with Iraq and Afghanistan war veterans indicates that trauma arising from being both victim and perpetrator of violence has contributed to unprecedented high rates of suicide among former and current military members.[55]

Cultural anthropologists who examine connections between trauma, violence, and political community show that traumas produced by wars and repression are inscribed and reinscribed in everyday narratives.[56] Brison writes that the undoing of the self in trauma involves a radical disruption of memory, a severing of past from present, and typically an inability to envision the future. Many veterans in this study found that reentering civilian society and college required them to find ways to reconstruct themselves and carry on with a reconfigured life.[57]

For some veteran participants of this study, race and gender were a source of alienation from the military as well as a disjunction between military and civilian collegiate institutions. Culturally, the practice of soldiering in the U.S. military is racialized (white) and gendered (male).[58] Even as the current all-volunteer armed forces rely increasingly on racial and ethnic minority male and female recruits and consciously and explicitly portray themselves as race and gender neutral, scholarship confirms that military practice is infused with the social construction of whiteness and hegemonic masculinity.[59] With the understanding that gendered and racialized perspectives shape institutional and informal military practices, I found that some gendered and racialized practices carried over into collegiate settings.[60]

There is a broad consensus among scholars that military institutional practice and wars are masculine social endeavors.[61] Enloe writes that nationalism and militarism typically spring from "masculinized memory, masculinized humiliation and masculinized hope."[62] Because it is not possible to study military practices without also understanding the male perspectives that historically shaped both institutional and informal conventions, this book explores experiences of both men and women soldiers and veterans through processes of basic training, deployments, and veterans' organizations.

The Study

Developing commonsense understandings of the world entails processes of learning and teaching in which individuals, groups, and institutions learn to adopt agreed-upon understandings as fact. This study focuses on multiple sites of learning to answer some key questions: How do civilians learn to become soldiers? What happens when soldiers leave the military, return to civilian life, and enroll in colleges as students? How does the presence of student veterans on campuses affect our understanding of veterans and the wars in which they fought? In what ways do veteran support efforts and relationships between campus actors (veteran advocates, college staff and administrators, academic instructors) and noncampus actors (community veteran support groups) shape discourse about the military? Answering these questions requires that we consider the broader implications of academic-military relationships.

This book uses ethnographic methods to explore the experiences and identities produced at the dynamic intersections of civilian, military, and student practices by focusing on processes and practices that socially make and unmake soldiers. In the context of military training, I examine sociocultural processes used to make soldiers, including participation, inculcation, sensemaking, and the legitimation and delegitimation of cross-border violence and racialized and masculinized nationalism. I examine what happens when soldiers return home and enter college—a site where their militarized identity is unmade and remade as civilian-veteran—and the ways that combat-related physical and emotional trauma affect student veterans' lives.

Laura Nader writes that tracing the less-visible ways in which complex systems of power operate within societies is a daunting task.[63] She calls for scholarly investigation into environments where individuals conduct their daily lives within systems that are designed, operated, and maintained by the institutionally powerful. The ethnographic method is appropriate for this type of inquiry. Ethnographies of power require that the researcher represent complex personal experiences without losing sight of the broader connections between the social and the individual. Ethnographic observation can be used to identify processes through which institutional power is exercised and normalized in the interplay between social structure and individual agency.[64] Ethnographies of power require the examination of unequal relations to identify what Nader calls "controlling processes"—the mechanisms through which ideas are taken up by individuals and institutions and become accepted relations of power.

Similarly, Catherine Lutz suggests that in ethnographies of empire, scholars may draw on the anthropological ethnographic tradition of person-centered contextual analysis to examine the processes through which imperial power is configured, reconfigured, maintained, and reinforced. Lutz argues that "empire is in the details," as power takes root through lived, daily interactions.[65] Drawing on this tradition, I look at the production of militarized common sense in quotidian disciplinary practices, such as training to comply with commands from superiors or the application of the "Military Friendly" designation to particular campuses.[66] To understand how militarism operates culturally in daily life, I studied the relations between veterans, instructors, and veteran supporters in multiple sites. My analysis focused on the practices of unofficial knowledge production—knowledge that is assumed and naturalized, rather than officially quantified.

All individuals, institutions, and locations noted in this book are identified pseudonymously. While some participants said they would be happy to have their real names and affiliations used, others felt they could speak more freely knowing that their identities would not be made public.[67]

Over the course of three years, I attended public and private veteran support events and spoke to veterans on and off college campuses. To examine institutional military teaching practices, I spoke with recent veterans about their experiences in basic training, supplementing veterans' recollections with a close study of Army training manuals. Next, to understand how college campuses receive recent war veterans, I spent three years in classrooms, veterans' club meetings, and meetings with school administrators and community service providers. To learn about veterans' perspectives on these support initiatives, I conducted over two hundred hours of open-ended, semistructured interviews on college campuses, in cafés, and in veterans' homes and by socializing with veterans in bars, at formal campus events, and at conferences. Participant observation in these contexts allowed me to examine the social and cultural processes of veteran reentry in civilian colleges.

Veterans had highly varied experiences with the enduring effects of military service on their college academic and social lives. Attempting to present a bounded portrait of veteran participants' experiences risks losing the full diversity of thought, personality, motivations, needs, opinions, and political orientations. Just as the population of civilian college students represents a wide diversity of backgrounds, aptitudes, opinions, and beliefs, so does that of military veterans.

This book focuses on higher education because college is the institution most closely associated with the promise of educational opportunity made by military recruiters. Colleges are institutions that conform to a specific set of civilian social norms. The content and structure of college courses are intended to educate students about how to conduct themselves in the adult world; at best, higher education can serve to teach students to think critically and function as autonomous members of civilian society.

The majority of the ethnographic data presented in this book were collected at two sites in California: a community college in a semirural agricultural valley town and an elite university in a cosmopolitan urban area. These two sites, which I call Central Community College and Southwest University, offer a study in contrasts. They represent the metaphorical bookends of the tiered U.S. public system for higher education, offering distinct pedagogical, cultural, structural, and social opportunities and constraints for military veterans. While Central College and su were my primary research sites, I also conducted ethnographic observation on a third college campus referred to as Los Olmos Community College, and interviewed students from six additional colleges.[68]

Historically, community colleges have served as open-access portals into postsecondary education. These colleges serve many nontraditional college populations, including first-generation college students, low-income students, immigrant students, and older students returning to college. Large research universities, as institutions conferring advanced degrees and producing scholarship for academic publication, historically serve a student population that is trained in college preparatory courses during secondary school.[69]

At the time of this study, both Central College and su offered benefits to veterans that included priority registration, priority hours for financial aid appointments, authorization for reduced course loads, and increased time to take exams.[70] Yet despite these basic commonalities, the two campuses offered very different veterans' services.[71]

Because the majority of student veterans begin their post-service college careers at a community college, I chose to study community college as the initial contact zone between the military and postsecondary education.[72] As institutions of learning, community colleges differ markedly from the military; they are open-access institutions that inculcate civilian social and academic norms. In these social spaces, returning veterans learn about conduct in the adult civilian world and have the opportunity to think critically about their place in society. These lessons about civilian adulthood contrast with the lessons inculcated by basic training, which teaches soldiers to follow explicit orders without question, subsume individual identities to group affiliation, and maintain a constant state of alertness.

In contrast to the broad-based educational approach of Central College, su was an elite civilian institution, representing a best-case academic scenario for many aspiring students in the United States. Nevertheless, for many veterans who transferred to su, military academic and cultural norms clashed with civilian ones, making their college experience difficult.

Central Community College is located in a majority Latino—primarily Mexican immigrants and their descendants—agricultural town that was hit hard by the 2008 economic recession. In this respect, it is typical of many towns from which the majority of military recruits are drawn during times of war.[73] Central College is on the outskirts of Orchard Valley (approximate population 50,000), a rural valley town and former agricultural hub in California.[74] Like many rural communities, Orchard Valley is currently in transition away from agriculture and toward housing subdivisions and retail stores. Large swaths of stone fruit orchards and root vegetable farms were paved over for housing tracts in the 1960s, a development pattern that accelerated during the real estate boom of the 1990s and early 2000s. Yet by 2010, abandoned half-built housing developments littered the adjacent country roads, skeletal reminders of failed economies of expansion. Manufacturing and business services in the area declined beginning in the early 2000s, as did electrical assembly jobs. Low-wage sales jobs were common, and big-box retail stores were the town's major employer. Yet agricultural labor remained a major source of employment in Orchard Valley, with at least six migrant worker camps run by private parties for profit.

Southwest University has a reputation as a prestigious research university, and admission is highly competitive. Promotional materials for su describe the campus as home to top scholars, accomplished writers, star athletes, and prize-winning scientists.[75] It is located in Los Santos, a cosmopolitan and densely populated city with a reputation for liberal leanings and antipathy toward military projects and militarism in general. The SU campus has become nearly synonymous with progressive and antiwar activism. Yet various military support organizations have designated the university one of the nation's top "military-friendly" schools, and SU boasts of having maintained its ROTC program even as other campuses were discontinuing them during the Vietnam War. It is expensive to live near SU: the university is located within a metropolitan area with high concentrations of wealth, which has become a factor in the high cost of living for students.

I interviewed fifty military veterans (thirty-three male and seventeen female) who participated in the campaigns Operation Enduring Freedom (Afghanistan) or Operation Iraqi Freedom (Iraq), or who had been stationed internationally as part of the U.S. military initiative titled the Global War on Terrorism. Because I was interested in the effects of war trauma on veterans' subsequent college experience, I invited participants who had participated in combat; however, I did not exclusively seek participants with combat-identified military occupational specialties, such as infantry, explosives specialists, or combat engineers. Instead, I chose a broader range of participants under the assumption that in conditions of insurgency and counterinsurgency warfare, anyone in zones of conflict (including U.S. military personnel and civilian nationals) can be subject to combat-related violence. Because I was also interested in everyday military practice unrelated to combat, I did not exclude participants who had never served in overseas zones of conflict.

I did not prescreen participants for family educational level and socioeconomic class, but many came from family backgrounds that did not consider college an expected educational goal; all but 10 were in the first generation of their families to attend college. All veteran student participants were between ages twenty-three and thirty-three. The racial and gender demographics roughly approximated the demographics of the current U.S. military (see table I.1).[76]

Participants enlisted in the military for a variety of reasons: to fund postsecondary education, to serve their country, to access job training and employment, to experience life outside of their hometowns, or to get out of difficult or dangerous social situations (some were offered enlistment as an alternative to jail; some wanted to distance themselves from criminal involvement in their hometowns; and some did not see any other available opportunities). Most participants noted a lack of economic or social opportunities in their preservice lives as influencing their decision to enlist.[77] Several participants (both women and men) came from military families and wanted the same experiences as their

TABLE I.1 IN-DEPTH INTERVIEWS:
Iraq and Afghanistan War Veteran-Students by Race, Gender, and Site ($N=50$)

	Southwest University		Central Community College*	
	Male	Female	Male	Female
Total	21	6	12	11
White	14	5	6	3
Hispanic/Latino/a	3	0	4	3
Asian/ Pacific Islander	2	1	1	2
African American	2	0	1	1
Native American	0	0	0	2

*Participants drawn principally from Central Community College, but also from six additional college campuses.

fathers, grandfathers, or brothers. With the exception of two officers (one who was commissioned after completing ROTC and the other who had attended the naval officer training school), all participants enlisted in the lowest ranks (E-1 or E-2 equivalents).[78]

Methodological Challenges: Researcher Positionality

Scholars in the areas of feminist studies, cultural studies, and critical theory assert that the researcher's subjectivity shapes and is shaped by the subject of study.[79] There are clear epistemological challenges to doing research in communities in which one is not a member.[80] As a researcher in anthropology and education and an outsider to military cultures, my goal is to understand and analyze how participants live and experience particular cultural dispositions in their military and postmilitary academic lives. I use ethnographic description and extensive quotations from interviews to reflect veterans' experiences and perspectives as accurately as possible.

My interview method was based on an open-ended, semi-structured interview protocol. I told participants at the beginning of each interview that I would ask questions about their experiences in military training and in college. I decided not to ask participants directly or explicitly about their combat experience because this was not the focus of my study and because I did not want to open topics that might leave them psychologically vulnerable when they left the interview, sometimes returning directly to their college classes. However, I decided that if participants brought up the topic of their combat experience, I would not avoid taking about it, and that I would ask follow-up questions.

The methodological tools at my disposal—observation, in-depth interviews, and participation (as an outsider)—seemed inadequate to fully capture their experiences, so to supplement my in-person research, I also relied on scholarly and popular literature (particularly war memoirs) and popular films, and I asked veteran participants to provide corrective critiques of these materials.

I came into this research prepared for the possibility that my position as a white, middle-aged, university-trained civilian woman might influence military participants' decision to talk to me—positively or negatively, though I assumed negatively. I wondered whether my civilian status might lead some veterans to be less forthcoming in their responses in formal interviews and informal social gatherings. As a situated other I attempted to mitigate this situation by demonstrating that I was dedicated, persistent, and genuinely curious about veterans' experiences in college.[81] As is common with longer-term ethnographic projects, I came to feel a great respect and affection for many of the participants. In the hope that participants might accept my presence as a researcher, I attended veterans' group meetings, answered questions about my research whenever asked, accepted social invitations, and joined, by invitation, a veterans' online community.[82] As a researcher, my outsider position undoubtedly influenced interactions with participants, yet I believe that my outsider status also provided a lens that rendered visible dispositions and practices not often considered by civilians. My social distance may have enabled a type of critical examination different from that of institutional insiders.

Terminology

A Marine is not a soldier. . . . A soldier is a soldier. A Marine is a Marine.
Anonymous poster on Military.com

This study's participants came from four U.S. military branches: Army, Navy, Marines, and Air Force. Each branch of service promotes its own identifying nomenclature: soldier (Army), sailor (Navy), marine (Marine Corps), airman, and guardsman (used for both male and female Air Force and Coast Guard members, respectively).[83] In the chapters that follow, I introduce individual veterans by noting the military branch in which they served. However, when referring to military members in general, I use the generic term "soldier," which commonly denotes "one engaged in military service" or one "who fights as part of an organized land-based armed force."[84] I chose this term for its inclusivity and because it stresses a gender-neutral, practice-based, and institutional relationship with the U.S. armed forces. I also wished to avoid military naming practices, which ascribe essentialized identities to members based on their branch of service.[85] I chose not to use the branch- and gender-neutral term "warrior" that is currently favored by the U.S. armed forces as a contemporary general term for military members because that term implies that service members are engaged primarily or exclusively in warfare. This implication conveys an ideological valence, framing and thus naturalizing the identity of military service members solely in terms of their function in war.

Plan of the Book

Militarized common sense is produced through everyday efforts to support veterans on college campuses, but how does this happen? The chapters that follow trace the production of militarized common sense on multiple levels and focus on multiple sites of learning.[86] In basic training, individual recruits are socialized into military life and trained for combat through explicit pedagogies that teach them how to think, talk, and act like soldiers. Veterans leaving the military and enrolling in college experience the social, cultural, and pedagogical norms of civilian campuses. In civilian life, we are also trained to support military projects in more subtle ways, informed by collective memory and the desire to respectfully care for veterans.

While it is important to understand how military valorization is produced on a societal level, it is equally important to understand how individual recruits are trained and socialized in the military milieu. Chapter 1 looks at individual processes of militarization, through veterans' reflections about their experience in basic training, where civilians learn to become soldiers. Through specific rituals of preparing uniforms, gestures of hierarchical relations, and complying with reward and punishment systems, civilian recruits learn to identify with the military institution, military mission, and fellow soldiers. The pedagogical techniques of basic training, which include isolation and separation, regimentation, enforced group participation, gendered group identification, enforcement of hierarchy, and the naturalization of violence, endured for the veterans and informed their subsequent college experiences. Embodied disciplinary practices teach recruits to shed their previous self-definition as civilians to identify as members of a military corpus. Through veterans' descriptions of basic training as a gateway into military life, we can see how military pedagogy informs and is informed by broader discourses of war, social mobility, and service.

The experience of basic training was profound and enduring for veterans, yet the processes of militarization did not end when soldiers left the military and became veterans. When veterans enrolled in college, the highly situated lessons of military training were transposed onto civilian academic settings. These distinct educative spaces—civilian college and the institutional military—are spaces of difference and contestation wherein disparate cultures meet, engage, and struggle with each other. Student veterans returning from war often encountered difficulties in the transition to college, finding that military training and combat experience complicated their ability to function in civilian schools. Chapter 2 explores how student veterans' military training intersects with civilian academic practices on college campuses, creating disjunctions between conflicting teaching, learning, and cultural norms of military and civilian institutions. Drawing on experiences of recently returned war veterans in college classrooms, I show that conflicting pedagogical and cultural expectations and practices create a disjointed experience for student veterans, and that these disjunctions may interfere with veterans' ability to succeed in college.

On college campuses, militarized common sense is organized ideologically through the best-practice literature for veterans' services that promotes a valorizing discourse that conflates support for veterans with acceptance of military actions and objectives. Chapter 3 examines how military support is introduced on two college campuses by offering an analysis of campus veteran support initiatives. Campus initiatives were marked by military-inflected relations, as trainings, meetings, support programs, classroom practices, and campus-wide events were designed to achieve the designation of being military friendly. Some educational initiatives promoted an exceptionalist view of the veteran student as more disciplined, dedicated, and serious (and by implication, more deserving) than his or her civilian counterparts, creating barriers to interaction with civilian students. These forms of military exceptionalism also had the unintended effect of alienating some of the very veterans they were designed to support.

Chapter 4 turns away from institutionally sponsored programs to explore the diverse strategies veterans used to adapt to postmilitary life as college students. These strategies included efforts to sustain and re-create military bonds, as well as efforts to distance themselves from military relationships and ideologies. Social bonds forged in military training and combat both re-created and contested militarized socialization on college campuses. Personal histories of men and women veterans offer a window into the affective nature of military bonds, how these bonds differed for men and women soldiers, and how gender relations were reproduced, codified, and enforced through cultural practices based on an ideology of male supremacy.

Chapter 5 provides some theoretical and historical context about ways that the legacy of the Vietnam War shapes contemporary understandings of veterans' needs and societal obligations by exploring campus discourse about military veterans and the current wars. This chapter argues, based on historical narratives of campus antiwar protests of the 1960s, that college campuses are portrayed as inimical to military interests and to veterans. The shared public imaginary of campus hostility toward veterans gives rise to what I call protective and valorizing discourses of care that conflate support for the veteran with uncritical support for military projects and have the effect of silencing debate on campus about contemporary military conflicts.

This discourse of care positions veterans as underrepresented minorities, beleaguered victims, and heroic figures, laying the foundation to increase military displays and military-valorizing discourse that ultimately represent and serve the interest of the militarized state. Stuart Hall argues that commonsense understandings of the world can be constructed through articulation, or the manner in which social relations, attitudes, and beliefs are related to broader societal forces that produce collective practices.[87] The process of articulation creates new relations among relatively autonomous social, cultural, and economic elements. These elements—such as discourses of militarism, social inclusion, civil rights, and veteran support—are structured as an ideological unity that defines and produces social meanings and practices. These newly formed social meanings include positioning veterans as underrepresented minorities and using ideological discourses (such as language and political strategies adapted from lesbian, gay, bisexual, and transgender [LGBT] and immigrant rights movements) that allow for the creation of programs that valorize and celebrate military projects on campuses. By positioning veterans as both victimized by and superior to the civilian population, these discourses conflate support for student veterans with support for military projects.

Chapter 6 returns to the voices of the student veterans and shows us that lessons learned through military service have important implications for veterans' identities and reincorporation into their postmilitary lives. Using extended excerpts from interviews with veterans, we can see some of the unintended consequences of support initiatives that rely on uncritical esteem for the military and societal silence about the current wars, as veterans struggle to make meaning of their combat experience and educate a society that has been shielded from the consequences of a national policy of war. Engaging deeply with the voices of veterans allows us to hear that ritualized public gratitude and suppression of public debate about the wars can leave some veterans feeling silenced, rather than supported.

Military valorization on campus ebbs and flows, tacking with shifting social trends and political currents. It is important to understand veterans' experiences in civilian colleges because it is important to improve their access to higher education, but also because this information can teach us about our country at war. The conclusion reexamines distinctions between what it means to strive to be veteran friendly as opposed to military friendly, and attempts to separate the conflation of the two. This begins with the recognition that what might be helpful for student veterans is not necessarily the promotion of a national military project. The chapter calls for meaningful dialogue around the wars generally, but also in particular about veterans' military experiences, and makes clear that the veterans interviewed for this study wanted to be welcomed home from war. These veterans wanted their voices to be heard and their experiences to be understood by society. It is also clear that many, and likely the majority of, U.S. civilians want to support veterans returning from the current wars. But it is the mobilization of that inclination to acknowledge and support returning veterans that deserves more focused attention.

Taken together, these chapters focus on the educative aspects of military activities—pedagogies of warfare and practices of schooling—to explore the links between military training and civilian education. Tracing the effects of wartime military experience on veterans' academic lives provides a more complex understanding of the gap between recruitment promises and their contestable fulfillment. When veterans return home and enroll in college, they bring the war, which is inscribed in their bodies and consciousness, into civilian college, a space that is generally assumed to be non-militarized. This book argues that civilian institutional spaces, and particularly civilian colleges, are not, in fact, non-militarized. They are simply militarized in a different way.

· 1 ·

BASIC TRAINING

Making the Soldier, Militarizing the Civilian

This book begins where the formal militarization of new recruits begins: in basic training. The institutional military milieu encompasses diverse learning environments for soldiers: basic training, daily life on the base, deployment in war zones, and combat experience all represent different sites of learning. This chapter looks at methods of teaching and learning in basic training as a site of educational processes intentionally structured to inculcate military ideologies, norms, and practices. As such, basic training can be understood as a standardized institutional curriculum of inculcation and behavioral modification. Later chapters highlight educational aspects of combat experience through the voices of student veterans.[1]

Military recruits typically enlist shortly after high school. New civilian recruits become soldiers through basic training, where they are prepared for combat through highly situated processes of physical and psychological resocialization. Basic training represents an initial point of contact between civilian recruits and their military trainers, a conflictive social space formed where transculturation occurs. Different cultures meet in and through asymmetrical power relations, so that cultural boundaries can be broken and reorganized in a complex educative process of learning and unlearning norms, practices, and identities.[2]

From psychological studies, military training manuals, military memoirs, and popular films, basic training is well known as a process where military trainers replace recruits' existing habits and norms through methods of domination and subordination. Sociologist Erving Goffman described this process as resocialization within a total institution, where a person's habits and personality are radically altered through total control of the environment.[3] Looking at the process of basic training as occurring within a total institution, we see that soldiers can be conditioned to behave and respond in certain ways through living in a highly regimented environment.

As totalizing as the institutional military might seem, the process of transforming civilians into soldiers is rife with antagonisms and contestation. Simultaneous to unmaking the civilian, the soldier identity is formed through the processes of indoctrination into military codes, rituals, and norms and practices. Because military training and combat experience are conflictive, they transform identities, practices, and subjectivities in ways that are contradictory and fluid, rather than fixed. Relations between pedagogies, systems of knowledge, and corporeal practices are codified for the exercise of behavior modification, social control, and identity formation.

This chapter examines the processes and pedagogies involved in training civilians to become soldiers to lay the groundwork for my larger argument: that enduring effects of military training and combat experiences—rather than a campus culture that is ostensibly hostile to military veterans—contribute most saliently to veterans' difficulties in college. Drawing on in-depth interviews with recent veterans, I explore how recruits make meaning of basic training indoctrination and examine former soldiers' attempts to understand, comply with, and resist military commands.

Moving from civilian to soldier (and back) is a complex process of learning, unlearning, and relearning norms, identities, social roles, and ideologies. Many aspects of veterans' military training, including learned discipline, physical fitness, task identification, and the ability to complete tasks transfer positively into their postmilitary lives. But the techniques and methods used to train soldiers to become expert practitioners of combat and military occupation sometimes produce feelings of alienation from civilian society. Depersonalization, the use of force and humiliation to establish relations of domination, to train recruits in the suppression of emotional affect, and to inculcate a dichotomous worldview of good allies and evil enemies, all have the potential to impede soldiers' reentry into civilian life, creating challenges for veterans in college.

The institutional system of basic training exerts a totalizing but not total control over new recruits. Individual recruits learn to function as a group, obey commands, and acquire the skills necessary to become proficient soldiers. Through embodied practices, recruits learn to shed their self-identification as civilians and to identify as members of a military corpus.[4] Military social relations inculcate a military habitus, a set of internalized dispositions that leads veterans to respond to their environments in militarily structured ways even after they have left the institutional military.[5] This chapter describes some lessons of basic training as told through the experience and memories of former soldiers.

The first point of initiation for new recruits, officially referred to in military training manuals as Initial Military Training, begins with what is commonly known as basic training or boot camp, which lasts from eight to twelve weeks depending on the military branch.[6] The *U.S. Army Training Manual* describes the goal of basic training: "Initial Military Training (IMT) provides an orderly transition from civilian to military life. It is the first step to transforming volunteers into Soldiers. It teaches Soldiers the tasks and supporting skills and knowledge needed to be proficient in required skills at the first unit of assignment. Initial entry training produces technically and tactically competent Soldiers who exemplify Army Values, live the Warrior Ethos and are prepared to take their place in the ranks of the Army."[7]

Basic training is a spatial-temporal-practice relationship between civilian recruits and their military trainers. It is the first point at which civilian individuals become military subjects through spatial structures, temporal rhythms, and body movements. Military training involves pedagogical processes intended to create group identity by dismantling new recruits' individual, civilian orientation through sustained sleep deprivation, depersonalization, humiliation, physical exertion, and ideological indoctrination.[8] Simultaneous to unmaking the civilian, the soldier identity is formed through the processes of indoctrination into military codes, rituals, and norms. This is achieved by subjecting recruits to taxing physical and emotional trials and by applying a pedagogical process intended to build intragroup bonds of mutual dependence. This pedagogical process is based on what Belkin calls military masculinity, or a set of beliefs, practices, and attributes that enable recruits (both male and female) to claim authority on the basis of affirmative relationships with the military or with military ideas.[9] The ideal of military masculinity, Belkin says, includes but is not limited to the masculine disavowal of feminized weakness and subordination.[10]

Basic training involves physical, mental, emotional, and cultural conditioning. It introduces recruits to the practices that will allow them to manage the relationship between their civilian individual identities and the military group, in particular, by submitting to authority based on rank. This training has both immediate and longer-term effects, inculcating institutional norms and the skills for combat survival. The mode of behavior learned in basic training lingers even after soldiers leave the battlefield. Habits and notions of discipline, respect, obedience, authority, and violence are corporeally instilled in soldiers, and they endure and resurface in civilian environments. The following sections look at how these skills are taught and developed while subsequent chapters examine what happens when soldiers leave the military and enter civilian classrooms with a militarized set of dispositions.

Basic training creates bodies that are physically fit and orients new soldiers to military norms, combat techniques, the operation of arms, and an allegiance to nation and command structure. Army training manuals describe basic training as an "orderly transition" away from civilian life to that of the military, but from the soldiers' perspective this process is chaotic, disruptive, and inherently violent. Gulf War veteran Jonathan, who received his PhD in sociology from SU, described the violence involved in erasing a civilian identity and replacing it with a military one: "In the first four weeks of boot camp, every single thing that you took as real—about your cultural reality and your identity—is not just called into question, but is raised and then erased. Norms about *everything*. Your norms about violence, about conduct, about role certainty, about moral reward. All the way down to spatial proximity between people. Every single one of those things is redone. And then your new identity is rewarded continually, for a longer period of time."

Goffman studied the moral life of inmates in large, disciplinary institutions that he called total institutions: prisons, mental asylums, military barracks, and boarding schools.[11] Goffman used the word "total" to refer to the comprehensive ways in which an institution organizes all activities—working, eating, sleeping, socializing—and to the strategies that incorporate the institution into residents' inner lives. Goffman's theory of institutionalization provides a useful lens to analyze specific pedagogical methods of basic training. In particular, having to shed one's civilian habits and identity, or what Goffman called role dispossession, came up repeatedly in veterans' narratives of basic training.

Role dispossession begins as soon as recruits physically enter the control of the military. Many veteran interviewees remembered the bus trip to the training base as a defining moment when they left their civilian "before" phase and entered their military "after." Several saw the bus trip as a portal into an alternative world where the polite conventions of civilian society were abruptly replaced by rigidly enforced commands, disciplinary rules, and customs. This radical transformation in social relations was made clear to them by a sudden change in their drill instructors' demeanor. Central Community College student Abel noted,

> I remember getting to the airport not knowing what to expect. And I'll never forget the drill sergeant. He was, I guess you could say, bipolar [laughs]. When we were out in the airport, he was very nice, like he said,

"Okay, just sit over there." Then he was walking us outside and putting us on the bus, and as soon as the bus left, then—[he became] *drill sergeant* [speaker's emphasis]. It turned out that's because he couldn't yell at us in public, in front of civilians; so [in the airport] he was all like, "Oh, okay, you can stand over here" because he's not going to scream "Get your ass over here!" in front of civilians.

Boarding the bus represented the moment that Abel realized he was in a situation in which he had no control. The drill instructor's courteous attitude, which Abel realized had been on display exclusively for civilian audiences, evaporated as soon as he boarded the bus and was out of the public eye. "It wasn't until [the drill instructor] got on the bus that we realized [what we had gotten into], and then from that point on it was just constant, constant yelling-type deal." Southwest University student Jessica also remembered that the transport bus served as the site of a blunt transition from the civilian world (when she was not yet "really in the military") into the unknown military world of basic training:

I don't think anybody forgets [the moment of transition]. From the first moment you're there, you're in-processing, so you're standing in long lines. That's not really the action part, right? This is before you're really in the military. You're buying your equipment and your supplies, standing in tons and tons of lines, filling out forms, going to briefings. Then all of a sudden you get onto a bus one day. They tell you to put your head down. This is when it starts getting real. You put your head down, and you're going on a bus ride. Then they just start yelling at you like, "Get yourself out, get out!" Then you go out there [on the base.] You're like, "Where the hell am I?" And you just run wherever you run to. It's not even organized. It's like mad chaos.

In the liminal space of in-processing, Jessica was the subject of bureaucratic coding and standardizing procedures: standing in lines for equipment, briefings, and forms. These activities are part of what Goffman calls identity trimming, coding and shaping recruits into subjects that are more easily processed by the military administrative apparatus. For Jessica, the excruciatingly slow lines and boring briefings led up to what she calls the "action part," when she was "really in the military."

On the military base, role dispossession and identity trimming continue as recruits are stripped of personal possessions: phones, electronic devices, and cigarettes. Recruits are taught to respond to their superiors and to focus on commands while ignoring extraneous environmental stimuli. They are no longer called by their full names but rather by their last name and rank.[12] At the base, recruits are isolated from the civilian world for the purpose of orienting to their new roles. During the basic training period recruits are not allowed to leave the base. In the barracks, recruits are contained in a controlled and monitored environment, without access to civilian newspapers or other media. Recruits interact with primarily one another and with their drill instructor; contact with family and friends is restricted. Southwest University student Mark, who went through basic training at a naval base in San Diego, said that new recruits were punished for receiving mail and contraband treats such as candy and baked goods. Punishment for these infractions included humiliation for the individual and forced physical exercise for the group. This decontextualized group punishment for individual infractions is what Goffman calls the "disruption between actor and act." Mark recalled, "People would get candy or something like that [in the mail], and [instructors] would just dump it all in the trash. There was this rule that, if you got mail, [the recruit] would have to read it out loud to everyone while the whole class had to do push-ups for the whole time he was reading it. So it was really like this huge humiliation, and you actually started resenting the people who got mail from their families." By publicly dumping the contents of packages sent from home, instructors performed the separation of recruits from their former family-affiliated civilian selves. Group punishment taught group members to ostracize recruits who failed to sever ties with civilian life.

New recruits are required to adopt deferential stances and postures to establish their position of inferiority and subservience within strict military institutional hierarchies. Recruits must request permission from superiors to speak, to enter and exit rooms, and even to move. Abel, who left the Army with the rank of master sergeant after eight years and three tours in Iraq as a military police officer, viewed the authoritarian training style as rational, necessary, and functional:

> They tell you when you go to the bathroom; they tell you when to eat; they
> tell you when to sleep, how to sleep, how to eat, how to sit down. This
> makes a lot of sense—if you're talking sixty people coming in, there's
> sixty different personalities, sixty different ways of doing things, and you
> can't have that. Being part of the military, you have to have a structure;
> you have to have a certain set way. And so my understanding is that they
> are going to break you down completely, strip away your identity, but then
> they're going to rebuild you with your identity intact, but as a soldier,
> with a certain way of doing things.

Brian Lande notes that soldiers learn to navigate daily activities and social relationships through bodily movements and processes, and thus the body is an essential foundation of the military domain. As Lande writes, in the process of militarization, when the civilian becomes a soldier, "the body not only takes on new meanings (as a 'weapon,' 'vehicle,' and 'protective armor') and value (physical performance as a principle of hierarchy), it is lived differently and thus changes form."[13] Interview participants found military training effective because it utilized structured, didactic, and practical techniques to teach tasks that were incorporated into daily practice and became habitual.[14]

Military pedagogy also trains the mind to respond reflexively through rote memorization. Army veteran Erica, an su student and former journalist for the Department of Defense publication *Stars and Stripes*, said that to prepare for promotion up the enlisted ranks, recruits memorized regulations and procedures. Erica called this memorization being trained "not to think": "The standards for promotion are you have to study to go before a board, and you're asked all these very specific questions. You're given the questions and the answers, and most people study by writing out flashcards. They say you need to know where to find the answer, so you need to memorize where all of the answers are in the field manuals, and know which field manual to go to."[15]

Erica felt that memorizing material in this way—with what some anthropological and business management literature calls "low-context" details[16]—was intended to inculcate obedience and to keep recruits from critically analyzing military policies: "I feel the reason that enlisted members are given all this stuff to memorize in this way is because it keeps them from asking questions. Because when your brain is full of basically what amounts to trivia, and you're not using all of this information on a daily basis—when you're filling your brain with that, you're making it too busy to think about what's actually going on. You're being trained to spout information and to follow orders. You are being trained to answer to people." Erica struggled with being trained not to think. Her military lessons clashed with her journalism training, which taught her to be curious, inquisitive, and analytical: "That [rote memorization and uncritical obedience] was something that I could not really buy into because (a) I wasn't very good at memorizing and (b) I didn't see the point. So that didn't work well for me. Also, that didn't work well for me because I was not very good at following orders without asking why. I was a journalist, so it was my nature and my training to ask questions. Of course, it was my other [military] training to *not* ask questions at all, just to say, 'Hooah!'"[17]

Learning to follow orders without question required recruits to accept relations of dominance and subordination as normal and necessary. Connor, an su student and Army veteran of the war in Afghanistan, said that the deferential posture he was required to adopt was one of the things he remembered most vividly about his first day of basic training:

> They put you there, all lined up, and then the drill sergeants would all come out in a pack. And they would just [psychologically] rip everyone to shreds. You're in PT [physical training] clothes, a short-sleeve shirt and these running shorts, and you're up against the drill sergeants who are wearing combat boots, the full combat uniform. They have the duty belt, and the hat, and all those symbols of power and authority over you, and so you're conscious of your physically lower status. You're just like this peon, this little ant scurrying around, trying not to get run over by people.

Connor's memories of being a newcomer in basic training centered on the enactment and embodiment of power relations: uniformed drill sergeants approached new recruits like wild animals ("in a pack"). His feelings of powerlessness were exacerbated by his underdressed vulnerability in gym shorts and a T-shirt as he attempted to avoid getting run over by other soldiers and the more powerful drill sergeants, fortified by combat gear.

With time, individual bodies are disciplined to become self-governing and obedient to military norms. Because all living, working, and training exercises are conducted in groups, every move is observed by the group, and each activity is broken down into minute segments, which are subjected to regulation and judgment from superiors. Disciplinary coercion through surveillance augments direct force. Training conducted in high-pressure conditions showcases the trainees' incompetence, placing recruits' mistakes and doubts in full view.

This training is intended to provide recruits with the skills they need to perform under pressure. It teaches recruits to avoid shame and humiliation by not being noticed, by not stepping out of line, by "flying under the radar."[18] Connor learned this lesson in basic training: "I remember I was just so stressed out and having a horrible time just trying to unlock my combination lock. God, I just could not do it! And I had the drill sergeant standing there yelling, 'Hurry up, we're all waiting on you!' And then they make everyone do push-ups, because you can't do your stuff right. It's that responsibility, that you're killing the whole group [by your incompetence]." Connor's failed attempts to unlock his combination lock resulted in his exposure to the group as incompetent. Connor was made to feel responsible for metaphorically killing the entire group, which was punished with push-ups, but the intended lesson was that this kind of failure prefigured a literal killing, where one soldier could potentially be responsible for the deaths of others in a combat zone.[19]

Basic training creates an environment of total control over participants involving specifically embodied rituals: breathing exercises, call-and-response techniques, a reward-and-punishment system, and gestures of hierarchical relations (such as saluting and march-and-parade commands). Recruits are subject to regulation of minute details of activity and conduct that under normal circumstances are left to individual judgment and planning. Verbal deference forces recruits into undignified verbal postures signaling subordinance, and soldiers are trained to comply with orders accompanied by name calling and physical intimidation. Because recruits are not able to physically remove themselves from the training situation, they cannot shield themselves from superiors' demands, verbal assaults, and physical punishment. This creates a relationship of powerlessness on the part of the subordinate toward the superior, and by extension toward the institution. Connor described the physical experience of subordination: "The drill sergeants are just these big-ass muscle-bound guys. They've got their Smokey Bear hats, and they get up like right in your face— I mean, they're just cussing and screaming. They're so close to you that they're spitting in your face and they'll hit you with their hat as they're talking to you." Connor experienced the instrumental violence of the drill sergeant's overbearing proximity, the assaultive nature of his language, and the act of spraying his face with saliva as intimately terrorizing and demeaning. But he also experienced these things as educative. Through processes of intimidation, Connor learned that his performance would be ranked, classified, and standardized, that his behavior would be constantly evaluated in terms of conformity or deviation, and that deviation would result in punishment.

As basic training progresses, correction ceases to be the sole purview of the drill sergeant, and fellow soldiers become "supervisors, perpetually supervised," as the enforcers of military norms through supportive counsel and informal mentorship as well as scapegoating and physical violence.[20] Scapegoating is a central element of American military culture because military masculinity requires that the fear of failure is projected onto outcasts who are blamed for contamination and excluded from the warrior community.[21] Violence plays a normalizing function in the practice of hazing, and ritualized punishment by peers may be administered as initiation rites or as correctives for deficiencies. Despite recent U.S. Department of Defense avowed efforts to curtail hazing, veterans across military branches reported that hazing remains common enough to be considered an informal part of the core curriculum of basic training. In particular, veterans who served in the Marines described "fixing people" who deviated from the military norm through violence. This practice was characterized almost as a duty. Southwest University student Mack said, "I remember in boot camp, getting hazed—I'd be angry. I'd say, 'I don't deserve this. I didn't do anything wrong,' but then later I found out it didn't matter [what I thought or did], so there was an acceptance. I guess a sense of fate, too, that things are how they are. I think that's what I learned; it's a sense of fate." The lesson to submit to relations of power and domination as fate and to accept one's powerlessness to challenge authority or to change an unjust situation naturalized relations of domination.[22]

Many veterans spoke about peer-administered punishment in which a recruit would be taken to an isolated location and beaten. Another remedial intervention was the blanket party, administered when a recruit was deemed deficient and in need of fixing: a group would cover a fellow recruit with a blanket, restrain him, and beat him with improvised cudgels made of hard objects (such as bars of soap or batteries) wrapped in socks or towels.

Keilani, a former marine and student at Central College, said that she experienced ritualized injurious physical force from peers, though she did not identify it as violence. This force was administered in a celebratory fashion when she got promoted to the rank of sergeant. Describing an initiation ritual that sounded reminiscent of being jumped-in by a gang, Keilani did not recognize this initiation practice as hazing but saw it as natural—"just an old tradition that happens": "When we got promoted, we used to go down the line and get punched or pinned. [It was] just an old tradition that happens. I mean, it was an initiation that was expected. And no one ever thought it was considered to be hazing. But it's gotten so bad in the Marine Corps where it happens all the time, like blanket parties."

A primary goal of basic training is to create patterns of behavior through ritualized practice. The Army training manual (AR-350) states, "The basis for training standardization is executing training using approved Army standards. While ensuring tasks are performed to Army standards, commanders encourage trainers to exercise initiative and to create realistic and challenging conditions for training within the context of mission, enemy, terrain, troops, time, and civilian considerations."[23]

Soldiers must train not only in the daily rituals of military life but also in specific combat skills. Command compliance is fundamental in combat situations, so basic training teaches infantry soldiers to obey orders without question. They also learn, through repetition and operant conditioning, to shoot to kill. Grossman argues that the main reason the U.S. military must train soldiers to respond reflexively rather than with a critical reflection is because human beings have a powerful innate aversion to killing, and soldiers must be conditioned to overcome this aversion. Grossman identified and analyzed operant conditioning techniques used by the U.S. military specifically designed to desensitize combatants.[24] These techniques begin with exercises linking everyday movement (such as eating and drinking) with rifle drills, and offering rewards for high kill rates in lifelike simulated target practices. Alongside behavioral modification techniques, ideological training teaches soldiers that their designated enemies are subhuman through everyday practices—marching cadences, jokes, and daily banter.

Southwest University student Mark, who was studying for a master's degree in education, spoke about his experience of basic training instruction as indoctrination and operant conditioning designed to produce reflexive action. He said that military pedagogy purposefully employed methods of infantilization even in the most mundane daily functions to teach subordination: "The first week is the indoctrination phase. That week you are the lowest of the low. You don't know anything. They teach you how to talk, how to walk, how to eat, everything." Through corporeal, practical activity in the military milieu, this instruction inculcates obedience and provides behavioral patterning and training for combat performance. Mark described learning to drink a glass of water at mealtime as preparation for a rifle drill:

> When you grab the glass in chow hall, you're told to shoot your arm straight out and put it down. You have to maintain the "thousand-yard stare" [vision fixed into the distance, not responding to stimuli] while you do this. They make you do this to brainwash you, but it's also to teach you the motions you'd perform for the rifle drill. It goes hand in hand. When you eat, you do the motions of the rifle drill, and when you do the rifle drill and marching, it's to teach you to unquestioningly follow orders.

Through constant repetition, daily activities like eating and drinking are linked to combat skills and to habits of obedience. Through habituated physical movements, recruits are psychologically trained to accept their subordinate position as "the lowest of the low."

In addition to teaching soldiers to function in a hierarchical bureaucracy and habituating conditioned reflexes for combat, basic training employs ritualized behavior to instill adherence to a social order. The tasks of military enculturation—standardizing physical performance, defining community, and adherence to authority—are carried out within a system of total institutional control. Rituals initiate and integrate recruits into a social order through daily relationships and collective events that define and bind the social group into a cohesive unit, affirm mutual commitment, and foster obedience to group rules.

According to Bourdieu, for any experience to become legitimized, arbitrary interpretive or conceptual models must appear necessary.[25]

For Connor, rituals surrounding uniforms and standing in formation were the primary practices that taught him to obey orders and gave him a sense of group identity: "Formations and uniform—that was something we'd do every single day. You have to be in the exact same uniform as everyone else. It doesn't matter how cold or how hot it is, how inappropriate wearing that jacket or not wearing that jacket is, everyone is standing there with you and you *will* look like everyone else and you *will* stand in that formation and if you don't, the consequences are very serious and immediate."

One of the first lessons learned by new recruits is that they should no longer consider themselves individuals guided by self-interest but should instead identify as part of a unified corpus. Connor noted that it was crucial for everybody to look the same and stand the same way, regardless of external environmental conditions. Soldiers learn that continuity must be maintained, whatever the external circumstances. Regardless of the heat or cold, one must stand at attention, in formation, in a heavy jacket. This demonstrated to recruits that undeviating consistency with the group was more important than personal physical comfort or sense of propriety. "Appropriate" came to mean whatever the drill sergeant ordered. Submission to arbitrary orders (for example, "raking rocks"[26]) and adherence to uniform dress and behavior did not simply maintain continuity—it provided the lesson that continuity must be maintained especially when civilian norms might indicate that it is inappropriate.

Soldiers are taught to tie authority and respect to names and rank, which are signaled visually and corporeally by the uniform. Central College student Brett, an Army veteran of two tours in Iraq, spends his summers on Army bases working as a basic training drill sergeant, where he teaches the significance of the uniform to new recruits. One of the first lessons he teaches new soldiers is that the uniform marks formal hierarchical relations. Putting on the uniform also signals a switch away from civilian relationships, which tend to de-emphasize hierarchy and value informality. He told me,

B: Going from civilian to military, it's tough, because you're used to saying, 'Hey Bob. Hey Joe.' In the Army, you have to snap back to 'Sgt. So-and-So. Yes sir. No sir.' But even on active duty, once you're off hours and you're out on the streets, you would usually call people by last names. But once you get back into uniform and you're on duty, it's rank and last name, or 'sir.'"

EM: Is it hard to keep that straight?

B: No, not really. As soon as you put your uniform on, it kind of snaps in, but sometimes it'll slip. Like my senior NCO [noncommissioned officer]—his first name is Guillermo—we usually call him G outside of work, but sometimes [on duty] we'll slip and say, "Hey G!—Oops, dang." But if it consistently goes like that and we see a pattern of it, then our form of disciplinary action will step in.

Putting on the uniform signals a shift in identity and relationships—when military discipline and respect for hierarchical relations "snap in" and are performed. Consciousness is compartmentalized and tied to practice, and the uniform signals how relations are negotiated through shifting circumstances. Wearing the uniform answers the questions: Which world am I in now? Which vocabulary and forms of address do I use? In which rituals am I engaged? For Brett, the uniform also signified a professional identity that caused him to take things "more seriously":

As soon as I put on the uniform, [I] take things a lot more seriously—it's a professional thing. You don't want to make an ass of yourself with the uniform on—you're held to a higher standard. When I put on the uniform, anyone I talk to, it's going to be name and rank. If it's an officer, it's going to be "sir or ma'am," "gentlemen, ladies" based on professionalism and respect. Even when I'm not wearing the uniform, [in the civilian world] it's going to be the same thing. Because people know that I am in the military, I'm not going to make an ass of myself. I'm going to be professional, courteous, and disciplined when I'm talking to others.

Brett's consciousness of the optics of military presentation in the civilian world offers a window into how he views himself in uniform: as someone who is professional, courteous, and disciplined.[27] But beyond the personal meaning that wearing the uniform has for soldiers, and the meanings that civilians may impute to soldiers in uniform, rules about military demeanor and apparel teach recruits lessons of compliance and hierarchy.

Within the institutional military, the uniform code forms part of authoritative discourse that exerts control over the recruits' actions.[28] For soldiers, the overarching lesson of basic training is that this military discourse is unquestionable: that military hierarchy and customs cannot be challenged on their own terms. While this does not mean that soldiers always obey the rules, military training gives recruits a dichotomous choice: they can reject military regulation or submit to it. But they cannot challenge the internal logic, rules, and hierarchy of the institution. Transgressors are placed in a position of marginality.

Connor described the consequences when recruits failed to keep discipline by breaking formation: "In formation, everyone is standing there, and if they see you walk away, it's a huge black mark against you. You don't want to be that one guy who walks in front of a hundred or more people." Group compliance is a powerful governing force that encourages recruits to avoid self-marginalization by stepping out of line. Military norms are maintained through peer surveillance, ranked judgment, corrective measures, and rewards. Compliance is also fostered by "making the slightest departures from correct behavior subject to punishment," or what Foucault calls the microphysics of power.[29]

According to Connor, drill instructors assert power through shame and humiliation. Shame attaches to acting as an individual; breaking rank is treated as an assertion of individuality and therefore a betrayal of the group. "[Drill instructors] would always say, 'Oh, so you want to be an *individual*?' It was like a jingle. We heard it since basic training: [sneering, taking on the voice and demeanor of the drill instructor] 'Private So-and-So wants to be an *individual*. Everyone go and do push-ups now, because *this* guy wants to be an *individual*. Rules don't apply to him. Everyone else has to do it, but he's *special*.'"

Drill instructors gain compliance by publicly shaming individuals, treating individuality as a kind of sociopathy: punishable and worthy of contempt. Repetition and public display, combined with group punishment for offenders, create powerful incentives to follow orders and act as a group. Because the assertion of individual needs poses a threat to the subordination necessary to maintain group cohesion, the term "individual" is deployed as an epithet to provide a social and behavioral corrective. By meeting the infraction of individualism with collective punishment, drill instructors raise the social stakes and heighten the contrast between a compliant group member and transgressive individuals.[30] When a drill instructor accuses a soldier of acting individually, he accuses the soldier of asserting a superior status over others in his group, of seeking to be special and thus better than the others. In the context of the group, individuality is an unwarranted claim of privilege that disregards the needs of the group. The fact that the drill instructor's taunt is "like a jingle" demonstrates that this repetitive slogan becomes woven into the fabric of everyday life as a cultural affirmation.

The public act of shaming is also linked to self and group valorization and superiority, asserting that soldiers, as individuals and as a group, are morally and physically superior to civilians by virtue of their association with the military and with war.

While individual physical prowess is valorized in basic training, there are advantages to remaining unnoticed or "flying under the radar." Recruits who draw attention to themselves often receive extra work assignments. In the experience of twenty-four-year-old Iraq war and Army veteran Bridget, any distinction, positive or negative, served as an invitation to extra duty:

> You keep your head down and you fly under the radar. That's the thing in basic [training]—you don't want to make a name for yourself. You don't want to draw attention to yourself in any way, because it's going to be bad, regardless. Even if they think you're good at something. Then they're just going to call on you to be in a leadership position and everything's gonna come down on you and you're going to have so much more work to do. And you're already really tired and really stressed out and you just don't need it.

Where deficient performance results in punishment, humiliation, and increased duties, demonstrations of above-average competence result in praise, acknowledgment, and increased duties, creating a punishment in the guise of a reward. Thus, flying under the radar is a multipurpose strategy to avoid any kind of individual distinction. But this evasive path is not an option for all soldiers. Bridget continued, "So [we tried to] just fly under the radar—don't stand out and don't be an individual. And even the drill sergeants tell you that. They say, 'Don't be an individual.' But I *am* an individual [speaker's emphasis]. I'm tiny and I am [female]. . . . There's just no getting around it. I'm not going to *not* stand out in a group of guys or whatever."

As Belkin notes, since the dawn of the republic Americans have glorified warriors as the epitome of patriotic masculinity.[31] The ideal of military masculinity, which encompasses being simultaneously tough and compliant, is an archetype of the ideal citizen. Thus, when soldiers learn that they must be both singularly outstanding and an indistinguishable member of a community, they embody the contradictions structured by military training. In a system that structures authority through a paradigm of military masculinity, the collective subject—the antithesis of the transgressive individual—is normatively and observably male. Female soldiers do not have the option to seamlessly blend into the corpus. They have no spaces of imperceptibility and no social or behavioral trajectory that can effectively keep them under the radar. Moreover, the reviled individual male subject who cannot or will not comply with the physical and psychological demands of basic training is gender-coded as feminized and emasculated.

Much of basic training focuses on mastering the small components of daily life on the base: how the uniform is put together, the details of cleaning and maintaining weaponry. This pedagogy of detail helps establish the soldiers' habitus. Ritualized attention to detail produces what Bourdieu calls the "ontological complicity" of "cognition without consciousness" and "intention without intentionality," through which soldiers learn to perform in combat without dwelling on the bigger-picture consequences.[32] Adherence to procedural details—such as those involved in making beds or folding underwear to exact specifications—trains recruits to function in chaotic combat situations without thinking about the activities in which they are engaged, such as shooting at people and avoiding being shot. Beyond serving as a focusing technique, for some veterans, attention to detail becomes a habit. It instills the kind of cognition without consciousness that allows them to accept military rationale and to respond in combat.

Southwest University student Jessica said that basic training laid the groundwork for a new consciousness of intention without intentionality:

> For the first couple of days, it was just a lot of screaming, yelling, and briefings. They are teaching you how to fold your underwear. They are teaching you how to set up your locker. They teach you how to make a bed. They teach you how to clean a rifle, how to check it out, how to hold it, how to shine your boots. Attention to detail. These are the fundamental things you learn in basic, but I think it really does carry through. So attention to detail, and also just doing the best job you can do and not being afraid to fail. Like I said, in basic training, they break you down. You are going to fail, all the time, all the time, all the time.

As Jessica noted, performance failure is integral and necessary to recruits' learning process ("You are going to fail, all the time, all the time, all the time"). Failure provides a pedagogy of retraining. It pushes recruits to continually strive for an ideal, and strict adherence to procedural details serves to guide them toward that ideal. Memorizing procedures and following habituated patterns instilled through punitive methods of shaming (screaming, yelling) and didactic training (briefings) taught Jessica and her fellow soldiers to react reflexively to chaotic situations of combat.

Iraq war veteran and su student Jordan said that Marine boot camp felt like "controlled chaos" intended to destabilize recruits and teach them to function under the stress of combat. Like many other veterans, he considered basic training a form of theater:

> [Boot camp was] controlled chaos. The drill instructors—their job foremost is to be actors and to play a role. You're on stage, too, and you're a part of the act, but it's really not about you. It's not pleasant, and that's

the point of it. But they really are trying to show you something that is chaotic, where you are out of your element. They try and make everyone out of their element. The drill instructor's job is to disorient everyone, to create chaos, so everyone is destabilized and out of their familiar surroundings.

In Jordan's view, this performative, destabilizing pedagogy of placing "everyone out of their element" was intended to teach people to function instinctively in combat ("when things are crazy") to avoid the life-endangering consequences of stopping to consider contingencies. Jordan explained, "You have to learn to function in chaos, because [in combat] you're going to face chaos. [In war] there's a problem, and it's a shitty situation. When it devolves into different and even shittier situations, as it inevitably will, we [Marines] are called in to fix it."

The combat environment is fundamentally unstable, often deteriorating quickly and uncontrollably. Soldiers are trained to function in this chaotic environment by learning to pay meticulous attention to detail through activities like shining boots for hours or grooming the uniform. Concentrating intently on the precise details of a particular task allows recruits to tune out extraneous thoughts. Jordan continued:

> They made us do what seems like really ridiculous things, like shine our boots and make sure that there are no threads sticking out of any part of our uniform, to the point of pulling at every seam and burning them away. Staying up late at night to iron our uniforms. This comes back to the idea of attention to detail, and this is a phrase that's repeated over and over and over again. It worked. It really annoyed me and I thought, "There's no point. I can pay attention to something if I want to." But the point is not to be able to pay attention to something only when you want to. It's to pay attention to something whether or not you're thinking about wanting to. In that regard, that's helpful, in some situations. When you're in that [combat] situation, those details are sometimes the difference between a good day and a bad day.

A "good day," as Jordan meant the term here, is a day when few soldiers and civilian noncombatants lose their lives to battlefield chaos. Actions involving cognition without consciousness helped create good days in combat settings. Yet while the skills Jordan learned in basic training were useful in combat, they became a liability when he returned to civilian life and to college:

> [Paying attention to detail] was important, and it's something that I've only come to appreciate and respect after thinking a lot about it, because

it's not even something I thought about when I went through [combat]. It wasn't like, "Gee, I'm really glad I paid such close attention because if I wasn't polishing my boots so well in boot camp, then I wouldn't be able to pay such close attention [in combat]." That's not what went through my mind. I was just consumed with this task at hand, and that's what I did. But as a civilian [in college], that's not necessarily a very useful skill. In fact, I feel my brain being overwhelmed.

Like Jordan, other veterans I interviewed felt that in civilian life and college their brains were "overwhelmed" by too many details. While some veteran respondents said that some habits of military training, including discipline and the ability to focus on tasks, were helpful to them in college classrooms, others said that the need to focus on environmental details was a problem when they reentered civilian classrooms. Their combat experience made them think of environmental stimuli as possible precursors to an attack. This is one effect of military training—which is solidified corporeally and psychologically in combat—that veterans carry with them into college classrooms.

Basic training represents a highly orchestrated transition from civilian to military habitus, a structured program of cultivation and guidance intended to militarize the civilian subject.[33] Though the experience of basic training felt chaotic to recruits, the training followed a fixed curriculum, and all recruits were expected to learn the same standards and practices. Recruits lived, ate, socialized, and trained together according to set schedules; life in the total institution regulated habits and taught compliance.

Veterans' stories of basic training dealt with similar themes: the bus ride, the shock of initial encounters with military culture, navigating living arrangements and social interdependence, and settling into familiar and predictable routines. These routines served as a template for soldiers' lives on the military base beyond basic training.[34]

Through pedagogies of depersonalization, shame and humiliation, and attention to detail, military training is designed to produce reflexive action rather than reflective contemplation, producing cognition without consciousness that allows soldiers to react instead of reflecting on their actions in chaotic situations of war. The inculcation of military norms and practices leads many veterans to respond to their environments in militarily structured ways even after they have left the institutional military. The chapters that follow show that soldiers trained in pedagogies of warfare carry certain practices, assumptions, beliefs, and expectations (sometimes consciously, but more often unconsciously) with them into college classrooms.

· 2 ·

WHAT THEY BRING WITH THEM

Effects of Military Training on Student Veterans

One day I'm a soldier; four days later, I'm sitting in the back of a community college classroom, and I realize that none of the people in this room gave a shit about what I thought was important: what I thought was a good reason to be honest, what I thought was true, what I thought was worth caring about—they couldn't give a fuck.

JONATHAN, Southwest University

[Returning to civilian life] was complicated, extremely complicated. . . .
I've been trained to think and react in a certain way. But how do you untrain that?

CODY, Central College

Soldiers' military orientation does not end when they are discharged from their military service. Veterans carry military conceptions of time, comportment, jurisdiction, demeanor, social relations, prerogative, and duty onto civilian campuses. When soldiers leave the institutional military, there is no corresponding intentional process to "recivilianize" them; no comprehensive process analogous to basic training that allows soldiers to disengage from institutional military practice and prepare to reenter civilian society. The closest thing to a comparable transitional process is the Transition Assistance Program (TAP), a series of mandatory meetings developed for those about to be discharged from military service. Each branch of service designs its own TAP; they usually last from three days to one week and generally involve bureaucratic administrative requirements of separating from the institutional military structure. Sessions typically dispense information about how to fill out discharge forms and sign up for postmilitary benefits like the GI Bill education benefits and subsidized health care insurance.[1] These may be augmented by voluntary classes in civilian job skills: résumé writing, classes in how to dress for the civilian workplace, and job placement counseling.[2]

These transitional programs have been criticized as being overly bureaucratic and superficial, and there have been attempts to standardize TAPs across the branches of the military. The American Legion, a veteran support and lobbying organization, offered the following critique of the newest iteration of the standardized TAP, saying that insufficient emphasis was placed on the culturally inflected "soft skills" of functioning in civilian life:

> The vast majority of the personnel leaving the armed services after their first or second enlistment have not had significant experience working in a civilian workplace setting as compared to their civilian counterparts. They lack the "soft skills" that are most commonly learned by spending a substantial part of one's adult life in a civilian work environment. By "soft skills" we mean personal qualities, habits, attitudes, and social graces that can make an individual employable. . . . It is impossible for transitioning service members to quickly rid themselves of the habits they acquired in order to thrive in service. While many of these habits are also conducive to thriving in a civilian workplace environment, many are not. We, of course, recognize that a five day course cannot hope to inculcate etiquette and behaviors obtained by spending a substantial part of one's adult life in a civilian workplace environment. . . . We believe that TAP would be improved if accompanied by some kind of program that would allow the veteran to gradually assimilate to the civilian office environment or if it at least included private sector companies to discuss office and/or workplace culture. The American Legion cannot stress how crucial it is that more emphasis and instruction be provided to the service member on this matter.[3]

In this uncharacteristically critical public appraisal of institutional military practice, the American Legion acknowledges that some aspects of military culture can be maladaptive in civilian environments, and the group advocates for a more prolonged, practice-based reentry into civilian life, somewhat akin to a gentler, less-punitive basic training in reverse.

All soldiers leaving military employment are required to attend a TAP, regardless of their job posting. However, in a separate but related process, all soldiers returning from combat zones are also required to complete a Post-Deployment Health Assessment questionnaire, which screens for physical and mental health issues commonly associated with deployments in which "concerns and referral needs will be documented and available resources discussed to help resolve any post-deployment issues."[4] This cursory mental health screening, often administered on a computer tablet, includes questions about whether the soldier has contemplated suicide. Most veterans I spoke with said they automatically answered "no" to this question because they wanted to avoid having to speak with a military psychiatrist. As one veteran said, "If you say yes [to the suicide question], they will send you to a shrink. At that point, you just want to go home." This means that combat-related mental health needs are going undetected in many soldiers.

Upon discharge, soldiers returned to heterogeneous civilian environments to readjust on their own to the civilian habits and identities that they previously worked so hard to shed. This chapter examines veterans' transition into college, looking at veterans at Southwest University (SU) and Central Community College, paying particular attention to points of conflict between civilian and military practice.

Central College and SU are two distinct educational spaces, each comprising particular pedagogical, cultural, structural, and social norms and practices. One of the first points of disconnection is when soldiers leave military life and are confronted with what some veterans described as the chaos of the civilian world, where their lives are configured individually, separately from their fellow veterans. For many veterans using GI Bill education benefits, community college is one of the first institutional points of reentry into this civilian chaos.[5] In community college, veterans' military training often comes into conflict with civilian academic customs as well.

Some veterans' advocates argue that veterans struggle in college because civilian students and faculty create a hostile environment for military members. This chapter presents an alternative explanation. It argues that differences in military and civilian cultural and pedagogical norms and practices create barriers to learning for veterans when they return to civilian classrooms. These differences, or disjunctions, coupled with veterans' experience of war trauma and a silencing of discussion about the wars, complicate veterans' attempts to succeed in college.

What follows describes veterans' experiences moving from the military into college classrooms and identifies the factors that supported and impeded their success. Their challenges did not come from the antiveteran attitudes of other college students, faculty, or personnel; rather, the disjunctions between civilian academic and military cultures and teaching styles impeded the transition to civilian college. In addition, some war veterans experienced lasting effects of combat trauma that exacerbated cultural and pedagogical disjunctions.

Finally, in an effort to welcome veterans into classrooms, some school personnel discouraged classroom discussion of the wars, with the unintended effect of discouraging veterans from talking about the military experiences that were so critical to their emotions and identities. Silence about the wars hurt student veterans by rendering their experiences invisible and discouraging critical examination of issues that are important to many student veterans.

I begin by identifying aspects of military training that that veterans described as having a positive effect in their postmilitary collegiate lives. I then examine points of conflict between civilian and military norms and practices and trace the effects of disjunctions on veterans' ability to navigate the college environment. Next I examine the effects of combat trauma on veterans' classroom performance. I provide a detailed analysis of the experience of one student veteran, Cody, to illustrate the complexity of veterans' feelings about the wars, and describe how he and others sought spaces to talk about these thoughts. College personnel who discouraged classroom talk about the wars inadvertently erased the social and emotional realities of veterans, who identified as both victims and perpetrators of violence.

Just as basic training was a social space of collision and contestation, for many returning veterans, civilian college represented a conflictive transitional space. Yet unlike basic training, college begins with no explicit instructions on how to function within institutions of higher education.[6]

Military and academic environments operate with divergent logics, traditions, and missions. The everyday practices of military institutions are based on a command structure and involve disciplinary procedures, rituals, and the raison d'être to create soldiers prepared to carry out military missions. Everyday practices in academic institutions reflect the guiding mission of knowledge production, teaching, and learning. The most apparent difference between the two institutions is college's emphasis on the ability to read, comprehend, and synthesize academic texts and to write in academic English. But this masks more profound and competing cultural differences between military and civilian cultural practices, understandings, and identities. They include expectations about command structure and hierarchy, discipline, comradeship, and collective effort in a context where few other students have intimate knowledge of the military experience. These disjunctions made the transition to college challenging for veterans.

Many veterans spoke positively about what they learned in the military and the changes they underwent. Some described aspects of their military training as helpful in the transition to college, and they spoke with nostalgic fondness about friendships made in the military.

Some veterans said that the discipline, structure, and mission-driven focus of their military training helped them in college. Yet many felt that they were not sufficiently trained in critical thinking skills and had to develop these skills extemporaneously in college classrooms. Others said that they felt more prepared for college than civilians because of specific skills learned in the military such as punctuality, note taking, public speaking, and leadership. Veterans entered college accustomed to obeying external commands from authority figures, and many were already comfortable complying with requirements to study and to practice tasks until they were sure of proficiency. All of the participants spent at least four years living within the military's institutional structure and cultivating a bureaucratic military habitus, easing the transition to a college bureaucratic college administrative apparatus. Because the college administrative structure was less punitive than the military, veterans perceived it as more benign, less threatening, and easier to deal with. This placed military veterans at an advantage over students who did not have significant experience with bureaucratic institutions, such as first-generation college students, immigrant students, or older, nonmilitary reentry students. For many student veterans, negotiating the military bureaucracy served a useful enculturating function.

The formative lessons of basic training figured prominently in veterans' memories. For example, twenty-eight-year-old su student Oscar, who was born in Mexico and raised in California, remembered from his training: "[My drill instructor] said, 'If ever in life you feel like you don't know what to do, just remember what you learned in boot camp.' And to this day that's what I remember." Though Oscar's high school teachers had discouraged him from enrolling in college because they believed he would not be successful, after being discharged from the Marines, Oscar saw college as a mission to be accomplished. He likened his college classes to combat: "[College] is a constant struggle. Like when you're attacking the hill, you want to attack the hill going up, not backing down. With my academic studies, I know it's tough being here at su. I'm trying as hard as I can, so I don't have any regrets. I study a lot, and I don't feel like I'm the smartest person, but I feel like I'm a very determined person. I think that's what I got from the Marines, and that's what's been helping me here at su."

Other veterans spoke about military conceptions of comportment and demeanor in their discussions of college life, which many conceptualized and spoke of as a "mission." Their military orientation to the concept of mission—a critical goal, task, or duty, whether assigned or self-imposed—surfaced repeatedly during interviews. Many characterized completing their college education as fulfilling a mission. This came up in a conversation with Central College student Brett, twenty-seven, who was raised in Orchard Valley, a few miles from

Central College, by his Colombian father and Irish American mother. Brett did not feel ready to go to college after high school, so he joined the Army to "travel the world and go to combat." After eight years in the Army infantry and two deployments to Iraq, Brett said he learned to function well under stress, and he drew on his military practice of mental and physical preparation to cope with daily stresses of college life. Many of the lessons he learned in military training transferred into his civilian life in positive ways, as military structure and discipline prepared him for the work in his classes. Employing the language and conceptual framework of his military background, Brett viewed his job as a college student in terms of a primary mission to finish his associate's degree. That primary mission consisted of smaller daily missions of writing research papers, answering instructors, and meeting deadlines:

> I learned [in the military] how to be calm in stressful situations, how to prepare myself for the next day or the next mission, just always be prepared and always be relaxed for stressful environments. Even for things like research papers. I always set it up: I write it on the board; I have the dates; I always give myself enough time to complete it. For, like, a research paper, I usually have it done like a week prior. . . . I've become more disciplined in how to prepare myself, with everything from preparing a job interview to doing homework, to performing my daily tasks at work, even talking to an everyday normal Joe, or a customer, or my dad, or anybody.[7]

Brett's daily life and interactions with others (customers in his retail job at Home Depot, his father, or in random conversations with the "everyday normal Joe") were structured through military conceptualizations of time and discipline. The military trained him to expect that deviation from behavioral norms would be punished, and Brett leveraged his ability to follow rules to his advantage, consciously maintaining practices that would help him as a student. Brett turned in all of his assignments early, a reflection of the Army adage taught by drill instructors in basic training: "If you're early, you're on time; if you're on time, you're late; and if you're late, don't bother showing up."[8]

Southwest University student Terry, twenty-five, echoed Brett's view that college was a mission to be accomplished. Terry, an Asian American, joined the Marines because he wanted to emulate his father's experience as a Navy medic. He also wanted to find a career that would take him out of his industrial California city. When asked why he enlisted, Terry said that he had felt "this need to fulfill the exploration part of [his] life." He continued, "It seemed like the ceiling was too low," referring to the limited vocational possibilities available to him in his working-class city, noting that his high school classmates all had jobs as grocery store clerks, gas station attendants, and bank tellers. Terry credited military discipline, which he said instilled in him a focused "mission accomplishment mentality," with helping him succeed at su: "I try to show up early and build that punctuality. I think that's a good thing. That definitely transferred over [from the Marines]. I want to say it's the mentality of how to discipline yourself in whatever it is that you need to do, that mission accomplishment mentality, that bled over a lot. Sometimes it takes [different] forms, whether it's ignoring phone calls or ignoring e-mails or just ignoring whatever it is that's a distraction."

Central College student and Army infantry veteran Jack said that in the Army, he was constantly trained and called upon to demonstrate his newly acquired skills. Raised in a white, working-class, conservative Mormon family near Central College in Orchard Valley, Jack was taught by his family that military service was his patriotic duty. Jack's father, a Vietnam War veteran, encouraged him to join the Army because he wanted Jack to become "more responsible." "[My father] said the military offers a great jump start on your life. It helps you grow up, mature," recalled Jack. Jack was a self-described "adrenaline junkie" who felt that his life needed a jump start after high school. Jack enlisted during his junior year in high school and left for basic training the week following graduation.[9]

The military training model—a combination of didactic training and practical demonstrations of newly acquired skills—helped prepare Jack for the demands of learning and taking tests in his community college:

> I had some problems with [high] school. I wasn't going to school so much, getting in trouble. I guess I prioritized wrong. I never did my homework. I smoked a lot of pot when I was in high school and stuff like that. So I didn't like school, but the whole time you're in the military you're going to little schools in a way, little classes to train you on this and to train you on that and you get quizzed and you have to do all this stuff. There is actually quite a bit of schooling [in the military]. I just picked that up, and I use it, civilian-education-wise.

The "little schools" Jack was required to attend during military training, which involved a combination of didactic lectures, demonstrations, and quizzes, prepared him to be a college student. The subject matter taught in his college courses differed significantly from that of his military training, but Jack said that the work habits and trained obedience taught him to perform the duties of a student. What helped him most, he said, was his training to obey commands.

In the military, his superiors defined the expectations and consequences for participation: "[In the Army] you can't *not* do [homework]. That mentality carries over to civilian education, and makes it really easy in a way. The discipline, I think, is really what it was. This [attitude of] 'Just do it. Break it down, and then just finish it.' The instilled discipline just transfers over really well."

The theme of poor or indifferent high school students improving through military experience surfaced in many interviews. Southwest University student Jacob's story echoed Jack's in many ways. A twenty-seven-year-old Navy veteran, Jacob was raised in an African American family in an urban neighborhood in Northern California. His father, a civil servant, and his mother, a cafeteria manager, both wanted him to expand his vocational options by going to college. A self-described "knucklehead" in high school who was "just into hanging out, partying on weekends, drinking and smoking weed—nothing really constructive," Jacob worked the graveyard shift in a pipe factory after graduation. He decided to enlist in the Navy because his factory job "sucked." He enlisted partly because the military would provide funding for college, although he also considered the possibility of a lifelong military career. "I thought if I liked it, I might stay in," he said. "[I joined] just to get out of the situation I was in."

Jacob said that despite having professional goals beyond the pipe factory, he was limited by context and experience. He said that the work ethic he learned in the Navy helped him exceed his limits, pushing beyond the boundaries of what he thought possible:

> Growing up, I had lots of goals. I was like, "I want to be a journalist; I want to be a businessman." I wanted to be a lawyer, but I didn't know how to get there. The way to get there is hard work. There's no way around it. I didn't understand what hard work was. I felt like if I had a job and sat there and did nothing for eight hours that was hard work. You can apply yourself in that eight hours and get a lot done. You can't do that in a pipe factory, but in jobs where you use your mind you can really take it to the next level and really achieve that job. That's what the military taught me. That's why boot camp was so hard. You stay awake for three days working your butt off. You're never good enough, and it's really hard. That way when you get to the fleet and you're working just twelve hours a day [you think], "This is easy—it's cake."

In basic training, Jacob learned that he was capable of handling long hours and stress. Yet even as Jacob benefited from enforced military discipline, he had a nuanced view of the lessons he learned in the military, acknowledging that some others did not share his positive experience with military schedules and discipline. He credited his military experience with helping him put the strenuous academic regime of su in perspective: "Not everybody learns the same lessons. There are a lot of guys that leave the military and get on drugs and stuff, but it taught me that if I work hard, then [college] is easy. [The Navy] showed me what hard work is, because I had to work for three days straight with no sleep. That's why I say my hardest days at su might be frustrating, but it's not hard. Mentally it's harder, but I can put in the work easily."

Women veterans also brought up the theme of learned discipline. Thirty-year-old Central College student and former Marine Keilani said that she lacked discipline as a high school student in Hawaii, preferring socializing to homework. She had planned to join the Navy, but a teenage DUI arrest made her ineligible for the job she wanted in that branch. Keilani joined the Marines to honor family tradition and learn discipline: "My dad was a Marine," she said. "I decided to go in because my dad told me I needed to learn what discipline was, integrity and respect, and the only way I'd ever learn those things was by joining the Marine Corps like he did."

Keilani said that Marine boot camp made her more task-focused and less self-centered: "Boot camp teaches you a lot of things. When I was a young girl in high school, all I cared about was my social life. I didn't care about my family. I didn't care about anything else. Boot camp basically slapped a new reality in me."[10] Keilani proudly noted that she is now doing well academically, and attributed her current ability to focus on the habituated discipline and respect for hierarchy she learned in the Marine Corps:

> I push myself. If one of my professors tells me that I have to do something, I make sure that it gets done, and I make sure it's to the best of my ability. The Marine Corps has trained me to do that. So that's one of the reasons why I think I'm so good in school right now. I listen. I pay attention. I give good eye contact, which I learned [in the Marines]. You're supposed to give good eye contact, so when my instructor's talking to me, I give him good eye contact. I acknowledge that I understand what he's saying. I take good notes.

Focus, concentration, organization, punctuality, and respect can all be useful in college. But trained obedience can also create a kind of rote behavior. For example, the attention a student gives to maintaining eye contact with an instructor may indicate that the student is listening, but this attention is not necessarily directed at critically evaluating the information imparted in the lecture. In Keilani's case, this formalized behavior helped her to focus in the classroom, while for other veterans, like Erica (introduced in chapter 1), the formality of trained military behavior served to eclipse critical thinking, and with it the attention devoted to grappling with ambiguity and nuance. In this case, behaviors learned in the military can both assist and impede success in civilian academic environments. At a meeting of veterans on the su campus in the fall of 2011, one veteran spoke about the need for tutors to help student veterans learn the abstractly critical process of learning through questioning, what he called "a different way to think, or a different way to look at things" that was prevalent at su: "[A tutor for student veterans] doesn't necessarily need to know the subject, but just [needs to be able to teach] the whole thought process. Like in the military we're taught to think in a cookbook fashion. At su you're not. At su you're supposed to think outside the box and approach problems in a different way. I'm getting crushed now because the way I've been taught to think about problems and troubleshoot does not work at su."

Veterans' transition from the military milieu into college is marked by contradictions and conflicts between institutional demands. Student veterans framed military and civilian differences as dichotomous: they spoke about hands-on (military) versus abstract (academic) learning; competency-based versus comprehension-based instruction; structured versus unstructured time and assignments; explicit versus covert hierarchy; formal versus informal dress; and group versus individual orientation. Yet it was clear from their descriptions that their experiences were not bound by simple dichotomies; rather, the transition into civilian college was a complex and contradictory process, and individual veterans experienced the contradictions of this transition in diverse ways.

Pedagogical Disjunctions:
Kinesthetic and Abstract Learning Styles

How is it that I can get through all this stuff, throwing grenades and firing
rifles, but I can't get through community college?
EVIE, Central College

Basic training relies on personal contact and kinesthetic, hands-on pedagogies, placing intense emphasis on the relation between trainer and trainees. Interview subjects recalled basic details about their drill instructors—name, voice, mannerisms—with intensely negative or positive affect (usually negative, but sometimes both). Contemporary military recruits train for deployment into combat zones, and veterans said their military learning processes felt immediate and applicable to life-or-death situations. This immediacy and intensity was not present in college, where many experienced the content and process of learning as passive, abstract, without context, and, as some said, occurring in slow motion. They were unaccustomed to the expectations of civilian classrooms, where they were asked to absorb facts and concepts without being called on to immediately demonstrate the practical application of their newly acquired knowledge.

When we met in 2010, Evie, a thirty-year-old Central College student, was making her second attempt at college—she had tried before, immediately after leaving the Army, but had dropped out after failing her classes. Over coffee in an Orchard Valley café, Evie spoke about her reasons for joining the Army. She grew up in a working-class neighborhood in South Tucson, Arizona; in her family, going to college was neither an expectation nor a financial possibility. Her parents had recently immigrated from Mexico and could not pay for college. After high school, Evie joined the Army because "there was no other option to get out" of her neighborhood: "We didn't have money to go right into school. My dad was a laborer, and my mom didn't work. So we didn't have a lot of money. The recruiters come to the high school in your senior year and they say, 'Hey, we'll give you this, that, money for school, and you get to travel all over the world,' and it sounds good."

Evie enlisted as an Army medic. She was sent twice to Iraq to work in field hospitals. After leaving the Army, Evie enrolled in college, intending to continue her education in the medical field. But after her highly physical experience in Iraq, she said it was difficult to learn when she couldn't perceive any practical application for her coursework. She felt overwhelmed at the new set of skills her academic environment demanded, and she struggled with the sedentary learning conditions of college: "There wasn't any hands-on—it was all out of a textbook. There was nothing that got us out of the chairs or anything like that. That was so frustrating—I couldn't learn like that. . . . I just didn't have any confidence that I was good at any of that type of thing—like having to sit down and read a book and look for these little clues, and like study techniques, things like that—and how to read a textbook and follow it, or take notes, that type of thing. It was too much."

Evie noted a sharp contrast between adrenaline-filled applied training exercises, where failure to master a procedure could have fatal consequences, and the sedentary, extended accumulation of knowledge (the relevance of which she could rarely discern) involved in academic study. She said that her inability to master what she considered the basic skills of being a student (sitting still in a chair, decoding academic texts, and participating in discussions) made her feel incompetent. Feeling like a failure in her first attempt at college, Evie did not believe she could succeed in an academic environment. She sought to regain a sense of competence by returning to a more familiar learning environment, and reenlisted in the Army.[11]

Evie was accustomed to learning in the military training milieu, where corporeal, practical activity served as behavioral patterning for combat performance. In contrast, her civilian college program stressed abstract and deliberative learning based on concepts rather than actions. She had a highly developed, action-oriented skill set for emergency medical care in war zones, but she had not developed or practiced deliberative cognitive and theoretical skills.

In the collegiate academic environment, student veterans are expected to question established knowledge and beliefs. This type of measured intellectual practice was antithetical to the reflex-driven response required on the battlefield. While some veterans embraced the new discipline of critical thinking, for many, like Evie, the transition to college was a disorienting experience that produced feelings of incompetence: "That's what made me have low confidence. Because I was like, 'How is this that I can get through all this stuff, throwing grenades and firing rifles, but I can't get through community college?' I mean, some people don't even show up to class and they graduate with their degree. It really was like torture—it really was, 'cause I felt so incompetent."

Evie entered college a highly trained Army medic who functioned well in high-pressure combat environments, but in community college, where she was surrounded by what she considered (at best) half-hearted students, she flailed. Evie's feelings of incompetence in college echoed her feelings of incompetence in basic training. Yet in the Army, her incompetence was shared with other recruits, making her feelings more tolerable. Because her entire cohort of recruits felt similarly disoriented and inept, Evie did not experience her basic training struggles as individual failures. In college, Evie was surrounded by students who were adept at figuring out the unwritten rules, expectations, and codes governing college life, including those who figured out how to graduate without even showing up to class.

Veterans struggled with the expectation to interrogate meanings and develop their own analyses of complex issues in college. College students are asked to make connections among diverse perspectives and to develop well-argued critiques. In this sense, college required exactly what they were trained not to do, that is, to question authority and work without orders. If the college mission is to cultivate curiosity, follow insights, and develop imagination, this stood in contrast to the reflexive command practices of basic training.

These tasks were particularly difficult for another Central College student and Iraq war veteran, Julio, twenty-seven, who was raised in rural central California. Julio enlisted in the Army in the hope of gaining skills that would lead to a job and financial security. Julio's family, second-generation immigrants from Mexico, went through periods of homelessness that made it difficult for Julio to attend school regularly. After leaving the Army, Julio worked in retail, but he ultimately enrolled in college to challenge himself and because he wanted to take advantage of his GI Bill benefits. When asked to name the hardest thing about being in college, he responded, "Elaborating": "You know, finding scholarly sources, doing the research. Like [the teacher asks], 'What do you think of China?' [I say,] 'I think China is a good country.' [The teacher says,] 'What else do you think?' [pauses]. . . . It's like trying to get in too deep—having to break apart, break apart, break apart. It's hard for me—I can't do it."

Julio was asked by instructors to do what he found most difficult: to delve into a subject, weigh and formulate new perspectives, and engage in the fine-grained work of constructing and contesting arguments. For Julio, having to "break apart, break apart, break apart" was a painstaking process that was neither gratifying nor interesting after his experience conducting ground transport convoys through combat zones in Iraq. When we spoke, he was at the point of dropping out of school:

> If I get a job, I'm not going to finish school. I'm done with whatever I have. I don't even care if I have to pay it back—then I'm just going to have to pay it. But I'm not interested anymore because I don't have time for a bachelor's or master's. I don't have time for a thousand-word essay. I don't have time for the research. I just don't. I'm a hands-on person. I like to go experience stuff. I don't like to be in one spot for too long. And half the people in the military, I'm going to have to say, are just like me.[12]

Class and cultural issues surfaced in Julio's story. In contrast to many of his Central College classmates, Julio did not grow up in an environment in which college was contemplated. Like many working-class community college students—civilian and military—Julio entered Central College with little academic preparation. Julio was never an avid student, so his current discomfort with school predates his experience in the military. Moreover, Julio was not intrinsically motivated to get a college education. But he might have had a different experience in community college had he been given more academic and social support. Julio's statement that he is "a hands-on person" presents this as an essential part of himself, not simply a product of his prior training. Julio saw himself as the type of person who responds to experiential learning rather than abstract inquiry, and extended this essential quality to other military personnel.

Practical Competence and Theoretical Comprehension

When you're here in community college and you're learning about anthropology or history, biology, what have you, it's harder to see how that translates to real life, so I think that's why some [veterans] have a hard time taking it seriously.
BRANDON, Los Santos Community College and Southwest University

Student veterans viewed the content of their college classes as lacking practical applicability, making it difficult to take course content seriously. This was true of two SU student veterans, Grant and Brandon. Grant was raised in upstate New York by white working-class parents—a bus driver and a secretary. Lacking both the money and the directed focus needed to continue his education, Grant enlisted in the Army after high school, ultimately serving in Iraq on a bomb-detection team. After leaving the Army, he enrolled in a suburban California community college before transferring to Southwest University to major in engineering:

I knew I wanted to go to college eventually, but didn't know what I wanted to do right then. My brother [who was in the Army] was talking about how he threw grenades—he was living in Germany—and I thought that was cool. I wanted to be cool like him. But I think the major reason I enlisted was college. I actually have to pat myself on the back, 'cause they offered me the choice of a straight up [enlistment] bonus—$3,000 cash in hand—or an additional, like, a ton of money for college, on top of the GI Bill, which I took, and I paid a "kicker," so I was definitely thinking about school afterwards. I was thinking about throwing grenades and being cool, but I definitely was also thinking about school.[13]

During his military training, Grant felt most engaged when learning practical combat skills. He knew that knowledge of first aid or bomb detection could save lives during combat. He connected the process of learning to the ultimate use of that knowledge:

I remember the first aid training. I really took it seriously, just in case I needed to apply a tourniquet on somebody. I really took my time learning it, and I'd ask questions off to the side. I was an active learner when it came to the first aid stuff. And when it came to the bomb stuff, to the finding bombs, they had 100 percent of my attention when they were talking about this. [Studying in college] is not as riveting, because I probably don't consider this stuff as being [similarly] real. The sense of urgency is what I don't feel as much now. If I don't know this stuff, it's going to be all right. I can go look it up in a book. . . . So that kind of took the wind out of my sails a little bit, but I still get good grades.

Like other veterans, Grant perceived a divide between the active process of learning potentially life-saving course content, and the less riveting, and what he called the less "real" content of college textbooks. Similarly, SU student Brandon found it easier to take seriously his military competence-based training. Brandon was raised in rural Minnesota by fundamentalist Christian parents. Growing up, he was naturally curious and had an analytic nature. His parents homeschooled him, and Brandon taught himself by reading every book he could find. After discharge from the Army, Brandon enrolled in college, first at Los Santos Community College, and then at SU. He was successful in his major at SU, but his transition to community college after leaving the Army had been rough:

In the military, [training] is taken pretty seriously: like when you're shot, you're shot; when you're dead, you're dead. It's very clear that this [infantry] education is useful. [Soldiers] recognize that what we're learning has a real-world translation that we can recognize. And in [civilian] school, it's not readily apparent how learning the sum of all x over x bar— statistics, or whatever—applies to anything. Especially with abstract things. In the military we learn abstract things as well, like radio wave propagation. But I guess you could say that that has a very functional element too, because it helps you learn how to intercept signals better. In the military it's very easy to see that education is practical. And when you're here in community college and you're learning about anthropology or history, biology, or what have you, it's harder to see how that translates to real life, so I think that's why some people have a hard time taking it seriously.

This dichotomous distinction between what they saw as practical education and "less serious" college courses was voiced by many veterans. This framing was inculcated during basic training.

Cultural Disjunctions:
Battle Buddies and Individual Orientation

> If you see someone obviously make a mistake or if they have the potential to
> make a mistake, get 'em out of that situation, help 'em out,
> because if they go down, you're gonna go down.
> **ABEL**, Central College

One of the biggest disjunctions reported by veterans entering civilian schools was the stark change from the collective practice and common goals of the military to the individualized practice of the civilian student. Student veterans in community college confronted the financial burden of civilian living expenses after giving up the subsidized housing, food, and medical care provided by the military. After leaving the "Army bubble" (which one veteran described as a being like a self-contained biosphere where all necessities were provided), veterans felt themselves to be very much on their own. Not only daily living but also school success was now a personal responsibility. For recently returned veterans trained to affiliate with a group and to adopt a communal identity, this disjunction, coupled with the harsh financial realities of a recession economy, proved daunting. Most student veterans felt alienated from the individualism, interpersonal competition, and self-focus of civilian society. Many also viewed their civilian classmates as representative of an individualistic culture, overly preoccupied with individual desires and personal well-being. To them, individualistic civilian culture seemed like a grotesque inversion of the collective ethos they learned in the military. This led to estrangement from their civilian classmates and the sense that civilian life didn't feel real. Southwest University student Grant said,

> When I got back, I just didn't feel like anything was real, and I still have that problem. Things were very tangible in the Army—you do this because if you don't, somebody can get hurt, or die. So you have to just get over yourself because what's going on is so much bigger than you. Then you get to the civilian world, and it's all about *your* feelings and what do *you* want to do, and you learn all this stuff in school and then you graduate and maybe you don't even use it, so it's just a very fake world. So it's kind of hard to get motivated sometimes. [Speaker's emphasis.]

Central College student Cody also felt alienated from the individualism of civilian life. He struggled with depression in college. He felt lost without the purpose that guided him and his fellow soldiers, to whom he felt accountable:

I almost can't function as a civilian any more. I could do really well in the military—I had a purpose then. I don't see [my purpose in civilian life] as clearly as I did when I was in the military. I had a job. I was relied on. I was important to somebody because [fellow soldiers] relied on me. Now, what's my purpose, other than to myself? I rely on myself now, and only myself, and nobody relies on me but me. I would say that was my motivation in the military: you never want to let anybody down. I guess I lost a sense of purpose when I left the military, so I do think that I was better in the military than I am as a civilian.

Cody mourned the loss of what he considered the better military version of himself. A personal grief came from the loss of collective affiliation and group identity, and many student veterans with whom I spoke shared in this grief. Some said that they disliked interacting with civilian classmates because they lacked a shared experience. This aversion led many student veterans to avoid general campus activities. Student veterans referred nostalgically to the intensity of their military experience, where living in life-or-death circumstances heightened their sense of purpose, their sense of competence, and their awareness of being alive.[14] Many spoke about losing their acuity, saying that material excess in the United States created an ease of daily life that muted what they considered the best parts of themselves, forged through conditions of hardship. Grant explained, "When people get out of the Army, they say they'll go off to do bigger and better things, but that's just not the case. I just think, 'I'll never be better than that. I'll never be more important than that.' I think that's where the reality thing comes in. When you see what civilians care about, you think, 'This isn't real—this is such a fake world.'" The psychological consequences of military combat trauma include feelings of alienation, isolation, and the belief that civilians will not be able to understand the military experience. Some student veterans saw this gulf as an unbridgeable divide.

Veterans talked about their alienation from civilians in the company of other military members in campus veterans' club meetings, veterans-only classes, at bars, and on social media forums. Often these conversations involved a tone of superiority or even contempt for individualistic civilians. Yet in one-on-one interviews, where veterans were separate from the need to socially perform a military role, their tone was often wistful. What I heard most commonly from veterans was that they missed the camaraderie and support of fellow soldiers.

In basic training and in military service, soldiers support each other to comply with time and activity structures. But in civilian schools, it is the individual student's responsibility to figure out class enrollment, schedules, and requirements, without explicit orders from a command hierarchy or support from other soldiers who are sharing exactly the same experience.

Early in basic training, every recruit is assigned a battle buddy, a fellow soldier with whom one is mutually responsible for keeping on schedule, on track, and out of danger. The concept of the battle buddy acknowledges that some situations require more than one body and more than one set of eyes and limbs. In combat, the battle buddy system ensures that no soldier is alone in dangerous circumstances. Logistics are supremely important in military training and operations; meetings, meals, transportation, and training all require coordinated movement. Mutual accountability is integral to the military habitus and makes good practical sense on bases and in fields of combat where plans and schedules may change at the last minute. Changes are transmitted and coordinated through a chain of command, and each individual depends on others for information. On an operational level, one soldier's confusion or delay can hold up the rest of the unit, exposing the soldier and others to danger and threatening the military mission. On a social level, deviation from the group dynamic threatens one's ability to participate fully in the highly structured activities in everyday military life, and in the culture of mutual accountability. Central College student veteran Abel appreciated the military practice of mutual responsibility: "I think [the military] teaches you camaraderie and teamwork, where you always had to teach your buddy. If you see someone obviously make a mistake or if they could have the potential to make a mistake, get 'em out of that situation. You know, help 'em out because if they go down, you're gonna go down. It's that weakest link thing. You're only as strong as your weakest link— that's how it was. That's what it teaches you."

Mitchell, also a Central College student, learned this camaraderie and the life-or-death stakes of military relationships in basic training: "Something happened halfway through basic training where everyone started to realize that, 'Hey, this is your man to the left and right. If you don't help him, then he's going to get you killed or you're going to get him killed.' They beat it into us, not physically beat it into us, but through mental drills and whatnot." The knowledge that social camaraderie in the barracks might become a means of survival on the battlefield endured for veterans. The lack of a structured system of mutual accountability left many veterans feeling unmoored and lacking in motivation.

Explicit and Covert Formality and Hierarchy

You have to know your role. In the Army, the teacher's the teacher.
That's the boss. Some kids at community college will give lip or not take
teachers seriously or not listen, or pack up early and things like that—
that would just not happen in the Army.

GRANT, Southwest University

The unifying goal of military socialization is to transform diverse recruits into a disciplined group trained to respond to authority and the demands of rank and hierarchy. This contrasts with the informality of civilian colleges, where the student-teacher hierarchy is less pronounced. Informality is especially notable in community colleges, where many students tend to be older (in some cases, older than their instructors) and come with a diversity of life experiences. Conflicts sometimes arise around issues of respect and authority in civilian college environments. In particular, the misaligned cultural norms between instructors and student veterans can produce daily conflicts, even when both sides are attempting to demonstrate respect.

One such conflict is related to veterans' training in strict, hierarchical respect for authority. For veterans, the civilian instructor represents a higher-ranking authority figure, but some civilian instructors seek to mitigate hierarchical relations between teacher and students. For example, Evie's instructor asked Evie to address her by her first name. Evie refused, saying that she felt this would be disrespectful of the instructor and of her military training. In this conflict, both Evie and her instructor believed that they were promoting a position of mutual respect, but their understandings of what respect entailed came from divergent cultural reference points: "My instructor told me, 'Don't call me ma'am. Call me Rachel.' And I said, 'I won't call you Rachel' because I consider her my superior and that applies wherever I'm at. That's one of those disciplines that won't ever leave me, and that's important to me; that's very, very important to me." In this instance, both parties attempted to signal respect.

The instructor sought to demonstrate her respect for students, including Evie, by rejecting hierarchical norms and insisting on the mutuality implied by first-name address. Evie sought to demonstrate respect by holding to her military practice of deference to rank and refusing to treat her professional superior as a peer: "[Instructor] Harner was probably just as offended as I was that I refused to call her what she wanted me to call her. I think at that point it does become a battle of your morals versus their morals, or whatever the case may be, but I still call her R. Harner because I don't find it comfortable to call her Rachel."

Evie resolved the conflict of cultural norms—which she understood as a moral battle—by choosing to honor a disciplinary practice that is an important part of her identity and "won't ever leave" her. Her decision to call the instructor R. Harner is an everyday example of the conflict between ingrained military social habits and the expectations of a civilian instructor. Evie enacted her military habitus in a civilian educational site, and military law continued to hold sway over her practices. Unlike Evie, who found a mode of address that upheld her commitment to hierarchy, some veterans were not able to negotiate conflict with the social and academic system.

Some veterans became angry when their civilian classmates did not show respect for authority. Southwest University student Mack said that when he started at community college, it was difficult to keep his temper in class when he felt that his classmates were disrespectful to instructors. His military training led him to feel personally offended when civilian students held side conversations during lectures. On more than one occasion, Mack expressed his frustration to the class, which damaged his relationships with fellow students. He felt that his classmates saw him as short tempered and perhaps unstable.[15] But keeping quiet in the face of disrespect also exacted an emotional toll: "A couple of times, I would stand up in class and go, 'It's really rude when you disrespect [the instructor's] time like this. It's rude to me. It's rude to your professor.' I'd say things like that, but not that often. Mostly I'd just sit there and get mad in my own head and just get madder and madder."

The issue of perceived disrespect was especially pronounced among student veterans at the community college level. Veterans at su said that the culture was more respectful toward professors, instead raising stories of disrespect from their pretransfer colleges. But even at su, student veterans struggled with a lack of defined social roles and codified behavioral norms. Southwest University student Grant said, "You have to know your role. In the Army, the teacher's the teacher. That's the boss. Some kids at community college—you don't see it here [at su]—will give lip or not take teachers seriously or not listen, or pack up early, and things like that—that would just not happen in the Army. I still don't pack up early. I think it's very disrespectful. That's carried over for me."

Southwest University student Ricardo got into clashes with civilian students at his community college in Los Angeles. After he was discharged from the Navy following deployments to Iraq and Somalia, Ricardo felt personally offended by students' casual attitude toward instructors. He responded to this perceived disrespect as if he were still in the military and fantasized about addressing his classmates in the manner of a drill instructor:

I would sit in the front to learn the lessons, but hearing people talk in the background, there were times when I wanted to get up and say [to them], "Get up!" Or if people were sleeping, I wanted to tell them to go to the back of the room and stand up. In one of my speech classes, I was able to say that—I told them all they were dirtbags. It allowed me to speak how I felt about the class. It was great. I told them, "You—sit up straight. And you—stop texting."[16]

Relations of Formality and Informality

One thing that hit me was: there were too many colors.
I was so used to brown or green, gray or blue, and now everyone was wearing different
things and everyone is yelling and talking, and I wasn't used to that.
RICARDO, Southwest University

Many student veterans found the generalized informality of college distracting after the strictly enforced behavioral norms they adhered to in the military. Veterans came to campus having matured in asymmetrical, situationally specific ways. Many felt that they had more life experience than some instructors and certainly more than most other students. But this experience did not necessarily translate into skills for living in a socially heterogeneous civilian campus environment and interacting with classmates who have varied attitudes and beliefs.[17] Ricardo said that the shift to a civilian campus felt chaotic after the Navy's strict behavioral and dress codes. He felt disoriented by the diversity of clothing styles and expressions. The college campus seemed disorderly, and Ricardo felt adrift:

[Coming to college] was tough in the sense that it was chaos—every single day. One thing that hit me was there were too many colors. I was so used to brown or green, gray or blue, and now everyone was wearing different things and everyone is yelling and talking, and I wasn't used to that. It was tough—I didn't understand these kids. I would sit in the front, so I really wouldn't see much action; it was just the instructor and I. In one class I tried sitting in the back—but it affected my performance. I couldn't concentrate.

Ricardo's interest in the course material, specifically in his economics classes, and his appreciation for the professors' abilities to push his thinking helped him to do well in community college, and he transferred to Southwest University. By the time he arrived at su, he had come to appreciate the diversity he previously found so disruptive and disorienting. "[Southwest University] is much better than I expected. I thought this was going to be a crazy regime of studying, books, when I walked through the campus and I saw all these clubs and protests every other day. [But now I think,] 'Yeah, I can say I don't like this. I don't agree with that. I don't agree with this.' I find myself more and more being able to talk about how I feel about different subjects out loud. And that's something I know I couldn't have done before." Ricardo's experience of discovering his ability to express his opinions, of metaphorically finding his voice, was not uncommon among the veterans I interviewed. However, many veterans become discouraged before reaching that point, dropping out of college without making sense of the chaos.

Habituation to External Command

In the Army, you don't really think for yourself. You just do
what you're told, so you don't really grow as a person. Instead of my dad
telling me what to do, it was my first sergeant.
YESENIA, Fulton Community College

Military experience can have a maturing effect on soldiers, but it can also inhibit independence. Soldiers are trained to follow orders through ritual, repetition, and punitive behavior modification. For some soldiers, this created a conditioned reliance on imposed rules and structure. Student veterans struggled to move from externally imposed military time and activity structures to the self-regulation and internal structure required of college students. Central College student and Army veteran Brett said, "Throughout your military career, you're told by your chain of command exactly every minute what to do and when to do it. In civilian school, it's really up to you to go out there and figure out how to do stuff—no one's telling you to do it. No one's giving you a 4:00 A.M. wake-up call to get up and go to school. I think that was the biggest hurdle for me."

Brett's difficulty adjusting to individualized civilian schedules was common among community college students in particular. For many veterans, community college is their point of entry into civilian postsecondary education. Their previous experiences with schooling came from high school or community college satellite campuses on or near military bases where they were still subject to the structured discipline of military schedules. Community college presented a set of demands and expectations very distinct from these experiences. New student veterans had to learn to negotiate less formal school systems while also learning or re-learning how to function as an independent adult in the civilian world: shopping, cooking, renting an apartment, finding a job, and accessing medical care.

Habituation to external command posed a problem for Army veteran Yesenia when she enrolled in college after leaving the military. She had joined the Army with the intent of leaving her childhood home to be independent from her overbearing father, a Vietnam War veteran who ran their home "like an Army base." Yesenia said she joined the Army because "I wanted to *be all I could be*; travel, get paid, get the college money, make something of myself, and get out of town."[18] Though she spoke about her desire to go to college as a prime motivation for enlisting, Yesenia struggled to adapt in community college, because she was unable to identify the courses she wanted to take. When I last spoke with her, Yesenia had recently transferred to a four-year state college, but she continued to have trouble choosing an academic major:

> In the Army, you don't really think for yourself. You just do what you're told, so you don't really grow as a person. Instead of my dad telling me what to do, it was my first sergeant. Or Uncle Sam. Uncle Sam became my dad. And when I got out it was like—okay, now what do I do? What am I going to study at school? I changed my major like ten times. Now I have to hurry and finish my degree—but what do I study? I'd go around asking people what I should study. I want somebody tell me what to do! I'm still trying to figure this out. I'm going back to school now and I still don't know what I want to study. Why can't I figure out what I like?

Yesenia attributed her indecisiveness to being habituated to following orders, and she was concerned that her time-limited military educational benefits would run out before she completed her degree. Because Yesenia could receive educational benefits for a period of no more than ten years, she felt that her indecision cost her crucial time that she needed to finish; the clock on her GI Bill benefits had been ticking since she first entered college.[19]

Class Contradictions

> I hate the snobby kids that are here, the ignorant kids, kids who just think
> they know everything. . . . I guess I don't really like civilians.
> **BRETT**, Central Community College

The issue of who fights in wars and why is important because it speaks to an underlying class bias of an all-volunteer military during times of war: low-income recruits are disproportionately represented in the troops deployed to Iraq and Afghanistan.[20] Proponents of the all-volunteer military downplay the idea of a poverty draft, but by Department of Defense statistics, the majority of recruits come from poor and working-class families, increasingly Hispanic/Latino/a. While 86 percent of lower enlisted ranks are white and come disproportionately from the southern United States, Kleycamp found that enlistment within some U.S. minority populations rises with increased economic and citizenship incentives.[21]

The theme of socioeconomic class repeatedly surfaced in interviews with student veterans, the majority of whom came from working-class backgrounds and would not have been able to pay for college without the GI Bill. For example, SU student Oscar grew up in a high-poverty, high-crime neighborhood in a major urban area in Northern California. Oscar grew up witnessing and participating in street violence. He said he knew that he did not want to follow the path of his older brother, who was involved in selling street drugs. Oscar enlisted in the Marine Corps after the U.S. invasion of Iraq in 2003, but the war was not a major factor in his decision. Rather, he hoped to escape family problems and take advantage of signing bonuses and the promise of college funding. Enlistment enabled Oscar to interrupt a path that might lead to incarceration or death: "Growing up in this city, there was a huge potential of passing away at any given moment. I knew it was a risk [to enlist during wartime] but I wasn't too worried about it. I knew if I died in the streets, my mom's not going to get anything. If I died in Iraq, my mom will get $400,000. That's a lot better."

Oscar's high school teachers never encouraged him to consider college; in fact, they actively steered him away from that possibility, predicting that he would not do well. The son of recent immigrants from Mexico, Oscar had never imagined being successful at school, much less at an elite university like SU: "I grew up around here, but I never knew the prestige SU carried. I was very ignorant. I didn't know the difference between a community college, state, and a university. I didn't have any idea what was going on. I just remember my teachers telling me that I would never amount to anything."

Oscar's self-perception as ignorant was reinforced by his high school teachers, and after entering college, he felt awkward and out of place around younger civilian students whom he viewed as having been born and bred for college.[22] Other veterans went beyond awkwardness to express disdain for civilians they saw as privileged, spoiled, and selfish. Central College student Evie said she struggled with the disparity in life experiences between herself and her classmates based not only on military experience but also on age and socioeconomic class. She said, "[It's difficult] going to class as a thirty-year-old and sitting next to kids right out of high school, or the kids that are maybe a little more privileged; they're riding around in brand-new cars and they show up to class in their pajamas—you know, that type of thing. Seeing that, I was like, 'Wow, are you kidding me? I mean, what's going *on* here?'"

Like most of the student veterans, Evie referred to her classmates as "kids," a term that drew on not just age but socioeconomic class and life experience to describe civilian college students as infantile and spoiled. For Evie, identity and notions of respect were tied to wearing a uniform, so college students' attire of pajama pants (especially for students who could afford to drive new cars) represented a stance of social entitlement, superiority, and disrespect.

Many veterans expressed resentment that civilian students led lives completely untouched by the hardships and sacrifices they faced as combat veterans. After two combat tours in Iraq, Central College student Brett left his position in the Army infantry to go to college. He found it difficult to relate to his fellow students, who failed to recognize his expertise, experience, or authority. Brett felt that being in civilian college represented a move backward in his development: "I hate the snobby kids that are here, the ignorant kids, kids who just think they know everything. It's kind of like that high school scenario all over again. And I wasn't a big fan of high school, with the kids and drama. It's kind of annoying. I guess I don't really like civilians."

Brett's use of the term "kids" to describe his community college classmates signaled his disdain, as well as a separation. Brett viewed interpersonal exchanges with civilian students through the lens of his class background, which he recoded as his military background. Unlike Oscar, who accepted the label of "ignorant" that came from his teachers in high school, Brett considered civilian college students to be the ignorant ones because their economic privilege had limited their life experience. Brett considered his classmates kids even though he was roughly the same age as most other students. Brett generalized his negative feelings about his classmates to all civilians, coming to the conclusion that he didn't like civilians.

Traumatic Response in the Classroom: Cody

In Iraq it was easy: just stay alive. Honestly, coming back here is a whole other war.
CODY, Central College

Many of the psychological mechanisms that helped keep soldiers alive on the battlefield became maladaptive in a college setting. Many veterans experienced enduring symptoms of emotional numbing or detachment, and hypervigilance or constantly being in a state of high alert. Some veterans had long-term, pronounced experiences of these symptoms and were diagnosed with psychological syndrome known as post-traumatic stress disorder (PTSD). Symptoms include reexperiencing traumatic events through intrusive, upsetting memories (flashbacks), nightmares, and intense physical reactions to reminders of the traumatic event (such as racing heartbeat, rapid breathing, nausea, sweating).[23] The syndrome also includes symptoms of avoidance and emotional numbing such as the inability to remember important aspects of the trauma, loss of interest in activities and life in general, and feeling detached from others. Combat veterans suffering from PTSD may experience symptoms of increased anxiety, including insomnia, irritability, difficulty concentrating, and hypervigilance.[24] These symptoms can create difficulties for combat veterans returning home.[25]

Academic environments are designed as a space apart from the everyday working world, organized to minimize distractions and facilitate intellectual inquiry and analysis. But when veterans bring with them into college classrooms battlefield responses such as hypervigilance, fear, paranoia, and heightened sensory awareness of auditory and visual cues, these spaces no longer feel separate or safe. For Central College student Cody, for example, habits instilled through military training and psychologically embedded through combat resurfaced in civilian classrooms, presenting an obstacle to college success.

Cody grew up in a white, working-class family in Central California. He described himself as a rebellious teen who did not get along with his parents in high school. Despite having "spectacular dreams and wants and goals in [his] life," which included going to college, he felt that his life had stalled out after graduating from high school. Cody was arrested and convicted of drunk driving shortly after turning eighteen. While on probation, he worked at what he called two "dead-end jobs" in a warehouse and a skateboard shop. Feeling that his life was "going nowhere," Cody joined the Navy in 2004 because he needed money to go to college and because he wanted to "get the hell out of my situation," which included excessive drinking and intermittent periods of homelessness. Cody scored well on all of his naval aptitude tests, earning scores that qualified him for even the most selective naval occupations: nuclear engineer, special operations, or medic. He wanted to become a Navy corpsman (a medic), but because of his DUI conviction, he was only allowed to enlist as a yeoman, the lowest-ranking administrative-clerical job.[26]

In the Navy, Cody was assigned to guard and transport prisoners at the prison camp Bucca, in Iraq. As a prison guard, Cody learned to pay attention to the smallest details in order to detect potential attacks: "You get used to a certain lifestyle, especially in Iraq, where you're just on alert twenty-four hours a day, seven days a week. The habit gets drilled into you, and that habit becomes your lifestyle. Sometimes [life in a combat zone] was bad—Baghdad was the worst. We were getting mortared left and right up there. The first day that we got to Baghdad, a mortar went through somebody's pod [tent] and killed a guy."

Through continued exposure to attacks, a sense of pervasive danger became ingrained in Cody's psychological makeup: vigilance began as a trained habit, but over time it became what he called a "lifestyle." Eventually, the "mind-set" that helped Cody survive in Baghdad became woven into the fabric of everyday life, where it remained even after leaving Iraq. Cody described living in a state of constant alert and feeling that an attack was imminent and inevitable, viewing anyone unfamiliar to him as a potential enemy: "You just never knew. You always had [the possibility of getting killed] in the back of your head, but you just never thought about it, because if you thought about it, you'd just freak out. You're out there—it could happen—but you're going to die if you [freeze up and] don't do anything. If you freak out—that's when you're going to get killed. If you can figure out how to put that behind you and just do your job, you have a lot better chance of surviving."

This state of constant alert, known to psychologists as hypervigilance, is a common symptom in trauma survivors. The mind continues to perceive threats even after the actual threat is no longer present. Because Cody's mind was accustomed to anticipating assaults from unknown attackers, he continued to respond to groups of unfamiliar people, including civilian classmates and instructors, as if they were potentially hostile enemy combatants. In Iraq, what he called "just do[ing his] job" entailed being constantly vigilant and avoiding dwelling on moral dilemmas or weighing the potential consequences of his participation in war.

After leaving the Navy, Cody enrolled at Central College, where his intense awareness of details in his surroundings made it difficult to sit comfortably in a college classroom. Cody didn't know how to respond to the college environment and his civilian classmates without the support of other soldiers:

How do you go from that mind-set where you're waiting—you know something [violent] is going to happen; you just don't know when or how—or how bad it's going to be? You go from living that mind-set for a year, where you knew who was who, and you knew the good guys and you kind of stuck together with those guys because you trusted those guys literally with your life. Now you take that group of guys, whose job is really to rely on each other, and you throw them out into the civilian life and say, "Okay, here you go!"

Cody failed his first semester at Central College, and he believes this was due to his PTSD symptoms. Sitting in classrooms in a state of high alert, surrounded by people unknown to him, made it difficult for Cody to tolerate being on a civilian campus and nearly impossible for him to concentrate on the course material.

CODY: You just looked at people and paid attention to little things about them so that you had that upper edge, so you knew what to expect.

EM: Who would you think might be a threat?

CODY: I wouldn't respond necessarily to any specific person, but I would respond to the threat, you know? Maybe it is the kid with the button-down and the tie—who knows? He was low on my list of possible threats, so my eyes would go other places. Everybody would be on a [different threat] level, and it would be like—"Okay, this guy's near the top, and this guy's down where the petite girls are." You know that you could flip them and they'd break a bone.

EM: So the thought is, if things turned, you'd be prepared?

CODY: Yeah, you're constantly [pauses]—I might not be calculating stuff out in my head, but I'm using more of my senses. My hearing has gone up because I'm focusing on listening to things, like I want to know that the door behind me is opening up. How is it opening up? Is it opening up really quick and fast? That tells me that, hey, this guy's coming in really hot and something might be going on. Is [the door] creeping open? Can I hear it creaking? Okay, is this guy trying to pull a fast one on me or not? Is [the door] opening like normal, and is he just trying to walk through the door? Who knows? You're doing that and then you're paying attention to details of everything. Okay, what time is it on the clock? Who knows what's going on, and at what time? What's going on with this guy over here? What's going on with this other guy over there? There's light projecting over there. What could I use as a defense mechanism? How heavy is this table? Oh, there's a fire extinguisher over there. You could use that on somebody. You're just looking, [thinking,] "Okay, if a bomb does go off, where would it explode?"

Cody's tangential thought process indicates his experience of battlefield fear and chaos, even as he sat in an Orchard Valley community college. His mind transposed conditions of combat onto his college classroom. In retrospect, he was able to acknowledge that his fellow students posed no actual physical threat, but Cody spent most of his time in class trying to detect potential threats. Cody's focus on detail created a situation where his brain had to function "in multiple different directions" at once, which made it difficult for him to track the instructor's lecture:

> You're constantly trying to think of possible situations that could happen. When most people are only thinking of what the teacher is saying, we [combat veterans] are trying to be proactive and think about all the situations that are going on. Not only are your senses heightened, but your brain is functioning in multiple different directions because you just don't know how severe [a potential threat] can be. It could be nothing or it could be a nuclear bomb. Who knows what it is, and you have to be ready for anything that could happen. Because if you're not thinking ahead, well, then they are. If they're thinking ahead then they have the upper hand on you. . . . I've been trained to think and react in a certain way. How do you untrain that?

Because each new class was populated by unfamiliar classmates, every college classroom felt unsafe to Cody. His question—"How do you untrain that?"—deserves careful attention, especially in an era when many young men and women go to war in order to pay for college. The college classroom is an important social site where veterans reintegrate into civilian society. It represents a space where students can develop intellectual and emotional understandings of their differences and increase their capacity to critically engage diverse worldviews. Yet this was not possible for Cody in his first semester of college. Unable to concentrate in class, he gave up, stopped going to school, and failed his classes.

> CODY: You can't pay attention in class because you're too busy paying attention to everybody else. At home, I had insomnia for the longest time. I was exhausted but I just couldn't go to sleep because my mind would not stop turning. Even when I'm lying in bed, I'm thinking of tomorrow. I'm reevaluating what happened today and then I'm thinking about tomorrow and how I can make tomorrow better. When you do that every day, all day, all night, you get to the point where you're just beat. You're not paying attention in class; you're not really doing the work at home

because you're just exhausted. Now I'm overwhelmed on a daily basis. So I just shut down. I just locked myself in my room pretty much.

EM: That was your first semester here?

CODY: That was about ten weeks into it, because I didn't go to my last six weeks. I just stopped going to class. I kind of just gave up. I was like, "I just can't do this anymore. I'm so stressed out on a daily basis that I don't know how to live a normal life anymore." It was the point where every day I wished that I was over in Iraq. I still have those times; I still wish I was over there. I might be getting shot at or mortared or stabbed or whatever, but that's simpler than being here.

Cody felt overwhelmed and cut himself off from others. He did not respond to his instructors' e-mailed messages of concern. He felt ashamed and saw his inability to function in class as a weakness. He could not face his instructors and could not give them a reason for his absence.

Depressed, anxious, and suffering from panic attacks, Cody tried to reenlist to get sent back to Iraq. Instead, he ended up at the Veterans Health Administration emergency room, where he was given medication and counseling. While he was grateful to get help, Cody was also frustrated that the effects of his military service made it difficult for him to redeem the enlistment promise of education: "I couldn't even do the simplest thing like go to class and pay attention in class. But this is why I joined the military—to go back to school. It's not like I'm not [going to class] because I don't want to do it. I want to do it. I sacrificed four and a half years of my life to go [to college], and I'm not able to do it now?"

I heard similar stories from other student veterans about the effects of combat trauma on their ability to function in college. Veterans coped with the effects of traumatic stress in various ways and with varying success. Southwest University student Francisco had trouble concentrating in class due to his condition of tinnitus, or chronic ringing in his ears.[27] As a result of repeated exposure to loud explosions, Francisco is now very sensitive to noise. Like Cody, Francisco was distracted by "every little thing that's going on, every click of the clock ticking, someone slamming a door, or a chair moving. I think, 'Okay, well why did that happen so suddenly? What's going on out there?'"

Francisco learned to adapt to his new surroundings by wearing earplugs on campus to filter out unnecessary noise, and he developed other strategies to calm himself down before entering a classroom. For instance, he would arrive early at class to give himself time to lower his heart rate and body temperature, which helped him to stay focused in class: "I kind of think about [calming down] before class while I'm waiting. I'm always early, just kind of relaxing. Especially when it's hot—I want to make sure that I'm not hot when I go into class because then I'm just that much more agitated. I try to take notes as well as I can because then I'll focus on just the notes."

In the course of this research, I observed firsthand traumatic stress reactions in some of the veteran research participants. For example, I conducted some interviews in a small, windowless research office on the su campus. Veterans walking into the darkened room would noticeably recoil when I opened the door. One veteran told me that the darkness reminded him of rooms he entered during military raids in Iraq. I quickly learned to warn veterans in advance that the room would be dark and to let me enter the room first so I could turn on the lights. Though it may seem small, this example represents the common and enduring effects of war trauma.

Silences and Erasures

Though the effects of military training and experiences were often present with veterans as they sat in civilian classrooms, instructors and civilian classmates often rendered these experiences invisible. As a result of the shift to an all-volunteer military, the majority of U.S. civilians live their lives untouched by the current wars, and some veterans felt a social distance from civilians because they felt that civilians lacked understanding about the conditions and consequences of combat. For many civilian students, veterans' war experiences are unknown and irrelevant. Other students feel uncomfortable bringing up the topic of the war or asking about veterans' experiences because they are afraid of saying the wrong thing and inadvertently offending veterans.[28] Whatever the reason for their classmates' silence, it produces the social erasure of veterans' wartime experiences.

For many veterans, the distance between their military-identified world and the civilian student world was both self-imposed and socially constructed. Southwest University student Kevin said he felt like an outcast by virtue of age and experience when he first enrolled in community college: "Having tattoos and looking older, I felt like kind of an outcast, especially when I was first starting in [community college]. I was in class with sixteen-, seventeen-, eighteen-year-olds. I was only twenty-four, but it was like a big jump. I didn't really get along with very many people. I just kind of did my own thing. I mean, I just felt no connection with people. I tried to be friendly, but it was just—[pauses] nothing ever happened, connection-wise. Everything just dissipated." As a new student, Kevin wanted to connect with civilian classmates but was unable to bridge the divide, and retreated into social isolation. Rather than feeling that his experience was actively disregarded, Kevin sensed that he just did not fit into the social milieu of the college.

Southwest University student Grant was frustrated when he returned to college after a sixteen-month deployment leading a bomb-detection squad in Iraq. He said that his civilian classmates were not interested in hearing about his experiences or opinions: "I'm kind of a wealth of knowledge about what's going on over there [in Iraq] and [students] wouldn't ask me questions. They didn't care. I thought I had some insight, but nobody really cared about it." It bothered Grant that the knowledge he accumulated during his military experience—knowledge he considered central to his identity—was ignored in the classroom context.

Grant described an incident in an English class at his former community college in suburban central California. Students had been assigned to choose a poem to read, and Grant found many of his classmates' choices frivolous. When it was his turn, he chose to read a poem about the death of a solider:

> I definitely remember saying in class, "This is really stupid." We were reading poetry. I brought in the poem "Death of the Ball Turret Gunner." It's really graphic: basically this guy gets killed and they wash his body out [of his gunnery turret] with a hose. I read that poem because of how simple it was and because there's no thought to when people get killed over there [in Iraq]. They make it out to be some heroic thing, but you just get blown up, and you're just dead, and that's just it. So I'm trying to tell everybody, "You think you're so important, but if any of you got hit by a car this morning, we would all still be in class here, learning today's lesson." And maybe ten people in this world would care, like your parents, and some family and friends, and most of them will actually get over it within the year, and only some affected for a very long time. You know how . . . [pauses] how insignificant you are. When they want you to be very significant, but you really don't matter.[29]

In reading this poem to the class, Grant was attempting to make his experience with death and war visible, to make himself visible in the civilian classroom. He was attempting to introduce the painful reality of war—and the ephemerality of life—into the consciousness of his civilian classmates. For Grant, death in war was not "some heroic thing" as "they" (presumably U.S. society) would have the class believe, but simply, and brutally, the end of life. He wanted civilian students to realize that as they sat reading poetry, soldiers were dying on unseen battlefields.

Despite a public discourse about the heroics of dying in war, Grant felt that he and his fellow soldiers were rendered insignificant by a societal denial about the current wars and soldiers' experience. For students like Grant, silence about war made him feel alienated from his fellow students. Because there is a generalized silence about the wars on college campuses, it is difficult to know if Grant was correct in assuming that fellow students did not care, or whether they simply did not know whether it was appropriate to ask him questions, but in either case, his experience was made invisible.

Grant and Kevin felt invisible in classrooms, disregarded or outcast because they could not bridge the experience gap with civilian students. Grant wanted that difference and his wartime experience recognized, and Kevin was unable to connect with the younger students. Yet other veterans were reticent about sharing their former military status. They felt that aspects of their military experience were painful, personally conflictive, and potentially controversial, so sharing basic facts of their lives in a classroom represented a risk to their emotional health. Some student veterans said that the most foundational experiences of their lives—being in the military and fighting in war—were precisely the experiences they could not or did not want to claim. This resulted in a process of self-erasure that widened and reinforced the distance between veterans and civilian students.

Southwest University student Jordan's experience illustrates this tension. Jordan was raised in a white working-class family on a farm in the foothills of the Sierra Nevada. He joined the Marines in 2003 because, though he was a good student in high school, he didn't have money to attend college immediately after graduating. He was also looking for adventure and wanted to get out of his small hometown. "I wanted to see the world," he said. Jordan applied to SU from his military outpost in Iraq and learned that he had been accepted while still on active duty. Within days of being discharged from the Marines, he began classes at SU. He majored in linguistics, to study a field related to his work in Iraq as a military intelligence analyst, a field that would make use of his Arabic speaking and comprehension skills.

Jordan had completed two tours of Iraq working as a cryptological linguist, where his job was to listen to intercepted messages and determine who should be classified as an enemy and targeted for arrest or assassination. Jordan expressed deep conflicts about his participation in the war. His job was to secretly monitor Iraqis as they went through their daily lives at work, in marketplaces, and even at home with their children. Jordan said he felt "like a hunter" stalking human prey. He was not prepared to talk about his military background with new acquaintances at su, but when other students discovered he was studying linguistics, they usually asked him a typical introductory question for linguistics majors: "What languages do you speak?" For Jordan, the answer inevitably led to unwanted conversations about his background:

> Of course when I said I spoke Arabic, [students] wonder[ed] how is it that I speak Arabic. I'm just some random white guy from California. I grew up in the sticks, and I speak Arabic. So I felt this burden: either I have to be deceptive, or I have to be honest. Unless I want to create some fictional story, I was having to go through this whole thing of explaining my story. So here's all of this shit that I didn't want to deal with that just comes with my major. I didn't know it was going to be emotionally such a burden to be some certain major. We say things like, "You're not defined by your major." Bullshit. It depends. Maybe [addressing the interviewer] *you're* not, but I was, and it was overwhelming.

Jordan correctly pointed out that a white female student of anthropology and education could pass as an unremarkable member of those academic communities and so would rarely need to reveal the history or motivations for choosing her course of study. Jordan did not enjoy the same privilege. A seemingly innocuous conversation starter forced Jordan to reveal his military history, a complicated and painful topic. This inhibited him from forming relationships with civilian students. Whereas Grant was eager to be asked about his experience and recognized for his expertise, Jordan did not want to reveal his military past to fellow Arabic language students, many of whom were from the Middle East. Because Jordan could not manage this social dynamic, the situation became untenable, and he dropped out of his linguistics major and out of su.[30]

After leaving military life and entering college, veterans must learn, unlearn, and relearn various sets of norms, identities, and customs. Many veterans find that the habitus of military life is unhelpful in college. The clash of pedagogical and cultural norms and practices creates disjunctions that impede soldiers' reintegration into civilian life and college success.

· 3 ·

CAMPUS VETERAN
SUPPORT INITIATIVES

In 1945, S. H. Kraines wrote of World War II veterans, "the returning veteran, even more than the usual college student, needs the best and most that can be offered."[1] Today, many Americans continue to hold dear the belief that it is incumbent on civilian institutions, particularly colleges, to repay a debt of sacrifice incurred by the nation for sending soldiers to war. This belief has been the basis for numerous educational programs designed to help veterans succeed in college. Between 2008 and 2012, more than 500,000 veterans of current wars enrolled in college, and the number of contemporary veterans enrolling in college is rising.[2] Yet many veterans still struggle to make the transition into civilian social worlds and into college.[3]

Many veterans drop out of college without fully utilizing their GI Bill education benefits, a fact that raised concern among educators and veterans' advocates and that produced a body of scholarly literature on the needs of veterans in college. In line with this literature, this chapter discusses institutionally generated initiatives to support veterans. These initiatives are academic spaces that translate and express the perceived needs of student veterans. The chapter begins with a discussion of the foundations of popular ideologies regarding veterans followed by a brief review of contemporary practices, widely considered to be what are known as "best practices" for veteran support programs on college campuses.

Military Superiority and the Student Veteran

We call on the warrior to exemplify the qualities necessary to prosecute war—courage, loyalty and self-sacrifice. The Soldier, neglected and even shunned during peacetime, is suddenly held up as the exemplar of our highest ideals, the savior of the state. The Soldier is often whom we want to become, though secretly many of us, including most soldiers, know that we cannot match the ideal held out before us.

CHRIS HEDGES, *War Is a Force That Gives Us Meaning*

I use the term "military superiority" to describe an ideology that treats veterans as representatives of the U.S. military project. Within this ideology, soldiers and veterans represent a unique and distinct subset of the population; they are considered superior in physical prowess, in moral fiber, in civic spirit and engagement, and in less-tangible individual attributes like discipline, honor, righteousness, and maturity. A fundamental underlying assumption of the ideology of military superiority is that veterans are to be admired principally for their affiliation with the military and more so than civilians, who are positioned within this ideology as weaker, less civic minded, and less disciplined. Military superiority is a prominent social force throughout much of U.S. history, especially during times of war.[4]

The notion of military superiority is not new, nor unique to the United States; throughout history warriors have been portrayed as possessing superior moral and physical attributes. Dating back to ancient Sparta, when mothers refused to swaddle their babies in the hopes of creating young warriors able to withstand harsh conditions of battle, and bathed their infants in wine instead of water to test their resilience, warriors have been depicted as a class above and apart from civilian nonwarriors.[5] Throughout U.S. history—from Theodore Roosevelt's mythologized Rough Riders to Hollywood depictions of John Wayne's Leathernecks and Green Berets—the ideology of military superiority is inextricably bound to the ideology of military masculinity, shaping cultural consciousness and providing a template for a mythic American identity. Archetypal attributes such as bravery, stoicism, sacrifice, and loyalty seen by society as essential characteristics of warriors are projected onto veterans after they return from war.[6]

The ideology of military superiority relies on the maintenance of a sharp and seemingly impassible divide between civilian and military spheres. In the contemporary United States, the population of soldiers and veterans is declining, yet U.S. military presence continues to grow worldwide as issues of national defense and global military governance are increasingly prioritized by the U.S. government.[7] Peter Kraska argues that this growing prioritization of military interests represents a rise of U.S. militarism.[8] Anthropologist and Army veteran Steven Gardiner notes that since the end of the military draft after the Vietnam War, civilians have been increasingly separate from the lived military experience.[9] This raises questions: How is militarism in civilian life increasing while civilian society is becoming more distant from the military as an institution? Through what mechanisms does this paradox occur? To answer those questions, I look at how military practices and ideologies are embedded and reproduced in nonobvious spaces. This chapter examines the production of military systems of "categories and obligations, roles, rites and rights" in civilian spaces such as college classrooms, veteran support networks, and equine therapy programs.[10]

U.S. military veterans are caught in this paradox of ongoing militarization and growing civil-military alienation.[11] Functioning within this divide between civilian and military experiences, many veteran advocates on campuses promote programs for veterans that are based on the ideology of military superiority. This ideology has the effect of elevating the military mission but also of distancing veterans from their civilian classmates. One consequence of programs based on the premise of military superiority is that they allow civilians to separate soldiers' needs, and the soldiers themselves, from the wars they fought, which has the effect of obscuring the wars from public consciousness while also denying veterans' experiences of war.

This ideological orientation can be found in the literature developed to guide services to student veterans. Exemplifying the best-practice literature is a special-focus issue of the publication *Insight into Student Services* titled "What Makes a Military Friendly Campus?" An article within this issue employs the language of military superiority, embedded within a discourse of national sacrifice, to explain why veterans are tougher and more mature in ways that "set them apart from the non-veteran student": "Veterans are a complex group with a wide range of military experiences as they make the transition back into 'the world.' . . . Every veteran has had the experience where she or he was pushed to the absolute limit of physical and/or mental endurance and still kept going, putting one foot in front of the other. This experience gives them a toughness and maturity that sets them apart from the non-veteran student."[12]

It is undeniable that veterans are a complex group with a wide range of experiences, yet the statement quoted above provides a selective and essentialized representation of the effects of military experience. There is much evidence to suggest that combat can also be destabilizing or damaging to soldiers.[13] Veterans hold widely varied opinions about their military service and whether it helps young people to mature or inhibits them developmentally. Yet the ideology of military superiority embedded in this article reduces military veterans to essential qualities of complexity, maturity, and toughness gained from physical endurance. It also suggests that these qualities separate veterans from their civilian counterparts, even as many college instructors would argue that students who have faced physical and emotional hardships in their lifetimes—including older reentry students and immigrant students—possess similar qualities. Yet according to the ideology of military superiority, military experience renders these students exceptional and deserving of exceptional valorization.

The discourse of military superiority on campuses is promoted not just by military advocates but also by some veterans. Many veterans in this study viewed the narrative of military superiority positively because it enhanced their self-esteem and helped them feel that they had grown during their military service. However, the pervasive discourse of veteran superiority also creates barriers between veterans and their civilian classmates. Southwest University student veteran Oscar noted both positive and negative social effects of the identity of superiority that was drilled into him during his Marine Corps training:

> OSCAR: You have this phrase that, you know, "You're a Marine now. You have higher standards than a regular civilian." That's something that I live by. I feel like I kind of bought into what the Marine Corps fed me, but it's okay, because it made me a better person.

> EM: You say you bought into what they fed you. What is it that they fed you?

> OSCAR: The whole idea that you're better than the average person. That's something that, when you're in boot camp they're like, "Oh, you're no longer a nasty civilian. You're a Marine now. You have higher standards." Right? It's something they keep constantly reminding you. Or like, "Okay, that might be acceptable in the civilian world, but it's not acceptable here."

> EM: How do you think that affects you, being with civilians and studying with civilians?

> OSCAR: You start believing it. Sometimes it makes you look down on other people.

Oscar spoke highly of his experience in the Marine Corps and credited his military service with instilling in him a positive identity and personal habits that helped him succeed in college and in his subsequent civilian life. Even after he left military service, Oscar aspired to meet his drill sergeants' expectations that he should be better than the "average [civilian] person." Yet he also noticed that this form of military self-esteem created a distance from civilians. For Oscar, the ideology of military superiority acted as both boundary and barrier to relationships with civilian students.

The ideological practice of military superiority informed not only personal relationships but also services designed to support veterans. Conventional wisdom among veteran support organizations holds that the most appropriate people to support veterans—who are normatively understood as male—are male service providers and, more specifically, male veterans. As I observed in diverse veteran support spaces—classrooms, campus trainings, and off-campus support programs—service providers often preemptively positioned themselves as supporters of the military or as having a military background to establish their credibility.

I heard the assertion that male veterans were able to offer the most effective (and legitimate) support to other veterans in training and support meetings both on and off campus. For example, one therapist stated this explicitly during a veteran support event in Orchard Valley, the GWOT Veteran Ranch Days.[14] Hosted by an organization, part of a national network of equestrian-based veteran support organizations called Horses for Heroes, the program offered a day of horseback riding to veterans who served in the Iraq or Afghanistan wars. With roots in physical and occupational therapy, equine-assisted therapy (also known as hippotherapy) programs are an increasingly common form of therapy for war veterans as well as for people with physical and cognitive-emotional disabilities.[15] Historically, equine therapy programs described their benefits using cognitive scientific and medical language, but contemporary veteran-supportive equine therapy programs instead draw on cultural archetypes to craft a symbolic argument for their worth.[16] Heavily concentrated in the western United States but also found in midwestern, eastern, and southern regions, these programs include Heroes and Horses (Montana), A Helping Hoof for Veterans (Utah), Equest Hooves for Heroes (Texas), Healing Horses and Armed Forces (California), Unbridled Warriors (Florida), Horses for Heroes—Cowboy Up! (New Mexico), and Back in the Saddle Warriors (Washington). These programs draw on nationalist symbols of cowboys and frontiersmen in their marketing of veteran support.

Richard Slotkin views the U.S. military mission through a lens of frontier mythology, which features the self-legitimizing use of violence by cavalry soldiers as agents of manifest destiny charged with bringing the American way of life to uncivilized others.[17] The symbolic frontiersman is closely associated with America's civilizing mission, currently framed and carried out as America's global democratizing project. The frontier archetypes of cowboy, cavalryman, and sheriff evoke an ethos of rugged individualism in the service of a greater project (such as staying alive, taming the wilderness, creating order out of chaos, or imposing and keeping peace).[18] Veteran equine therapy programs draw on Western imaginaries that harken back to a time when the military was an exclusively male subculture maintained with masculine relationships and symbols. In doing so, they suture nationalist military narratives to healing narratives of self-discovery.[19] The mission statement of one veteran equine therapy program draws on both of these narratives: "To use the remote wilderness, and the horse/human connection to challenge, and inspire growth in veterans suffering from mental and physical scars. We re-galvanize our nation's veterans so they can rediscover who they are, and what they can be after moving forward. [The program] focus is not about what happened, but what can happen if you choose to drive on."[20]

This is not the sterile scientific discourse typically found in evidence-based therapeutic interventions. The language of this mission statement vigorously evokes national interests and rediscovery of identity, promising to mobilize veterans into action and to return them to a previous robust state. This is done by invoking the Army motto "suck it up and drive on," which is used to exhort soldiers to move through a difficult past and present and into a more secure future. The following example illustrates ways that the discourse of military superiority was employed in one equine therapy program.

The Veterans Ranch Days took place in bucolic pastures at the base of foothills on the outskirts of Orchard Valley. Four male and two female veterans paired with the stable's staff members, riding teachers, and therapists to learn to groom and ride horses. The day included guided rides and a lesson on how to navigate an obstacle course on horseback. As a nonveteran observer, I was allowed to accompany a veteran who was paired with a volunteer therapist. My riding partner was Mason, a twenty-seven-year-old Connecticut native and veteran of two tours in Iraq. Mason was recently discharged from the Army with a 100 percent disability classification for physical and psychological wounds suffered in combat, which included symptoms of PTSD. After serving in the Army infantry and as a sniper, Mason returned home heavily decorated with medals, including two Purple Hearts—one for wounds received while evacuating U.S. soldiers under fire—and three Army Commendation Medals for valor in combat.

As Mason methodically cleaned the horse's hooves with a stiff bristle brush, Dirk, a therapist and Navy veteran, spoke about his work as a counselor visiting veterans at the military hospital at Ft. Lewis-McCord near Tacoma, Washington. Dirk said that he came away from that experience convinced that only other male veterans could appropriately counsel male veterans:

It takes a male vet to be able to talk to these guys. Because I shot competitively, when I sit by the bedside of someone who's been shot three times in the sternum, I can say, "What caliber did they get you with?" And he says, "I think it was an [automatic weapon caliber bullet]." And I can say, "Nah, that would have come from an automatic weapon. And you wouldn't have that kind of a wound. It must have been a [single-shot bullet]. You must have been hit by a sniper." And that's how I get their respect.

In this exchange, Dirk's bedside counseling techniques leveraged his masculinity, his military status, and his knowledge of weaponry to gain the respect of the wounded solider, which is what Dirk believed allowed him to be an effective counselor. The soldier's physical wounds became the medium for male bonding, establishing Dirk's masculine credibility and his right to support the wounded soldier. Based on what Belkin calls military masculinity, and formed in what Gardiner calls heroic masochism, these social processes construct soldiers in ways that inculcate an entitlement based on gendered identity and group belonging.[21] In the production of heroic masochism, Gardiner says, "pain as technique, discipline for the body and mind of the initiate . . . becomes *desirable*."[22] Gardiner writes that narratives of military masculinity reinforce the notion that the "toughening and hardening presumably required to endure the rigors of the battlefield construct not just gendered bodies, but gendered spaces, archetypically 'the front'—a space from which women are supposed to be absent." This gendered separation "underwrites masculine and feminine spaces as fundamentally different, creating a social warrant for the de facto zoning practices that make pediatrician's offices and elementary school classrooms into feminine spaces, while football stadiums and engineering colleges are masculine."[23] Likewise, veteran support spaces are constructed as different and fundamentally masculine through bonding practices rooted in shared experiences of physical endurance and pain.

Yet defining military culture and "veteran" as normatively male ignores the reality that multiple genders are represented in the military.[24] Moreover, this template of veteran support assumes that the outward manifestations of war and warriors—combat stories, weapons, military social relations—represent a singularly authentic military culture with which all student veterans positively identify. The assumptions underlying this model of veteran support elide many veterans' conflicted feelings around their participation in combat. As my interviews with student veterans illustrate, some go to college to distance themselves from, or to critically examine, U.S. military policies and practices rather than to valorize them.

Framing veteran support work as an exclusively male endeavor is not only problematic because such framing might discourage women from serving in support roles and diverts attention from needs of female veterans, but also because it is not always true that "it takes a male vet to be able to talk to these guys." My research yielded many counterexamples represented in the more than two hundred hours of wide-ranging conversational interviews I conducted with veterans. These included one with my horse-grooming partner, Mason, at his home in a small California town. Our four hours of conversation began with my standard interview questions about Mason's college experiences, and following that—at Mason's initiative—he spoke about his children, his combat experience, his multiple military decorations, his interactions with Veterans Affairs mental health counselors, and his episodic depression and suicidal thoughts.

While there is little doubt that the presentation and position of interlocutors influences conversations, the claim that male veterans are always more appropriate as service providers to male veterans forms part of the discourse of military superiority and can serve to maintain and increase the distance between civilians and veterans. Moreover, some veterans seeking to understand their conflicted feelings about their participation in the Iraq and Afghanistan wars may not feel comfortable talking with counselors associated with the U.S. military. For example, SU student and former Marine Jordan said that he left his military service disillusioned with the war and his role in it. In his attempt to distance himself from the U.S. military, he avoided seeking counseling because he did not want to speak to a therapist employed by the military. But when he ultimately decided that he needed to speak with someone, Jordan found his way to a local Vet Center, a federally funded mental health clinic for combat veterans that emphasizes peer support:

> Eventually I walked into a Vet Center. It took a little while. I saw a counselor I didn't really like for maybe a month. The Vet Centers try to hire vets, but it was my thought that vets are kind of too plugged into this whole [military] system and that whole way of thinking. I mean, I'm trying to get out of all that. So I actually requested [a civilian counselor] from the leader of the Vet Center. [I said,] "I want to talk to the counselor who is not a vet. I know you have one counselor on staff who's not a veteran, and I want to talk to her." And I lucked out because she's an amazing counselor. Incredibly caring and intelligent and professional. I saw her for about a year one-on-one every week, and it's made all the difference in the world.

While Jordan had great success with his female civilian counselor, other veterans expressed similar discomfort with seeking counseling from VA employees. Some were reluctant to talk to military-affiliated counselors because, like Jordan, they wanted to distance themselves from a military perspective. Others did not feel comfortable talking about certain aspects of their lives (for example, illicit drug use or other illegal activities) because they did not want that information included in their medical or military personnel files.

"Best Practices" of Veteran Support

Despite diversity among veterans in both academic needs and opinions regarding the U.S. military and the wars, much of the current literature on what are called best practices in veteran support services is based in perspectives that are wholly uncritical of the institutional military.[25] This literature is dominated by scholars and practitioners associated with the military (ex-military or individuals currently working for the VA or DoD) and emphasizes the role of positive military identities in veteran support service.[26] Much of this literature argues that support programs on campuses should reinforce student veterans' military identities and promotes veterans as exemplars of military superiority. This model of veteran support calls for campus celebrations of an ostensibly unitary military culture.[27]

The programs that are widely considered models for veteran educational support include strategies to create what are called veteran friendly (or military friendly) campuses.[28] These support programs rely on the assumption that veterans are generally uncritical of the U.S. military. The ideology of military superiority that constitutes veterans as veterans vis-à-vis their special status conflates honor and respect for veterans with the notion that military projects similarly deserve honor and respect. For some participants in this study, this position was congruent with their own views, and they experienced it as unproblematic. Other veterans felt alienated from their wartime military experience. For them, conflating honor and support for veterans with honor and support for military projects heightened, rather than diminished, their feelings of social disconnection on campus.

Military Identification in Civilian Support Groups

Veterans on and off college campuses are supported by large networks of civilian nonprofit organizations that offer an array of services related to housing and legal assistance, corporate employment opportunities, spiritual support, academic tutoring, and scholarships. Over the course of three years, I regularly attended meetings of civilian networks devoted to veteran support and found that civilian participants in these organizations were actively encouraged to claim a military affiliation. For example, at one meeting, the attendees were asked to introduce themselves not only by name and social service agency, but also by their personal relationship with the military.[29] For current or former members of the military, this self-introduction was relatively straightforward and involved a simple statement of the branch of service with which they were affiliated. The remaining participants—mostly civilian women social service providers—introduced themselves with statements such as, "My grandfather served in the Army in World War II" or "I had an uncle in the National Guard." Although the meetings consisted largely of civilian organizations, this ritualized declaration of affiliation enacted military allegiance and linked military affiliation with status as a service provider for veterans.[30] The politics of identification also acted as a disciplinary force: in publicly identifying familial military status, participants performed a ritual of allegiance in which family relationships were transformed into military affiliations, thus uniting the act of supporting veterans with allegiance to military institutions. Moreover, for the social service professionals, the act of declaring one's military connection carried the implication that familial military affiliation might render one more competent to provide housing assistance, job placement, or substance abuse treatment.

Services at the Sites

Veterans' services on college campuses reflect the diverse communities in which those campuses are located. Veteran support on the Central College and SU campuses was based on institutional programs and pedagogical practices that reproduced particular ideas about veterans, transforming them into collective common sense. Despite the diversity in campus communities and among student veterans, campus veteran support programs throughout the nation share similar templates of best practices for veteran support. Echoing the student services literature, many campus programs take patriotism, uncritical esteem for the military, silence about the wars, and reverence for veterans as the ideological foundations of their discourse of care.

Veterans' Services at Central Community College

In the United States, the majority of enlisted military recruits come from rural towns like Orchard Valley. And after discharge, the majority of veterans who choose to go to college enter two-year educational institutions like Central

Community College. Yet in early 2010, Central College offered none of the services that were becoming commonplace at other California campuses; there was no veterans' club, no designated financial aid officer, and, to the outside observer, no recognition that veterans might have specialized needs or could benefit from specialized attention. Veterans asking for services at Central College were starting from scratch.

By the end of 2010, a small group of Central College veterans had begun to advocate for services at the school. A group of student veterans joined a dean of student services to create a campus veterans' club in November 2011. Their first official act was to convene student veterans to discuss their needs on campus and to advocate for a designated veterans-only space on campus, which they envisioned as a veterans' resource center. The group gathered in the Theater Department's auditorium and handed out surveys designed to create a wish list of campus services, including peer tutoring and mentoring, counseling on academics, mental health, vocational rehabilitation, financial aid, and readjustment, help accessing VA records and benefits, and a private space where veterans could go to reduce their stress.

Over the next year, student veterans advocated for themselves, and there was incipient yet measurable progress to establish veterans' services at Central. As of 2012, Central College had a veterans' club that met informally every month. The Central College website prominently featured a section welcoming veterans to campus and providing links to an array of services. A regional Veterans Clinic sent a mobile clinic to visit the campus on a bimonthly basis.[31]

By 2013, three years after I began visiting the campus, the Central veterans' club had grown to include four faculty members, approximately ten active student veterans, and one administrator. Central College also provided a specially trained financial aid officer for student veterans.[32] Eligible student veterans were able to receive tutoring and academic and technical support from the school's Extended Opportunity Programs and Services (EOPS), a program that was also open to the general population of Central College students; however, few veterans enrolled in the program.[33] The Central College veterans' club was also given use of a small office to serve as a peer-staffed Veterans' Service Center, giving students a veterans-only space to relax and to receive peer counseling.

Many of the Central College veterans' club initiatives were self-funded. At a 2011 meeting of the veterans' club, student veterans gathered in a far corner of Central College to discuss ways to garner support from the broader Orchard Valley community. Club members and faculty supporters debated the relative merits of fund-raising barbecues, donation drives among local businesses, and a virtual fund drive via the Internet site Kickstarter. They spoke of themselves as social entrepreneurs attempting to crowd-source support for services.[34]

Services at Southwest University

Southwest University had vastly greater resources than Central College (money, space, staff, and the less tangible yet still salient resource of social prestige) and a much richer array of on-campus services available to veterans. Student veterans at SU benefited socially, financially, and academically from their status as transfer students. The majority of veterans enrolled as undergraduates at SU had transferred from community colleges, which made the SU student veteran population a subset of the school's transfer student population. Some services for student veterans were provided or informed by transfer student services while others were provided entirely separately. Most of the veteran support initiatives on the SU campus were directly or indirectly run through the Student Center designed to assist transfer students.[35]

The Student Center where veterans gathered was located in the SU Student Services Building, which also housed tutoring, psychological counseling offices, student service clubs, an LGBT resource center, and several student clubs. Because many veterans and other transfer and reentry (defined as age twenty-five years or older) students arrived at SU without the benefit of a rigorous college-preparatory educational background, the Student Center also offered semester-long courses as well as brief workshops on how to successfully navigate academic life at the university. In the political economy of resource distribution at the university, the size and physical layout of the Student Center indicated Southwest University's support for students coming from community colleges: on a campus where office space was at a premium, the Student Center occupied the entire southern wing of the two-story Student Services Building.[36]

The atmosphere of the center emanated an inclusive hominess that contrasted with Southwest University's highly competitive, rigorous academic environment of meritocratic achievement. It had the welcoming atmosphere of a well-used and well-loved community center. The reception area doubled as a lounge, furnished with comfortable sofas and overstuffed chairs where students sat or lay down, reading and talking to each other; some even napped in the lounge. Most of the students there were noticeably older than the eighteen-to twenty-two-year-old age range of typical SU undergraduates. Cubicles along one wall provided semiprivate spaces for drop-in advising sessions with staff and graduate student advisors. A coffeemaker and a bank of computers were available for student use. One corner of the large ground-floor space was taken up by the program for student-parents, where children's toys and books were strewn about on child- and adult-sized tables.

Behind the entrance, a large conference room accommodated larger meetings and beginning- and end-of-semester parties. When not in use for official events, this large conference room served as an informal drop-in center for SU veterans, who gathered there before and after classes. Student veterans met weekly for a brown-bag lunch, where they compared notes on strategies to get into graduate school, scholarships to apply for, and classes taught by what they called "veteran-friendly" professors.[37]

Established in 2004, the SU veterans' club had a permanent, dedicated office in a quiet corridor adjacent to the Student Center. It was furnished with a late-model computer and ergonomically supportive desks and chairs. Appointed with comfortable chairs, the office served not only as a quiet place for veterans to do homework, but also as a peer-support drop-in center. Stacked against the walls were flats of bottled water and boxes of energy bars, soda, and snacks for veterans who might drop in.

The SU veterans' club was funded as a campus club, and other expenses, such as food and incidentals for parties and other events, were funded by special university grants. University funding was also allocated for campus-wide events related to veterans, such as Veterans' Day events, ceremonies, and panel discussions. The local VFW also donated money to student veterans at SU on an ad-hoc basis.[38] The anchor of this comprehensive program was Rick, the veterans' services coordinator. Rick was held in high esteem among SU transfer students in general, and especially by SU veterans, as he served as their advocate, trusted counselor, broker of campus resources, and a guide who helped them decode the many unwritten rules of the elite university. Rick also acted as a liaison between the administrative apparatus of Southwest University and that of the VA, advocating within multiple overlapping bureaucracies on behalf of the SU veterans.

It was not always easy to reach Rick. A line of student veterans often formed outside his office waiting to talk with him; whenever an SU student veteran had a crisis, emotional, financial, academic, or otherwise, Rick was called on to help. Rick was the public face of SU veterans' services, but he was also intimately involved in the everyday work of veteran support as a mentor and advocate offering supportive counseling and referrals to campus and community services. Student veterans at SU spoke with reverence about Rick and his place in their lives. Their attitude toward Rick reflected a deep, abiding respect and devotion that by all accounts was mutual.

Peer Mentorship

The SU veterans' club offered extensive advising and mentoring, both formal and informal; such support was much harder to find at Central College. Brett was a Central College student who worked two retail jobs while going to school and who spent his summers as a drill instructor training new Army recruits. Staying in school was difficult for Brett because he struggled to decide on a course of study. He initially wanted to major in Spanish, the language of his Colombian father, but after taking some classes, he realized that they were geared toward a career as a Spanish language teacher, which did not interest Brett. I first spoke with Brett before the Central College veterans' club had its initial meeting, before any supportive services for student veterans existed on campus. Brett, who at that point planned to leave school at the end of the semester without an associate's degree, said that he wished he had been given guidance about which courses to take from a veteran who had successfully graduated from Central. When I asked what might have helped him stay in school, he replied,

> Talking to [a veteran] who's actually graduated, who can help provide a better guidelines [would help] because when I entered the military I didn't know what I wanted to do. Then I came back [to community college] because I promised myself I'd earn that degree. Coming here, I still kind of didn't really know what I wanted to do. The counselor was really great at helping me out, but it still didn't really define my path of where I wanted to go. But [it would have been better if there had been] just somebody who knows more about the field and can give better, a better pathway, like, "If you were to take this [course], this one and this one," as a vet going to school.

The peer mentorship that Brett missed at Central College was abundantly available at Southwest University, largely as a result of Rick's advocacy. While student veterans at Central College had faculty members who provided similar mentorship and advocacy, there were clear differences in resources and veteran support programs at the two colleges, and these differences affected veterans' experiences at the two sites. Veterans' academic standing seemed more precarious at Central College: of the nineteen Central students I interviewed, only ten planned to continue their studies beyond an associate's degree. Juggling part-time jobs and families, these students struggled with a steeper academic and social learning curve that made it more difficult to stay in school. Central College veterans spoke about negotiating multiple part-time jobs while also weighing options about changing majors, classes, and jobs—dropping out of school was typically included on their list of future options. Central College students were more likely to drop out because of difficulties relearning civilian and academic norms and practices but also because (in common with those in the general civilian community college student population) they lacked social and financial support.[39] Veterans at Central College, more so than those at su, spoke about feeling socially unrecognized. The tendency to feel isolated, alienated, and invisible was less common at su, especially and crucially because veterans' clubs and special classes were designed to orient veterans to the campus.

Southwest University student veterans reported fewer difficulties negotiating civilian college life, at least in part because they were transfer students who acquired skills for the civilian world in their previous education in community college. These students had completed all academic prerequisites with a sufficiently high grade point average and had applied to and been accepted by a competitive university. These veterans went through a process of selection before they reached su. The disparity between student veterans' experiences of su and Central can also be explained by su's strong veterans' group, which provided mentoring and informal guidance. Every su student veteran I spoke with had received extensive support and mentoring from instructors, family members, partners, or veteran service organizations. Once student veterans make it into su, most graduate. All of the su veterans I spoke with were on track to graduate but said that without coaching and support designed specifically to prepare them for the demands of the university, they would not have made it to su and would not have been successful there.

Veterans' Reentry Class

At Southwest University, academic enculturation for student veterans often took place within a context of esteem for the military. This esteem was reified in common practices (rituals at gatherings, ground rules for meetings, and jokes and banter) and celebrated in public events. The message that veterans were valued members of an elite institution was often reinforced by various faculty and staff, and many student veterans indicated that this message of meritocratic superiority resonated with their experience in the military.

A central component of veterans' services at Southwest University was a reentry class designed especially for veterans, introduced in the opening pages of this book. The class was offered to veterans in their first semester at su to introduce them to the university's social, cultural, and academic norms and practices. The class provided students with companionship and mutual support, as well as practical tips on time management and how to study, read academic texts, and write university-level papers. This course was optional and offered only one semester unit of credit, which helped to round out veterans' course loads so they could meet their requirement for full-time enrollment status necessary to receive full financial support from the GI Bill. The course was popular with veterans, who learned about it through the campus veterans' website or by word of mouth. It offered a classroom environment for veterans that was socially cohesive while teaching them practical academic skills.

I spent one semester as a participant-observer in this class, which served as student veterans' introduction to the academic and social norms of the university. The class was designed to help with academic remediation and to acclimate SU veterans to the expectations of student life at SU. As part of the class, student veterans were encouraged to identify with and take pride in their military service.

The following field note excerpt describes the first day of class, when twenty-five men and one woman began the course:

> The classroom is located in a Southwest University residence hall and tightly packed with tables and chairs arranged in straight rows, with all chairs oriented to the front of the room. Before class begins, the instructor, a man in his mid-thirties, announces that he wants students to be able to see each other when they speak in this seminar, so he asks the group to rearrange the chairs and to form a circle and to move the tables to the edges of the room.
>
> Immediately, the students rise in unison to comply with the instructor's request. Within twenty seconds, the room has been completely rearranged to the instructor's specifications: extraneous tables line the walls and the chairs are neatly arranged in a symmetrical circle. The instructor, smiling broadly, says, "You can tell this is a room full of service members. If you want something done well . . ." (A slight shrug and a smile substitute for the implied end of the sentence: "ask a service member to do it.") The instructor then formally begins the class by thanking the students for their military service and noting that while he did not personally serve in the U.S. armed forces, his way of serving the country is to give support for veterans' educational needs (excerpt, field note, September 1, 2011).

This vignette illustrates that the discourse of military superiority subtly imbued teaching techniques for military veterans. In addition to making an ideological statement, the instructor also voiced an observable fact: it was obvious that this group of students was trained to work together to accomplish a common goal. The students' immediate, efficient, and collective response to the instructor's request to rearrange the classroom chairs was clearly a result of their shared military training.[40] However, in this instance, the instructor's praise went beyond approbation for the efficient rearrangement of the chairs. It invoked the discursive power of military superiority, which marked the students as valuable by virtue of their military training and status. The instructor made this explicit when he began the class by thanking the students for their military service.

This course consciously built on members' shared military experience, which fostered a sense of commonality. In many separate conversations and in my observations, the instructor indicated that he did not subscribe to the idea that military veterans were superior to civilians, yet in subtle ways, the pedagogy of the class fostered this effect. The discourse of military superiority was the pedagogical keynote of the course.

After asking the students to introduce themselves by name, academic major, and branch of military service, the instructor began the class with a questionnaire about what was considered a unifying experience for all the students in the room: basic training. He circulated a sheet with four questions:

1   What about basic training proved challenging for you?
2   Were there any elements of basic training that you particularly enjoyed?
3   What helped you get through basic training?
4   Why did they yell at you?

The arc of these questions suggested a pedagogical journey for the class that specifically linked their military training with their new task of being college students by likening the first weeks of classes at su to their military initiation in basic training. To answer the questions, the class had to remember thoughts and feelings from the beginning of boot camp. Through this technique, boot camp was brought into the classroom.

While the course curriculum was based on participants' shared military experience, the instructor also held space for a diversity of opinions about military practice. For example, in response to the instructor's question about the difficulties veterans faced in basic training, veterans' answers ranged from the generic ("lack of sleep," "sharing a room with people with poor hygiene") to comments that pointed to a critique of military practices: "being around intolerant people," "losing who you were, destroying your sense of self," "the screaming in your face," and "smokings, beatings [group punishments for individual infractions]." The questions were designed to evoke collective social memory of military hardships and to remind the class that they had endured more onerous physical and emotional trials than the ones they faced in college.

The question regarding what they enjoyed about boot camp was designed to evoke the positive aspects of their collective military experience. Responses to this question included, "unexpected laughs with Drill Instructors," "All the diversity—different people of different ethnicities figuring out how to be soldiers together," "Having a brotherhood," and "Learning to shoot." The responses reminded students that while boot camp may have been onerous, it also provided social benefits.

The third question, "What helped you get through basic training?" then gestured toward resiliency. Answers included, "knowing it would end," "knowing that people stood up before me, gave their lives, and I had to stand up for them," and "finding one or two other people I can relate to." Answering this question recalled students' memory of the inner strength they used to manage adverse circumstances. It also drew on their sense of mission and of military bonds as motivation to confront present challenges.

The final question, "Why do they yell at you?" served, by effect if not by intent, to vindicate the authoritarian military style of training. Rather than asking the veterans about their affective experience of being yelled at, this question called for students to enunciate a rationale for authoritarian military training techniques. The students' answers ("So you can handle the stress," "It's a transformation," and "to build you up: brotherhood, relying on each other, military, discipline, trust") reaffirmed the group's military identity. Yet one dissenting voice wrote, "So they can spit on you," indicating that positive regard for the shared military experience was not unanimous.

This university class was not unique in containing an ideological orientation. Gramsci reminds us that there is no neutral outside from which we can compare our lived historical understanding with a theoretical or an ahistorical truth. This means that all educative space is ideological and that every social interaction or utterance contains politics. University classes carry valences from across the political spectrum, some more overtly than others. In that respect, the veterans' class was similar to other entry-level classes sponsored by different academic departments and tailored for unique student populations such as ethnic minority students or transfer and older reentry students. These classes are successful, in part, because they build on common experiences of members and promote feelings of unity and shared identity among classmates. Whereas the entry-level class in ethnic studies might use the lens of critical race theory to understand and decode university practices, this veteran-specific class built on military cultures and relationships to teach students to navigate the university. Using military relations as a template and lexicon, the veterans' class focused on peer support, skill building, and mentorship as well as resource referrals.

Student veterans' profound sense of mutual care and support developed quickly over the semester, partially because of the instructor's conscious effort to encourage student veterans to build on their common military experience, and partially because of the instructor's group facilitation skills. Pedagogy based on mutual support and group identification helped the group to coalesce in support of, rather than in competition with, one another. It was emotionally moving to observe veterans' demonstrations of fondness and tenderness, although these were often cloaked in avuncular bravado that resembled good-natured harassment. The mutually supportive environment was especially evident as veterans coached each other on how to maintain calm when they felt that they might lose their temper and "go off" in response to academic pressures, or in response to what some students called ignorant comments by civilians. Suggestions included breathing deeply and counting backward from ten. Some students advised the avoidance of "knife hands" (a flattened-hand, closed-fingered gesture, similar to the martial arts move known as "knifehand strike" or more popularly, "karate chop,") saying that civilians might perceive this gesture as aggressive. As one class member said, "People give us a wide berth. People are more cautious [around veterans]." The habit of using knife hands appeared ingrained, however, as it persisted among the group. Whereas the class cultivated mutual support, they also studiously avoided critical discussion of the U.S. military or the wars.

Service Providers

It is important to note that, just as there is wide diversity in the political sentiments, motivations, and practices of soldiers and veterans, similar diversity can be found among veterans' service providers. In both my personal experience and my research, I found that most service providers were not hawkish ideologues promoting uncritical support for contemporary wars. The majority of veterans' service providers I met on campuses—including Rick and others at SU and at Central College—were thoughtful and caring advocates for student veterans who held complex and nuanced views about military service and the current wars. But common sense is most often produced from assumptions embedded in the collective popular consciousness; it is typically not handed down through edicts from ideologues in the dominant classes. Common sense is taken up and promoted by a diverse range of actors whose ideas and actions are influenced by particular social forces. Many veterans' service providers neither professed nor believed in ideologies of military superiority, but they often delivered services shaped by that discourse.

Returning combat veterans have undergone intensive specialized training, and some have had traumatic combat experiences that may present challenges to learning in college classrooms. Combat veterans entering college need and can benefit from specialized support services. However, not all veterans feel a positive relationship to the U.S. military; for these veterans, programs that require uncritical esteem for the military may not be able to offer effective support. Some veteran support programs are based on explicit valorization of military institutions and military service, which contributes to the production and promotion of militarized common sense on campuses. Everyday militarism operates on college campuses through institutional programs and their pedagogical practices, as institutional and unofficial supporters of the co-constructed militarized common sense with the participation of students, professors, and the general civilian population. Yet this ideology is not force-fed to an unwitting public. The sincere desire to support veterans by valorizing the military and avoiding discussions about the war is not the product of a false consciousness implanted by propagandists but rather reflects a hegemonic social reality built on the articulation of ideological discourses and positions.

The power of an ideology of military superiority is informed by dualistic assumptions of good and evil. A recognition of soldiers' suffering and self-abnegation relies on a partial telling of the war story that involves the mystification of the military mission and the erasure of similar suffering by the enemy/other. For a narrative of military superiority to become dominant, it must feature the binary paradigm of good soldiers and evil enemies.[41] However, this is also a primary reason that the discourse of military superiority is problematic for many student veterans, as well as for our national understanding of the current wars. This discourse obscures the complex realities soldiers face and their contradictory feelings about war. For soldiers who actually experience war, idealized concepts of honor, dishonor, heroism, and cowardice are necessarily complicated by the realities of combat.

Because many veterans have conflicting and contradictory feelings about their military service, supportive interventions that rely on unquestioning support for U.S. military policy and the wars is not sufficient to address their needs. Thus, even as campuses strive to meet the needs of recently returned veterans, some student veterans are organizing separate self-help interventions.

· 4 ·

VETERAN SELF-HELP

Embracing, Re-creating, and
Contesting Gendered Military Relations

Previous chapters have shown that military sensibilities, ideologies, and habits are embodied by veterans and reenacted on college campuses. Social bonds forged in military training and combat are important to soldiers during their time in the military and after they leave military service. Many veterans in this study said that the aspects of military culture they found most enduring and powerful were the social relationships they developed with other military members. These social relationships offered important pathways for individual veterans to seek and receive support on college campuses. While veteran social networks served a supportive function for student veterans, they also maintained and re-created militarized socialization on college campuses.

Chapter 3 examined veteran support initiatives created by campus administrators and staff; this chapter examines how student veterans conceptualized and created supportive interventions. Veterans used social relationships formed around shared military histories to both reproduce and contest militarized socialization. The chapter begins with a detailed discussion of the social bonds forged during military service. I then describe how these bonds maintained and re-created military-based socialization on college campuses. This chapter also explores the social affordances, limitations, exclusions, and contradictions military social bonds entailed. In particular, I examine how a culture of military misogyny codified and enforced gender relations. Different meanings assigned by males and females to gendered social bonds influenced adaptation to civilian life. Finally, I explore the diversity in veterans' strategies to adapt to postmilitary life in college, which involved attempts to sustain military bonds but also practices of distancing from military relationships and ideologies.

Functions of Collective Military Social Bonds

We few, we happy few, we band of brothers:
For he to-day that sheds his blood with me
Shall be my brother
SHAKESPEARE, St. Crispin's Day speech, *Henry V*

A single soldier is nothing. It's all about the group.
JEN, U.S. Army, quoted in Benedict, *The Lonely Soldier*

I didn't experience real camaraderie until I entered the PTSD treatment program—
it was 98 percent women who had gone through MST [military sexual trauma].[1]
SARAH, U.S. Army

Throughout history, the bond among soldiers has been extolled in literature, the arts, and popular culture. Twenty-five-year-old SU student veteran Ricardo said that he was inspired to enlist in the Navy to fight in Iraq after his teacher read him the St. Crispin's Day speech from Shakespeare's *Henry V*. One of two sons in a second-generation Mexican immigrant family, Ricardo was sent to a military-model continuation school because of his failing grades in his Los Angeles public high school. "I know it's one of the weirdest reasons to join," Ricardo told me, "but I had an instructor in high school who was a Vietnam vet. He started talking about this play, about the whole band of brothers, and I wanted that." Ricardo continued, "I had never belonged to something like [a military band of brothers]. The strongest thing I could identify with myself was with my family. But I couldn't imagine being in a bond with other men, going through something like [combat]. I wanted to know what it was like. Part of [the speech] says, 'Those who stay, you will tell my story.' To me, that was like, 'Seize the day. Take it. Do it.' "

Ricardo's epiphany led him to join the Navy, where he worked as a cryptological technician and analyzed signals. He said that the relationships he formed in the military were almost familial and endured over time: "We were just one. Even to this day, I can't break that. It's a bond. It's the strongest bond I've ever had next to my family. . . . There's nothing that can compare to that [military] relationship."

These collective social bonds did not simply end when veterans left the military and made the transition to college. Some veterans relied on and incorporated these bonds while others distanced themselves from military relationships and developed relationships with civilians.

Veterans contested and reproduced not only military relationships but also military socialization on college campuses. Some veterans worked to replicate military structures and social patterns while others rejected military practices and ideologies. And for yet other veterans, a successful transition to college involved actively organizing against the increasing militarization of society and taking a public stance against the wars.

Sociologists note that enduring social relationships serve multiple functions.[2] Social bonds allow individuals to work in concert toward a single goal. Bonds support social unity and cohesiveness, and they serve to clearly differentiate who is within the group and who is an outsider—or, specific to the military, who is an ally and who is an enemy. In addition, social bonds facilitate the development of collective resilience, enabling individual members of a group to better withstand psychic and physical assaults. Veterans' social bonds are naturalized through the intensely affective experience of combat, and over time, military bonds are incorporated into the soldier's identity.[3]

Erikson called this type of mutually dependent relationship *communality*, or a primary group that serves as the locus for activities normally regarded as the exclusive purview of individuals. Communality provides a group context that creates meaning for individual members. Erikson uses the metaphor of a "communal store" of emotion to describe the function of these relationships, writing that within the bonds of communality, "It is the community that cushions the pain, the community that provides a context for intimacy, the community that represents morality and serves as the repository for old traditions. In effect, people put their own individual resources at the disposal of the group—placing them in the communal store—and then draw on that reserve supply for the demands of everyday life."[4]

Erikson stresses that communality is based not on territorial affiliations (as in village communities) but on the "network of relationships that make up their general human surround."[5] Likewise, communities of veterans on college campuses develop a fictive kinship system based on a shared military past rather than regional, ethnic, or cultural characteristics. The communality practiced among veterans is conditioned by the intense relationships formed during military service as well as the lingering effects of military frameworks for social bonding.

In the masculinist social world of the U.S. military, this intense social bonding most commonly occurs among men in the absence of women. Scholars observe that the ideal of military masculinity rests on the enforced negation of the feminine.[6] The contemporary U.S. military no longer officially excludes women from most occupational categories (including combat roles), but official status has a limited impact on ingrained cultural norms. In the military milieu, femininity is coded as weakness, subordination, emotionalism, dependency, and disloyalty. Belkin writes that these traits are "framed as dangerous aspects of the unmasculine that warriors must reject at all costs if they are to acquire the strength necessary to defend national security." He argues that the annihilation of the feminine is treated as central to protecting against the annihilation of the nation and its military defenders.[7] As Gardiner observes, "the hard masculine body of the military qua military is always under assault from the feminine softness of the civilian sphere."[8]

Interviews with women veterans confirm gender-specific patterns of social bonding. In particular, women veterans form bonds with one another as a result of being treated as outsiders and transgressors in the military.[9] In her generative social history of women and militarization, Cynthia Enloe argues that women's essential, yet socially marginalized, supportive roles during wartime militarized women's lives and provided the emotional, logistical, medical, and sexual human infrastructure for male soldiers to carry out military campaigns. Even in the contemporary era when women are increasingly active and visible in U.S. military conflicts, the normative image of what and who is a soldier is still firmly heterosexual and male.[10]

Military rituals and practices—exercises, call-and-response techniques, reward and punishment systems, and gestures that signal hierarchical relations— are designed to teach soldiers membership in a normatively male military corpus. Drill instructors gender their shaming practices "such that service members who fail to conform to archetypal understandings of military masculinity such as bravery, stoicism, sacrifice, and loyalty are punished through gender shaming."[11] This makes military bonding a complex and contradictory process. Because many of the male soldiers in this study were raised to understand emotional caregiving as the exclusive domain of female intimates, encountering intimate emotional support from other men within the masculinist military community was a revelatory experience that heightened the power of the masculine social bond.

As a white heterosexual man growing up in rural Northern California, Army veteran Connor learned what he called "traditional rural values, like stereotypical masculinity, you know, like this is what a male should act like." Connor described his experience of interpersonal intimacy in the military as distinctly masculine:

You know, the whole feminine idea of like compassion and understanding was completely gone [in the Army]. It was like *Lord of the Flies* [laughs]. It was very much a male dog-eat-dog world, like, you don't have feelings. You don't cry. You get your shit together and just do it. It was my stereotype of being male: being tough, physically, not whining, being strong, stoic, that kind of thing. And because of that, that's how you bond with the other guys, and that was big. But because everyone's away from their girlfriends, they'd bond with their fellow males, like they'd talk at night in their bunks and stuff. It's a very powerful experience, and I can recall just pouring your heart out to people. And having people pour their hearts out to you, and that's what made it all tolerable, really. It was like being able to share it with someone and to know that someone was going through exactly the same shit as you were.

Goffman notes that the intimacy created within total institutions forces a subject to "engage in activity whose symbolic implications are incompatible with his conceptions of self."[12] For Connor, the intimacy of the bedtime barracks contradicted, yet deepened, his self-concept as a masculine soldier. In the hypermasculine, heteronormative, *Lord of the Flies*, dog-eat-dog world of drills and training, emotional intimacy was suppressed. But it was not eradicated. The close quarters of the barracks created intimate, emotionally sustaining relationships that made military life tolerable.

Other veterans also formed emotional bonds in the barracks. For example, Ricardo described intensely intimate relationships with other soldiers: "I lived with these guys. It wasn't living like people live together. We *lived* together [speaker's emphasis]. We were within arms' reach. I remember reaching into the bunk under me and I would slap the guy. We were together. There were no boundaries between our private [lives and functions], no boundaries between even us going to the restroom or showers. We were just one." The shared experience of basic training and combat created intense physical and emotional relationships among soldiers, but it also created social and emotional distance from civilians who did not share in this experience. Ricardo emphasized that men soldiers really "*lived* together" in "arms' reach," unlike mixed-gender civilian others. The lack of boundaries between private and public selves signaled the erasure of individual identities and their replacement with group membership.

Military interpersonal relationships often form quickly and with great intensity, especially during basic training, when communication with family and friends is severely restricted, and when recruits are put under extreme physical and emotional stress.[13] Yet women and men have distinct experiences of bonding during basic training.

Raised in suburban Los Angeles in a Korean immigrant family, twenty-four-year-old Jessica described her father, a veteran of the Korean military, as authoritarian and a "scary individual." "I guess maybe he had wanted a son," she said. "He gave me a little too much discipline, so I avoided him." Jessica joined the Army after high school because she needed money for college and she was looking for what she called "balanced discipline" in her life. She said that her closest military friendship began in basic training, when another new recruit lost her way and followed Jessica. This paring quickly became a battle buddy partnership and a deeply bonded friendship. Jessica said, "My battle buddy was [pauses], really we're soul mates. We really just complemented each other very well. She was someone I don't think I could have survived basic without."

As newcomers, and as women, Jessica and her battle buddy were treated as deficient.[14] In a world set up for men, female soldiers like Jessica and her buddy relied on one other for social, emotional, and physical support. Jessica told the story of how she relied on her battle buddy to make up for an additional deficiency caused by a previously undiagnosed vision problem: "I had an eye disorder, which I didn't know at the time, but I couldn't see at night. One time [during a night march], I had to hold onto my company commander, which is the most embarrassing thing. A company commander is not going to deal with a young, lowly private. But I had to hold onto his arm during one of our ruck marches. After that, I was like, 'Never again. This is really embarrassing.'"[15]

Jessica's failing eyesight required that she complement herself by pairing with someone with better visual acuity. Jessica coped with her vision problem by holding onto her buddy, who served as her guide during night marches:

> So I always stood behind her, and I held onto her bootstraps. So, even if we were going in the middle of the night and I couldn't see crap, I knew if she went down[hill], I was about to go down. If she went up, I was going to take a step up. If she tumbled, we tumbled together. And I think that's why I will always be indebted to her. We don't talk often now, but when we do it's always like for really long periods of time. And I always tell her, "I couldn't have survived it without you."

The bond Jessica felt with her battle buddy extended beyond companionship and solidarity. She saw this relationship as a means of survival when the grueling physical demands of basic training were impossible to accomplish on her own.

Military women form relationships based on their shared position as outsiders navigating a world designed for men. Military masculinity forms the basis of official training procedures; for example, uniforms, weaponry, and auxiliary gear are designed to be worn by a six-foot-tall man. Melissa Herbert notes that given the masculine nature of the military, "female soldiers may be accountable not only as women but as pseudomen."[16]

This was the case for Yesenia, a twenty-eight-year-old Army veteran, who described the "fine line" between proving herself competent in the masculine arena of soldiering and demonstrating an acceptable degree of femininity:

> You always have to prove yourself. Not just with all the soldier skills, firing a weapon, but I had to prove myself physically, through PT [physical training]. But I also had to prove myself as a woman. If I had been really gung-ho and acted more masculine, then I would have been put into a category and people would have thought less of me. I felt I had to maintain my femininity while proving myself that I could do everything the same as men. It's a very fine line—you don't want to go too far and be a prude.

Yesenia had to display enough military competence to perform "the same as men," yet she also had to avoid appearing masculine to maintain the respect of male soldiers.[17] Yesenia needed to project a calculated degree of femininity that was competent yet sufficiently soft while maintaining an aura of sexual availability, so as not to be considered a "prude." The pressure to balance between masculine military competence and femininity encouraged close bonds among female soldiers, who shared a similar status as outsiders or transgressors.

In everyday relations with male soldiers, women's military social status was constructed as sexualized and deficient. Journalist and military researcher Linda Bird Francke noted that in the military, "if the measure of a man was in his contrast to a woman, then she, by definition, had to display the feminine attributes for which she was derided."[18] Women in Francke's study of gendered social relations in the military, like the female veterans I interviewed, had to appear militarily competent without threatening men's self-confidence.[19]

Former marine and Central College student Keilani enforced military constructions of femininity among her female subordinates. Though she was a highly decorated noncommissioned officer, Keilani said that part of her job as a sergeant was to teach women marines to "take care of themselves" and to appear attractive and unthreateningly feminine.[20] Keilani showed woman how to dress appropriately so that they and other women would not be singled out for maltreatment: "Just being a woman marine, if you look bad (disheveled, out of uniform, or insufficiently feminine), you make all the other women marines look bad."

An official language reified masculinist relations whereby women acted as the feminine standard bearers by which male Marines could distinguish their masculinity. While men were called "marines," women were called "women marines."[21] This term took on even more derogatory and sexualized forms in colloquial use: "I always made sure that my female marines took care of themselves. Because in the Marine Corps, we're singled out all the time for being women. [Women marines] are called WMS, walking mattresses, wasted money. Wookiee monsters. That's what these guys would call us."[22]

In their study of male sexual offenders, Diana Scully and Joseph Marolla found that the sexual objectification of women "must be understood as an important factor contributing to an environment that trivializes, neutralizes and, perhaps, facilitates rape."[23] This has been borne out by contemporary research on female military and ex-military members.[24] Army veteran Sarah described this link between a military culture of objectification and her own rape perpetrated by male soldiers in her unit.

As the daughter of an itinerant white Southern Baptist pastor, Sarah spent her childhood moving around the United States. When Sarah joined the Army at age seventeen, she believed she was following a spiritual imperative: "At the time, I thought that God wanted me to join. I think it was a calling for me. At the time, I believed it very firmly, but now, looking back, I'm not sure I believe that God called me to join the military, or how my involvement in the military helps or hurts anything—I just don't know." Sarah's ambivalence about her military involvement did not arise from her participation in the war in Iraq; instead, it came from the treatment she received from military men. Sarah said that her Army experience never matched the highly touted masculine myth of the idealized brotherhood: "The problem I had was that I understood basic training to be a time where they break you down from your individual self with all your bad habits and build you back up into a soldier. I don't feel like the build-you-back-up part ever happened. Right up until graduation time, we were all pieces of shit, and so I never got that feeling of accomplishment, of, 'Now you're a soldier! Congratulations, you did it!' or anything like that. It was purely negative throughout the entire thing."

Describing herself as "idealistic" and "naive" when she joined the Army, Sarah said that she wanted to believe in military bonds of comradeship, but that she never experienced them. She had a particularly difficult time interacting with people who did not share her values of hard work and individual responsibility: "I was lucky that in Iraq, my group was a fairly honorable group of people. I mean, we weren't all best friends, but we did our work well. So that was fine. But for me, the Army values were something that every person internalizes; this is how we do our jobs. And for other people, they're ridiculous slogans on the walls of the halls. And I really didn't understand that until something traumatic happened to me. It was a very egregious learning process." This "very egregious learning process" was rape. On a two-week mission to Korea, three soldiers in Sarah's unit sexually assaulted her and another woman soldier. Sarah filed charges against her assailants, but, during the trial, advocates portrayed Sarah as responsible for the rape because she had gone out drinking with the men in her unit: "The process went to trial, and it was a three-year-long trial, at the end of which [the assailants] were all acquitted, and my career was absolutely defunct. So you get a gang rape, plus your reputation being tarnished, plus no more career that you built yourself around. It was really devastating for me."

Because she tried to hold her rapists accountable, Sarah lost her career, her faith in the military justice system, and her identity as a military service member. Sarah's deep sense of loss was made even greater by the idealization of military relationships. The band of brothers and sisters ethos of mutual dependency for safety and survival sharply juxtaposed with her experience of gang rape by men who were supposed to be her comrades.

Sarah felt betrayed not just by her rapists but also by military culture. The walls of her barracks were marked with the slogan "Do the right thing, even when no one is looking," but the Army fostered a culture of sexual violence against women. After she left the Army, Sarah did not maintain any military relationships. She refused to identify with the military or associate with veterans' groups, which she characterized as male-identified spaces hostile to women. Sarah did not experience the masculine military camaraderie as supportive as she was excluded from it and ultimately victimized by it.

This slogan, "Do the right thing, even when no one is looking," was mentioned often and with bitterness by women veterans. Most of the women I interviewed had been sexually harassed or assaulted while in the military.[25] Marine veteran Keilani was sexually assaulted by a male superior officer. She told me, "To this day, I feel like nobody understands the whole picture. You know, this [assailant] is a man who had drill instructors underneath his charge. He was a man who was supposed to turn these recruits into United States Marines. He was the one who was supposed to teach them about what integrity was, about doing the right thing when nobody is looking."

Francke writes that because military cultures are driven by "a group dynamic centered around male perceptions and sensibilities, male psychology and power, male anxieties and the affirmation of masculinity, harassment [of women] is an inevitable by-product."[26] Gender equality and respect for women conflicts with a military culture predicated on male dominance such that "the masculine forces driving the military culture make the enforcement of sexual harassment policies impossible. The systematic degradation of feminine attributes in the making of a military man required the very harassment the directives were supposed to eradicate."[27] Through a review of military court cases, Francke demonstrates a lack of institutional interest in enforcing codes against sexual harassment and assault. Equal opportunity advisors, who are charged with investigating complaints, may tacitly accept sexual harassment by ignoring complaints or promoting cultural rationalizations of harassment.[28]

In line with the findings of journalists, social scientists, and congressional inquiries, veteran students told me that sexual harassment (though not necessarily sexual battery or rape), was more rule than exception in military gender relations.[29] Sarah explained how the institutional military supported a culture of derision and disregard for women's sexual safety:

> There is lip service [paid to addressing sexual harassment]. Every unit has an EO [equal opportunity] officer, so we'd occasionally have these little trainings or meetings around this, where somebody says, "Okay, you can't say 'chink,' and you can't say 'whore.'" . . . It's like, "Ha-ha, oh and you know you can't rape anybody." So it's kind of like a joke. Occasionally you'll get somebody who's serious about it, but [other soldiers] roll their eyes and are like, "Oh geez, here he goes again." On the lowest levels, this is not taken seriously.

Sarah noted that before her rape, she participated in the culture of contempt for mandatory equal opportunity training, viewing it as superfluous "little trainings or meetings." She considered the content irrelevant because she did not imagine that she would be attacked by her fellow soldiers: "And I have to say that for me, I didn't take it all that seriously because I *knew* that the soldiers I was with weren't going to hurt me. They had my back. We're going into battle together. I'm not worried about them. I'm worried about these people I don't know. And it turns out that the people I trusted were the ones that raped me. So the whole culture makes it so that the equal opportunity stuff is laughable." Sarah said that her current antipathy for the EO training stemmed not from a belief that the content is irrelevant, but from her belief that the trainings were insincere.

Sarah's case illustrates the complex and contradictory nature of intense social bonding for military women. Women confront a social system that portrays them as sexualized transgressors in a social and professional world for men. Gendered social bonds played a critical role in veterans' post-military college life and in the transition from military and to civilian life, where many veterans depended on social relations developed in their previous military experience. Yet this option was rife with contradictions for women who experienced the institutional military as hostile, unhelpful, or abusive.

Both male and female veterans developed strong interpersonal relationships through the adverse conditions of living in combat zones, and they relied on companionship to ameliorate the physical and emotional hardships of military life. But when these bonds disappeared, veterans experienced a crisis of individual identity and profound social dislocation.

Some veterans spoke about the disappearance of military relationships as a loss similar to the death of a loved one. Some attempted to ameliorate this loss by hewing more closely to military ideologies and structures and by seeking to re-create military milieus within civilian colleges. Some sought familiarity in quasi-military social groups and professions, while others enrolled in courses in law enforcement or emergency services, and others participated in veterans' clubs and support organizations.

Some veterans chose careers in military-related or law enforcement fields because the paramilitary structure of these jobs resonated with their military experience. Central College student Brett said, "When I first got out [of the Army], I wanted to go to the academy and become a police officer 'cause it has that same basic structure as the military. It's very strict. They're very disciplined. You have to know your job and be able to perform it proficiently, so that was what I chose to do."

Other veterans sought careers in law enforcement, emergency services, or with the growing Homeland Security sector, because they felt these fields would allow them to use skills they acquired in their military training.[30] This was Central College student Jack's motivation for studying law enforcement:

> I decided I can go to school to be a cop. I decided about a year before I got out of active duty. I joined the military just to serve, just to do my part or whatever. I knew I was going to get out, and I wanted to be a police officer because a few people in my family are police officers, and they said [being in the military is] the perfect jump start for it [and that I should] go do that. It'll teach you discipline and all the things that they are looking for to get you a job.

Jack used his training to "jump start" his career path. He also enjoyed the criminal justice major because the learning process resembled the hands-on learning he experienced in the military: "All my criminal justice teachers are great. I love [the instructor]. He's an awesome guy. He's very practical and can relate things down to your level, not just read from a textbook and say these are the rules and this is how it happens." Jack's favorite criminal justice instructor was also a military veteran. Like Jack, other student veterans at Central College (and, less commonly, at SU) tended to gravitate to professors who were ex-military or supportive of the institutional military, and said that they would steer other veterans in the same direction.

Campus Veterans' Clubs: School-Based Military Networks

Much of the published veteran support literature notes that veterans' clubs provide helpful social, professional, and academic support to ease the transition to college.[31] According to DiRamio, Ackerman, and Mitchell, student-led campus veterans' groups are "one means for veterans to connect with peers and to develop a sense of camaraderie," and "a visible, campus-based student veterans' organization could provide opportunities for veterans to meet with students who have had similar experience while also serving as a point of connection to the campus."[32]

Campus veterans' clubs provided a place of connection in the midst of an otherwise disorienting entry into an unfamiliar system. Veterans' clubs were intended to address veterans' desire for camaraderie and their need for more practical services, such as logistical support, rides to events, tours of the campus and the surrounding area, and job referrals. They provided a structure for relationships of interdependence like the relationships veterans developed in the military. Yet unlike military life, the daily reality of college did not include forced interaction, grueling physical training, or life-threatening work conditions. Instead, veterans' clubs invoked positive memories of military relationships to facilitate campus-based yet military-influenced friendships.

These affinities surfaced in various venues. Group loyalty and familial relationships were fostered among veterans' club members through ritualized gatherings. For example, SU graduate student Joaquin issued a standing invitation to a monthly dinner at his house for all single SU club members. One veterans' club member told me that Joaquin wanted to offer veterans "without families and girlfriends" a place to experience a home-cooked meal. This statement reflected the male-focused heteronormative culture that dominated the SU Veterans Club. As with all campus clubs, membership changed each semester, but during the two years I observed club events and meetings, the group's active membership stayed at about twenty-five, with only one or two female veterans regularly attending.[33] Other ritualized gatherings included campus tailgate parties hosted by the Veterans Club before every major football game played at the su stadium.

Relationships developed in these clubs reinforced veterans' military connections and identities and provided networks that proved highly instrumental after graduation. Large corporations tended to recruit heavily from the veteran population, and campus veterans' clubs offered prime recruitment pools.[34] Recruiters from technology industry corporations regularly spoke at the su veterans' club meetings and the club hosted regular meet-and-greet events and field trips to tech firms in the area.

For some student veterans, campus clubs offered peer support and a reminder that they were not the only veterans at the school. Terry said that joining the su Veterans Club helped him to feel that he had his own community within the large urban campus. This kept him from feeling overwhelmed by the large body of civilian students:

> The su Vets Club for me was a very necessary thing. I don't know why any [veteran] who came here wouldn't join. 'Cause you walk around [su]—and I heard there's like forty thousand people here—and so you're just by yourself. But [after joining the club], I know there's the su Vets, and now I see them everywhere. Now that I've seen them once, I see them all the time, so that helps, even if we don't know each other's names necessarily, but I know that there's people here. We don't even have to talk, but I know they're there.

The su Veterans Club offered crucial social support for Terry, a male former marine who held positive military allegiances. Terry's comment that he did not understand why any veteran would not want to join the club reflected his position as a veteran who was not openly critical of U.S. military policy domestically or abroad.[35] Support for U.S. military actions was an implicit requirement to fit in at the su Veterans Club. The kind support Terry received was not necessarily available to other student veterans who expressed opposition to the U.S. military mission or who held conflicting feelings about their military service.

For some veterans, campus clubs provided supportive mentorship, with senior members serving as trusted cultural guides for navigating college norms and customs. This included advice on what classes to take, what labs, fellowships, and internships to apply for, professors to seek out or avoid, tips on time management and study skills, and strategies for managing traumatic stress in class.

Southwest University Navy veteran Jacob found what he called "a home" in the Veterans Club and credited club members with reaching out to him by phone after he had received his acceptance letter to su. "When I first got accepted to su, [a Veterans Club member] called me and said, 'Welcome to su,'" Jacob said. "He really made me feel at home." Jacob was invited to club events even before he started classes, which made him feel like he was part of a community. The mentorship of other veterans encouraged Jacob to think about expanding his own educational trajectory: "I really like [the Veterans Club]. It was really cool meeting a vet who started at a community college, then went to undergrad here [at su] and now he's getting his PhD. It made my own goals even higher and I thought, 'Maybe I can do that.'"

Like Jacob, Navy veteran Ricardo looked to his su peers for inspiration and motivation to succeed academically. Ricardo especially sought out advice from veterans who came from working-class immigrant or first-generation college backgrounds like his own or, as he put it, from veterans "who aren't officers." Ricardo felt that these veterans could serve as effective role models for him:

I really like [su] because I meet veterans that are successful. And not just successful where they are doing good. No, very successful. I met a Marine Corps Gulf War veteran who had his master's from Harvard. That tells me I can do it. I met a veteran who's a lawyer. I can do it. I met veterans that go to different [graduate] schools that have multiple degrees who aren't officers. There is a chance. I could do it. There are people who work hard and get those rewards. That's a big motivation for me.

Veterans' meetings at su often invoked a narrative of upward social mobility. Most regular undergraduate members of the su Veterans Club had enlisted at the lowest ranks. Though many had been promoted to specialist, corporal, or sergeant, the atmosphere of club meetings and social events remained proudly, almost defiantly, noncommissioned.[36] Just as Veterans Club members contrasted their working-class roots with their perceptions of entitled civilian su students, they also joked about the privileged cluelessness of commissioned officers. Many su veterans referred with pride to their working-class backgrounds and their noncommissioned military status, which they characterized as involving physically rigorous and dangerous duties.[37]

Veterans on both campuses developed similar informal advising networks; these functioned particularly well for students who wanted to enter military-related fields. Students sought out their fellow veterans to recommend courses and instructors. At Central College, many veterans took courses in the administration of justice and police science departments. Informal veteran networks were actively employed to advise and guide student veterans in choosing classes, instructors, academic majors, internships, and jobs.

Central College students Mitchell and Alex re-created military social bonds on campus that eased their transition into college. Both Mitchell (twenty-four years old) and Alex (thirty-two years old) were raised in white working-class families and had fathers who were ex-military. Both served combat tours in Iraq, and both experienced long periods of social isolation after leaving the Army. Mitchell joined the Army because his father, a former marine, wanted him out of the house. While still in high school, his father drove him to the Army recruiting station and signed a waiver authorizing Mitchell's enlistment as a minor. Mitchell left for basic training at age seventeen, two days after his high school graduation. When he was discharged from the Army after two tours in Iraq, he was unable to even consider going to college because his experience in combat had left him depressed and unable to focus. He drifted around, taking and quitting jobs in Ohio and Florida and forming turbulent romantic relationships with women. The psychological aftermath of his experience as an infantry soldier included severe depression, panic attacks, and uncontrollable rages. He explained, "For the first two years after I got out of the military, I did not want to set foot on a campus, because I was kind of afraid of myself. I had some night terrors. I had problems."

Alex was also born into a military family. Both his parents were members of the Air Force, and his father was an officer. Alex was not a motivated student and had conflicts with his father as a teenager. After graduating high school and looking for direction, he enlisted in the Navy. "I was, for lack of a better word, lost at the time. I stumbled through school. I graduated, but not very well. Never dumb, but still I just didn't care to try. I knew—something told me I needed something to alter, to change. If I would have gone to college at that point of time I would have just floundered around and done nothing."

After leaving the Navy, Alex went from job to job, taking work where he could get it: he remodeled kitchens and bathrooms, and worked as a boiler technician. He had a five-year stint as a manager at FedEx, but relocated with his girlfriend and young daughter to a town near Orchard Valley, where he found that jobs were harder to get in the agricultural community. Alex's decision to enroll in Central College was influenced by the bleak economic landscape of his new hometown: "I needed to do something. The economy was pretty much in shambles. I had a GI Bill and [I thought] it's probably about time to use it. So I decided to come back to school."

Mitchell's decision to return to school was motivated by wanting to improve his living situation. Tired of couch surfing at the homes of his high school friends, Mitchell moved in with his grandparents in Orchard Valley. His grandparents' offer to house him came with the condition that he attend school, so Mitchell enrolled in Central Community College, but continued to feel socially isolated:

> [In] the transition to Central, I kept to myself. I didn't talk to anyone. Classmates, females, would ask me questions, and I would answer them and then go right back to what I was doing. I didn't really open up much at all for the first four weeks or something like that. Even then, I didn't really do it until after I met my buddy Alex. He walked into our psychology class and he sat a couple of seats behind me. He had the [short, military-style] haircut and everything like that and the first thing I thought [was], "He's walking like he has a stick up his ass." So I turned around before class started and I said, "Are you ex-military?" He just started to laugh. He goes, "How the hell could you tell?" I said, "By the stick stuck up your ass." And that's how we became friends.

Mitchell's ability to decode the physical signifiers of Alex's haircut and comportment allowed Mitchell to see Alex as an ally. In a separate interview, Alex also recalled that first meeting in the psychology class, describing it as helpful for him as well because it gave him the chance to break his self-imposed social isolation: "I didn't go to school when I first got out [of the Navy]. I was very depressed for a very long time. Also, I wasn't into meeting people when I first got here. The support structures [at Central College] didn't exist for me. So a big thing for me is that one of the first people I met when I got here my second semester was Mitchell. [He was] the first vet that I talked to. We talked to each other for awhile. And he's going through very similar things that I did."

At thirty-two, Alex was older than Mitchell and considered himself a mentor: "[Mitchell] can talk to me. He knows that I understand. Him being able to talk to me seems to be helping him push forward. [I'll say,] 'Come on, let's go. Whenever something goes wrong, let's make it a positive.' Sitting next to him trying to be positive. Turning a negative into a positive. I just keep going." Alex and Mitchell's friendship helped to form the basis for the Central College veterans' club. The two men, along with other campus veterans, and Faye, a supportive college administrator, formed the group around an initiative to bring a mobile service center offering mental health evaluations, benefits advocacy, and peer supports for veterans to Central College. The student veterans identified each other and formed a critical mass with a demonstrated need that enabled Faye to advocate for institutional support.

Like the SU Veterans Club, members of the Central College veterans' club coached each other on how to relate to the broader campus community. Student veterans offered advice and social correctives to steer fellow veterans away from behavior that might get them in trouble or reflect poorly on veterans as a group. In one incident, Faye and Alex "had to put the kibosh" on Mitchell's behavior at a faculty meeting where members of the veterans' club were scheduled to make a presentation. The veterans were slated to speak after another campus student group, and Mitchell became impatient during the preceding group's presentation. To signal his displeasure, Mitchell pantomimed opening a rifle case, assembling and loading a rifle, and aiming it at the speakers.

> FAYE: Mitchell was particularly irritated by [the students in the preceding group]. But all of a sudden he goes something like this: he opens this case up and he pretends to assemble a weapon and load it.

> ALEX: Yeah, for lack of a better term, he's locking and loading.

> FAYE: Afterwards, I go, "Mitchell, Mitchell, Mitchell, you can't lock and load."

> ALEX: Oh, I chewed his ass that night.

> FAYE: And [veterans] all do this [offer each other advice] because they take care of each other. And I go, "Mitchell, you're going to destroy everything we did here. Do you understand what's happened in some of the colleges?" And not necessarily [just with] vets, but locking and loading, stuff like that, shootings in college. . . .

> ALEX: You can't do that. Especially with our particular community, with the things that are out there. . . .

When Alex spoke about "our particular community," he was referring not only to the community of military veterans, but also to the town of Orchard Valley. Weeks before this interview took place, the small rural community was rocked by a violent incident. One of the town's residents—an Iraq War veteran— shot and killed his mother and eleven-year-old sister before fatally shooting himself.[38]

> FAYE: Oh my God yes.

> ALEX: And I'm like, "Dude, you don't represent yourself anymore."

> FAYE: [I said,] "Never do that again."

ALEX: I said, "If you're part of this group, you represent yourself, but you also represent our group. And you represent the college. You need to control yourself. I understand you don't like [the students]. And it's okay not to like them. It's your choice. God bless America. But you can't do that."

As Mitchell's mentor, Alex offered guidance about norms of behavior in civilian society and instructed him on how to appropriately represent the veterans' group on campus. Alex's message—that gestures that might be humorous in some military settings could easily be interpreted as threatening in a civilian faculty meeting—did not threaten Mitchell's sense of self, because it came from a trusted fellow veteran. Alex acknowledged the animosity Mitchell felt toward the civilian students, but forbade him from acting out a symbolically violent scene. Shared experiences enabled veterans to train each other on appropriate behavior among civilians.

Like Alex and Mitchell, student veterans at other community colleges experienced feelings of alienation that caused them to seek out other veterans and to create campus veterans' clubs. Southwest University student Kevin remembered feeling isolated during his first days as a community college student after leaving the Army: "There was no one to connect with. There were three hundred [veterans] on campus, and I didn't know any of them. There was just no network of people there to interact with for veteran issues, or to bring up issues." The veterans' club at Kevin's community college was formed after Kevin and others reached out to a student veteran known to suffer acute psychological episodes symptomatic of severe PTSD. Student veterans on the campus were concerned about this veteran's mental health and tried to get him help. Kevin said:

> One of my best friends [who also served] in Afghanistan, me and him, we'd always find this guy just flipping the fuck out and throwing shit, or barricading himself in the library. That's why I contacted . . . the web advisor person . . . like, "Hey, how come there's no veterans' officer? Who do I contact? There's nothing there." That led to me meeting up with my best friend, the Afghanistan vet. We were talking [to other veterans on campus] about how this guy was flipping out all the time. Me and him would be talking [to other veterans, saying], "Oh, when you see this guy, this is what he's dealing with. Maybe you can help him." It was word of mouth.

The word-of-mouth network Kevin and his friend used to support a veteran with psychological needs organized into an informal network of support, sowing the seeds for a more formal campus organization. Kevin continued, "Then we started the Vet Club. I originally contacted the president of the school and was like, 'The veterans need to be looked at.' They agreed and had all the board members sitting there. We started the vet group. They gave us our own office."

To address problems of isolation and psychological trauma, Kevin and his friend started a club where he and other veterans could re-create the atmosphere of camaraderie they experienced in the military. Kevin said that he identified with the veteran who suffered from PTSD, which is why he pressured the school to provide support: "I've had breakdowns at school too, and the school needs to be aware of that, if that's going on. They're dealing with mentally fragile people that are trying to restart their life. You need to embrace them and help them along the way. Veterans are so used to being told where to go, what to do, and how to act. Now, you're being thrust into community college or something like that where you're just another face. A lot of times, we come undone."

While not all veterans return from war and enter college exhibiting symptoms of PTSD, Kevin's words underscore the importance of peer and institutional support measures for newly arrived veterans on college campuses. Tensions arise when veterans move from the highly structured, group-oriented military environment to the civilian collegiate space, and veterans' clubs that re-create a sense of commonality and group identity can mitigate those tensions.

While some veterans worked to re-create military relationships, others sought to broaden their social circles, branching out and away from exclusively military support networks and identities. Many looked to create alliances with civilians in their postmilitary lives. Central College student Cody was one of these students who chose to look beyond a familiar circle of student veterans. When he enlisted in the Navy, Cody knew he wanted a career in medicine, and he began at Central College as a prenursing student. After getting to know some premed students at his school, he decided to finish the requisite science courses and transfer to a premed program at a four-year college. While Cody maintained friendly relationships with other veterans on campus, he came to realize that he had more in common with nonmilitary students who shared his academic interests and current life goals and began associating with civilian premed students rather than veterans:

> I'm really not as affiliated with [veterans on campus] as much as I am with Med Club [for medical school aspirants] right now. The veterans' club office is completely on the opposite side of campus from me. My classes are all over here because I'm taking all science classes, and all the people I'm

with are people that I want to be with in med school. It's easier for me to talk to them on a daily basis because I'm sitting right next to them in class. Not that the campus is huge, but it's a five-, ten-minute walk to get over there, and you're always running into people on the way over there, so it takes longer than you want to get over there, and it's like, "Man, I really should be sitting down working on my homework or something."

Cody realized that his aspirations were more in line with the Med Club but seemed somewhat apologetic about choosing to associate with civilians rather than veterans. Cody credited the members of the Med Club with exposing him to new perspectives and future career possibilities. He said the Med Club gave him the confidence to go after an MD degree: "When I first joined [the Med Club] I was like, 'I'm not going to med school. I'm going to go to nursing school. I'm going to get my BSN at State [University] and we'll call it good; then I'll re-evaluate at that point.' Now it's like, 'Okay, well, I *could* do med school.'" Cody attributed his confidence to his newfound relationships with like-minded civilian students. The college experience exposed ex-military and civilian students alike to new ideas, questions, and ways of thinking. For some student veterans, this process brought them closer to military affinities and relationships, but for others like Cody, it created distance from their military affiliations.

Some veterans who had complicated relationships with the military and the wars did not see veterans' clubs as welcoming spaces because they overtly valorized the U.S. military. Many veterans who struggled to make meaning of their experiences of war still identified support from fellow veterans as extremely important to their ability to integrate into civilian life, but they did not necessarily find that support in campus veterans' clubs. Instead, these veterans sought camaraderie from other veterans who did not support the wars or who openly disagreed with U.S. military policies.

Many student veterans felt strongly loyal to their fellow veterans after discharge. Many of these ex-military students wanted to help other veterans even though they did not necessarily endorse or embrace military ideologies. For example, during SU student Jordan's tour of duty with the Marines in Iraq, he developed a critical view of the war's rationale and tactics. In Iraq, where he was following orders and leading subordinates in combat, Jordan's critique was visceral and inchoate; in his words, "Sometimes you don't know what's right, but you know what's wrong." Without the language or detailed analysis to formulate his objections, he felt that his only recourse was to distance himself from all things military. When his contract ended and he left the Marines, Jordan attempted to sever all connections with military habits, dress, and identifications. To reclaim his civilian identity and repudiate his status as a "cog in the [military] machine," Jordan grew his hair long and took an extended backpacking trip through Europe. "My coping mechanism was denial. Grow the hair out, grow the facial hair out, because the first thing they do in boot camp is they take your hair away. It's an identity that most people don't realize and don't appreciate. They take your hair away and give you all the same clothes and then you're a cog in the machine."

To distance himself from the negative psychological effects of his difficult combat experience, Jordan briefly embraced a form of denial: "[I was] trying to just run, just get away from it as much as I could. . . . That's all I knew, is that my experience was not just unpleasant but miserable, you know? And so I was just trying to get away from it. Like, okay, I did what I was supposed to. And now I'm done with that. And I'm going to put that in a little box, shut it aside and forget about it forever." Jordan scrubbed his life of any physical identifiers that might mark him as a marine so that his external appearance would match his internal identity as nonmilitary. He said, "There are no stickers on my car. I don't have Marine T-shirts. I don't have stuff on my bag. I don't have tattoos and I wouldn't show them off. I was just trying to be as far divorced from that as I could."

But despite Jordan's grown-out hair, the experience of his job in Iraq was indelibly inscribed in his consciousness: "It definitely becomes a part of you that you can't get rid of, even if you want to. That's the realization I've come to recently, that—I mean, I described running from the experience, just trying to get as far away from it as I could. [pauses] And you can't. It's a part of who you are."

When Jordan left the Marines, he faced a task shared by many combat veterans: to try to piece together a cohesive understanding of the fragmentary and traumatic experience of war. Throughout ten hours of interviews over the course of five meetings, Jordan kept returning to the idea that "sometimes you don't know what's right, but you know what's wrong" to describe his reaction to his participation in what he came to believe was an unjust war. Jordan returned from Europe still grappling with these internal questions and conflicts, and he reapplied to su, this time majoring in cognitive science:

I also was looking for some, I guess the word is maybe "redemption." And I knew it would just click when I found it. So I started looking in school. [College funding] was one of the big motivating factors for joining the Marines, so that was pretty obvious. Like I could get paid to go to school, but really, what I wanted to do was find something that was meaningful to me and that was the opposite of the feeling [I had in Iraq]. I was looking for that sense of purpose, scholastically or intellectually. So the fact that I was able to come to su was like, "Wow! That's a pretty good place to go and look for something like that." And I was very appreciative for the room to grow and the room to explore, not just intellectually, but personally.

Like Jordan, many veterans entered college highly motivated, not simply to complete a degree, but also to make sense out of their psychologically disjointed experiences of war. Several veterans chose their course of study specifically to learn about global politics and about the diversity of geopolitical thought. Southwest University student Terry said that he chose to major in political science because his experience fighting in Iraq made him want to learn about international affairs. Being deployed in Iraq, he said, "definitely gave me a different view of the world from when I left home and went overseas. It really opened up my eyes and made the world seem like a much bigger place." Other veterans said that they believed that taking college courses would help them to contextualize their involvement in the wars.

Erica came to su specifically to learn about Iraqi history and culture. Born into a white Christian family and raised in a small town in upstate New York, Erica was studying at a local community college when an Army recruiter got her name from the school's financial aid office. "I got a call from a recruiter. He had gotten my name from the school, which I think should be illegal," she said, adding that she considered this practice of identifying potential recruits through the financial aid lists predatory and invasive. "I told him I wanted to be a journalist, and he said, 'I can offer you a journalism job in the military, and we'll pay you.'" Without any other funding possibilities on the horizon, and facing the possibility of having to drop out of college, Erica enlisted. After two tours in Iraq as a military journalist, Erica left the Army disillusioned about the U.S. mission in the Middle East. After her discharge, Erica settled on the West Coast and returned to her studies at a local community college before transferring to su. "I'm studying Near Eastern civilizations [at su] to get a little more perspective on my experience," she said.

Look, I spent two full years—more than two full years—of my life in Iraq, and I came back knowing nothing about it. I didn't know how to speak any of the language, know anything about the history, didn't know anything about the culture or the people, and now I want to know because I feel like I should, you know? It's not that, like, anyone is expecting me to, but once the idea was introduced to me of like, "Why don't you study the

Middle East?" it was like, "Yeah, why don't I?" Like that made complete sense.

Erica felt that she should learn about the language, culture, and people of the place that had so affected her life. She had been uncomfortable as a military journalist in an occupied country, where her task was to promote her superiors' point of view. Now that she was no longer representing military interests, her vocational focus had shifted away from professional journalism: "I wanted to be a journalist in the military, right? But I went in only knowing the military's point of view. So, you know, even though now I'm not really interested in going into journalism per se, I'm still very interested in being an information spreader and, like, being a voice of reason where I can be, and in order to do that, I need to have more knowledge, like I need to have more information at my disposal."

Though she did not use the same words, Erica implied that she was also looking for what Jordan called "redemption," or a reworking of her wartime experience. Erica intended to transform herself from a purveyor of officially sanctioned information to a critically informed "information spreader" and a "voice of reason." Her desire to recast her military role led her to join the off-campus group Iraq Veterans against the War (IVAW).[39]

Though Jordan sought to distance himself from U.S. military ideologies and from the wars, he maintained bonds with other veterans on campus because they shared a common history and because he identified with their struggles to reconnect to civilian academic and social worlds. Jordan was deeply loyal to other veterans, if not the institutional U.S. military. While he spoke against the war vociferously and eloquently in private, Jordan was not affiliated with any group organized to oppose the war, but he was also not a regular member of the campus veterans' club. On the SU campus, there were no formal groups or organized spaces for veterans who did not hold positive associations with their military experience.

One reason that many officially sanctioned campus veterans' clubs operate with a military-valorizing valence might be that these groups tend to be actively supported by military advocacy groups such as Veterans of Foreign Wars and the American Legion. These larger groups provide campus club members with financial support and hold celebratory events like barbecues, flag ceremonies, and other events marking Flag Day, Veterans Day, and Memorial Day.

Some campus veterans' clubs discourage critical examination of the wars or of the U.S. military. In these spaces, the perspectives of veterans who oppose the wars may be unwelcome. Moreover, because the gender dynamics in campus veterans' clubs can mirror the masculinist gender dynamics of the military, women veterans who oppose the wars may feel especially marginalized. In November 2011, a former U.S. marine and antiwar activist suffered a severe head injury after being hit with a metal gas canister fired by police at a street protest. When Erica (a member of both the su Veterans Club and ivaw) posted statements supporting the injured protester on the su veterans' Facebook page, the posts were removed without explanation. She said, "[Veterans Club members] just deleted it. When I messaged to ask why this got deleted, I didn't get a response." Eventually Erica was told by the moderators of the Facebook page that the Veterans Club defined itself as apolitical and that the group voted to prohibit her political statements on the Facebook page, calling them "controversial." She said, "That's when I was like, 'Look, this Facebook group needs some oversight because if you want to make rules and guidelines, then you have to stick to them. If somebody posts something that's controversial, if it doesn't violate the guidelines, then it's [simply] controversial. That's okay. I was like, 'This is Southwest University. Why are you guys acting like you're in the military?'"

Later, at a meeting called to discuss the club's Facebook policies, Erica contested the group's decision.[40] She described the interchange as follows:

[Veterans Club members said,] "You've got to keep your politics out of my vets' group." It was literally, "Keep your politics out of my vets' group." I'm like, "Do you guys even realize what you're saying?" I started getting really upset because I was like, "The way you're talking is like, what are you, still in the military?" It was very much still in the military mind-set. Some of those comments that they were posting, it was like, "She doesn't know how to fit into the group." I'm like, "Oh, really? Is it about *me* not knowing how to fit into the group? Why can't the group have room for all vets no matter what their stance and their politics?"

In the contested ideological terrain of the veterans' club, the accepted common sense held that engaging in politics meant taking a public stand against the U.S. military or the current U.S. wars, or supporting social causes such as the Occupy Wall Street movement that challenged the status quo. Erica heatedly challenged the club members' claim that the club didn't engage in politics. She asserted—in line with social theorists such as Antonio Gramsci and Stuart Hall—that there is no political neutrality in expressive acts and that all public gestures convey political meaning.[41] According to Erica, the Veterans Club's claim to an apolitical stance was a stance in support of a military-valorizing status quo. In the meeting, Erica argued that pictures on the Facebook page of su veterans shaking hands with George W. Bush and raising money for military causes conveyed the group's underlying politics of support for the current wars:

> I said, "If you want to say this su Vets Facebook group is for nothing political ever, then I better not see pictures of any former fucking *controversial* presidents, and I better not see pictures of that guy trying to raise money for his Marine Corps unit's ball by raffling off an assault rifle. How are you going to say that's not political? That is an extremely political statement: saying we're going to raffle off this gun for our Marine Corps ball. That is a political fucking statement. There are shootings happening all over the place but [offering a rifle as a raffle prize] is okay to post. Those things get approval. But as soon as I want to post something that refers to Occupy it's like, oh no no. Whose interests are you fighting for?'"

The discussion about the deleted Facebook post at the Veterans Club meeting devolved into a shouting match, and Erica said she was told to "get the fuck out." When Erica objected to the aggressive tone of comments directed at her, another member told her, "We're veterans—we're supposed to be aggressive." Through interactions such as this one, the su Veterans Club reproduced and defended the masculinized culture of the military and disciplined those who challenged militarized practices.

Female veterans were more likely than males to experience alienation from campus veterans' spaces. Erica's experience with the su Veterans Club was dramatic and uncommon, perhaps because most veterans who didn't agree with the club's positions and practices simply faded from the scene and stopped attending meetings and club events. But other female veterans on campus told me that they shared Erica's feeling of exclusion. While I don't know all of the reasons that individual student veterans chose not to affiliate with campus veteran support groups, one comment I heard often was that many wanted to disassociate themselves from the military; they just wanted to fit in and be considered students rather than veterans.

Sarah's rape by fellow soldiers who were subsequently exonerated by the military judicial system was the primary reason that she no longer identified as military and the reason that she did not seek to replicate military relationships. Her military identity was sharply and temporally divided into before-and-after periods, marked by her assault. Sarah refused to identify as a veteran anywhere but on VA benefits forms. She said, "[Being a member of the military] is who I was, and not who I am. I think if my military career had turned out better, I might have different feelings, but in my mind, today, there are two different militaries:

there's the one that I volunteered to serve in and the one that kicked me into the road when I was gang-raped. I can't reconcile those two militaries. So when someone says, 'Congratulations, you're part of the whole thing,' I've got mixed feelings." Sarah chose not to attend male-dominated veterans' meetings because of her deep alienation from the military milieu and her desire to rejoin civilian society: "I'm really trying to assimilate into a civilian environment, and it does not help me to surround myself with people who aren't able to function [in civilian spaces], so I've chosen to distance myself from those people. Some people just can't relate to civilians. I think that's a really sad state of being: they can't get back in the military, and yet they don't fit in this [civilian] world either."

When I spoke with Sarah in August 2011, she had left college without graduating and was working as an administrative assistant for a mental health agency. She had been considering the possibility of returning to college when she had what she called a "nervous breakdown." After a period of avoiding all things military, she entered a VA military sexual trauma treatment program: "At first I didn't trust the VA because it's part of the military, but I did four months of in-patient therapy with them and have experienced tremendous recovery since then. It's cheesy to say, but it's been life-changing, having gone through the program. If they would make me a poster child and give me a microphone I would tell people, 'You don't have to suffer anymore.' They [VA military sexual trauma unit staff] are very professional and very caring on a personal level."

At the time we spoke, Sarah was researching the possibility of returning to college. She had joined a peer support group for women veterans who experienced military sexual trauma. Her group met weekly to provide informal social support for each other as well as practical support, sharing advice on navigating the VA system and GI Bill college funding, and maintaining personal relationships in their postmilitary lives. Sarah's military sexual assault support group served many of the functions of campus veterans' clubs, in that it provided social support and guidance, but the group also provided acceptance that members may have conflicted or negative feelings about their military experiences.

As a man, SU student Kevin's experience was significantly different from Sarah's, but he also avoided social groups like the SU Veterans Club because his antiwar politics put Kevin at the margins of the tight-knit campus group. Kevin said he felt uncomfortable with what he called club members' overt and implied support for the current wars. The veterans club Kevin started at his community college called for increased veterans' services while also taking a public position against the war. Kevin said that he knew of several SU veterans who did not affiliate with the campus Veterans Club because their opposition to the war was unpopular with the club's more vociferous members. Like Sarah,

Kevin distanced himself from his previous military life because it did not reflect his current belief system:

> Another veteran who's here at SU, me and him have had the same kinds of run-ins with the rest of the [SU veterans'] group. We're kind of like-minded with our political beliefs [opposing the war] and stuff like that, and we're distancing ourselves from the military. [The military] was part of my life, but I'm not there anymore. I have that [veteran] connection with these guys, but that's about it. I am hesitant about the whole like, "Hooah!" thing and being part of the military thing still. A lot of these guys are still all about that, and I'm not. Me and my friend talk about it all the time. Why are there like 275 people [of the 300 veterans enrolled at SU] not in the group?

Kevin hypothesized that perhaps so few veterans on campus joined the club because the group's activities centered on social events reflecting interests that he and other veterans did not share: "All of the [social] events circulate around drinking and going to strip clubs or whatever it is. Not everyone's about that. Some people have got families." Kevin was referring to informal Veterans Club social gatherings; however, the club also organized philanthropic and service events like a golf tournament to benefit nonprofit veterans' service groups, home-building weekends with Habitat for Humanity, and a Valentine's Day fund-raiser to benefit breast cancer research. Asked what he thought the Veterans Club might do to help him and his like-minded student veteran friends, he said, "Maybe it could be like [organizing] a study session. I don't know—[pauses] I guess that sounds stupid."

Concerned that he would appear stupid for advocating activities that went against the dominant social dynamic of the Veterans Club, Kevin opted instead not to participate. Thus, while veteran-only clubs and classes can be very helpful to veterans making the transition to civilian college, these clubs may also serve to exclude veterans who have conflicted or negative associations with their military experience.

Of the fifty veterans I interviewed, many privately expressed views against the war, but only Erica publicly took an antiwar stance and openly claimed membership in IVAW. Other veterans who were not openly affiliated with groups opposing the Iraq and Afghanistan wars chose to offer support to fellow veterans in less public ways. For example, Adam, a Gulf War veteran, described how his community college art classes provided him with a medium for working through his war experience and laid the foundation for his current practice of supporting fellow war veterans through the arts:

As a young man, I thought being able to take somebody's life or to hurt somebody was power. But then after the [Gulf] war, you feel pretty weak when somebody gets shot and you can't do anything about it. So I got out of the Marines and was studying to be an EMT [emergency medical technician]. Then I snapped my ankle, couldn't complete the training. I had one drawing class [in community college], and I asked the professor if I could take his painting class as well so I could keep up the units. I took drawing and painting classes with this guy, who is Japanese American, was raised in internment camps during World War II. He said all art is political. He kind of encouraged me after the beginning classes to make work about my experiences and stuff.

Art classes that began as a way to fill his schedule with required units ultimately provided Adam with a way to express his feelings about war and to reach out to other veterans. Adam was drawn to artistic expression, which allowed him to make personal statements reflecting his opposition to war without appearing overly strident or confrontational. Creating art also allowed him to break out of what he felt were dichotomous stereotypes of veterans: "I started doing ceramics and that kind of just locked in. I think the [problem] with trying to talk about war is that I don't want to be vilified or made a hero."

Adam's reluctance to become a public spokesperson about war, coupled with his strongly held position that the violence of war should not be glorified, led him to his current job working in the Art Department of SU, running the campus ceramics studio and creating ceramic art in his off hours. His specialty was making ceramic cups decorated with images evoking his combat experience. About his art, Adam said, "I think clay is the right scale. And cups. I've been making cups, seriously, since 2000. I had my first show after undergrad in 2001. I'm at like fourteen thousand cups, now, that I've given away since 2001. I resisted the 'art is healing thing,' you know, but I realized it is about becoming clear, or something."

Adam's search for clarity involved finding a way to portray the humanity of soldiers and of civilian victims of war violence through art rather than rhetoric. His art allowed him to express pride in his service to fellow soldiers and his dissent from the current wars. Above all, Adam sought to make visible his feelings about the detriments of war.

"Working with ceramics is kind of a vocation. I feel it's what I've been called to do, and focusing on these issues of war and violence is what I want to talk about," Adam said in the clay-splattered studio at SU. After the Gulf War, he sent a thousand cups decorated with images of soldiers and combat to corporate and political leaders and to military leaders at the Pentagon. This was his

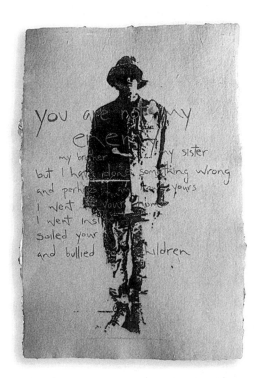

FIGURE 4.1 Drew Cameron and Drew Matott, "You Are Not My Enemy (Vol. IV)," poem and image on combat paper made from repurposed combat uniforms.

you are not my enemy
my brother my sister
but I have done something wrong
and perhaps so have yours
I went into your home
I went inside
soiled your
and bullied your children

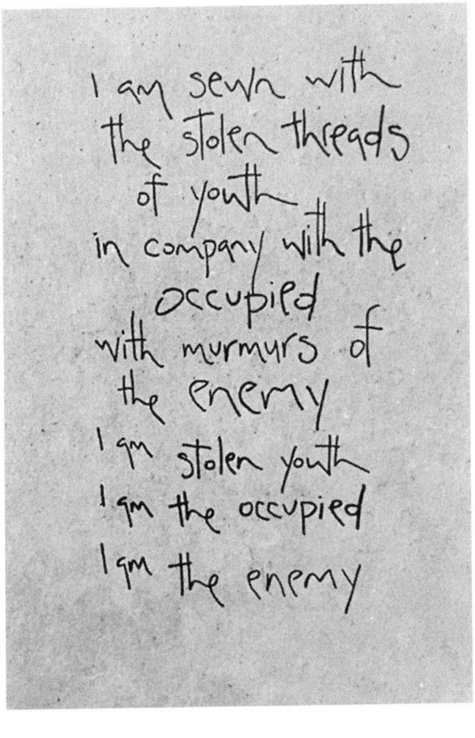

FIGURE 4.2 Drew Cameron, "Stolen Youth," poem on combat paper made from repurposed combat uniforms. University of Iowa Center for the Book.

I am sewn with
the stolen threads
of youth
in company with the
occupied
with murmurs of
the enemy
I am stolen youth
I am the occupied
I am the enemy

attempt to help leaders to see the human costs of war. "The cups are my version of humbly, quietly, making the thing, and letting it out into the world; of asking people to accept it, to recognize it."

In addition to developing his own art, Adam reached out to campus veterans when he heard they were having trouble adjusting, especially those who might feel alienated from other campus veteran support groups: "Now my own story is overlapping with the younger vets. I can't help but feel really protective. I want to help them, because it feels like I failed some way; that if I had succeeded, then they wouldn't have to be in Iraq." Adam got his department to sponsor art events on campus like the Combat Paper Project where combat veterans were invited to cut up their combat uniforms, put them through a pulping machine, and turn them into paper. Veterans then used the combat uniform–based paper to inscribe poetry, drawings, or other artwork to process—in a literal as well as figurative sense—their wartime experiences through and into art.

Veterans' particular responses to their participation in war will influence the kind of support they require after returning home. Veterans arrive on college campuses with varying degrees of affinity and disaffection for the military and employ different strategies to adapt to college. Some veterans reproduce military social relationships while others work to create distance from their military experiences. At SU and Central College, student veterans who sought to replicate military social relationships on campus tended to be men who were not openly critical of military policies and projects. Veterans who struggled with their military service may also attribute their disaffection and psychic pain to different sources. For example, Erica joined the Army to become a journalist but realized that she was instead acting as a propagandist for a cause she did not support; Sarah enlisted in response to a call from God but was raped by her fellow soldiers. Jordan entered the Marines to serve his country and left seriously objecting to the war. Support programs that do not take into account veterans' complex relationships to military service and war will fail to serve all veterans, privileging those who feel positively about their military service at the expense of those who do not. When support programs are built around essentialized assumptions about veterans, many veterans will feel alienated from the very services that are designed to ease their integration. Effective support for veterans requires programs that are built on a nuanced understanding of complex wartime experiences.

· 5 ·

SPECTRAL WARS AND THE
MYTH OF THE ANTIMILITARY CAMPUS

Common sense is not a single unique conception, identical in time and space.
It is the "folklore" of philosophy, and, like folklore, it takes countless different forms.
Its most fundamental characteristic is that it is a conception which, even in the brain of
one individual, is fragmentary, incoherent and inconsequential, in conformity with
the social and cultural position of those masses whose philosophy it is."
ANTONIO GRAMSCI, *Selections from the Prison Notebooks*

For any way of thought to become dominant, a conceptual apparatus has to be
advanced that appeals to our intuitions and instincts, to our values and desires, as well as
to the possibilities inherent in the social world we inhabit. If successful, this conceptual
apparatus becomes so embedded in common sense as to be taken for granted
and not open to question.
DAVID HARVEY, *A Brief History of Neoliberalism*

Before familiarity can turn into awareness the familiar must be stripped of
its inconspicuousness; we must give up assuming that the object in question needs
no explanation. However frequently recurrent, modest, vulgar it may be,
it will now be labeled as something unusual.
BERTOLT BRECHT, *Brecht on Theater*

When I began this study, I originally set out to explore war veterans' experiences and meaning making on college campuses. But as I explored what happens to soldiers after they return home from the battlefield and enroll in college, I learned that soldiers are not the only individuals trained in military ways of thinking. Civilians also receive training on how to perceive and relate to military personnel and projects. Historical narratives are strategically deployed by advocates of the military mission to produce an idealized narrative of veteran victimization that valorizes military projects on college campuses. These narratives can have negative consequences for student veterans whose unique experiences are rendered invisible.

This chapter examines the relationship between the social production of the idealized yet victimized veteran and the enforcement of loyalty to veterans and, by extension, to the contemporary U.S. wars. College veteran support programs, veterans' service agencies, high school programs, and other nonprofit community organizations produce idealized narratives of student veterans that tend to reify military discourse. I look to Gramsci's theory of hegemony to understand how military discourse is institutionalized on college campuses.[1] Hegemony creates a unified vision of an assumed natural order that universalizes the concepts of rule, aspirations, and culture to naturalize ideological conceptions—in this case, of what it means to care for veterans. This chapter examines how support for veterans is promoted as support for the military and taken up as educational "best practices" on college campuses. The formulation of militarized best practices of veteran support rests primarily on two assumptions: (1) that contemporary college campuses are hostile to the military, and (2) that veterans' programs should be designed to remediate this ostensibly hostile campus climate.

I begin by examining the mythologized image of contemporary college campuses as hostile to U.S. military veterans. This lays the foundation for a review of interventions designed to remediate this supposed antimilitary problem through the discourses of care that simultaneously frame student veterans as victims of discrimination and as heroes deserving public valorization. Interventions aimed at protecting veterans from alleged discrimination are what I call protective strategies, and those celebrating not simply veterans' military service but also the institutional military are what I call valorization strategies. Both protective and valorization strategies conflate support for the veteran with uncritical support for military projects, and both have the effect of silencing debate on campus about contemporary military conflicts.

Heroic Narratives

The practice of using heroic narratives about soldiers to rally support for veterans returning from war is as old as the practice of war itself. Marc Grandstaff notes that even before U.S. soldiers returned from World War II in 1945–1946, mass-market magazines like *Life* and the *Saturday Evening Post* ran full-page public service ads with rich narratives extolling the virtues of returning heroes.[2] Popular magazines, newsreels, and radio shows ran stories about "who the soldier was, what he had endured and what the veteran came to expect upon his return."[3] The treatment of GIS returning victorious from World War II set the standard for subsequent wars.[4] However, unlike soldiers after World War II, veterans today return from multiple deployments to multiple conflicts that do not enjoy similar widespread popular support.

In addition to the standards set by World War II veterans' services, contemporary veterans' services are informed by the narratives of Vietnam War veterans. The enduring image of campus hostility to the Vietnam War gave rise to veteran support services designed to counteract historical antipathies by actively welcoming military viewpoints on campuses.

The Specter of Vietnam

The trope of the antimilitary campus is rooted in historic narratives about the Vietnam War. Since the 1991 Gulf War, U.S. civilian society has shifted toward the militarization of public spaces, collective understandings, and discourses about wars.[5] Veterans are returning from contemporary wars in growing numbers, inspiring a burgeoning scholarship on the experiences of veterans in institutions of higher education.[6] As background to my claim that veteran support is conflated with military support, I look to the literature on the national mythos of the reviled Vietnam War veteran that influences current debates and practices on college campuses.[7] Over time, there has been a "gradual but continuous absorption" of heroic narratives about military missions and soldiering on college campuses, and these narratives have been institutionalized in campus programs and everyday consciousness.[8]

The Vietnam War was a bitterly contentious experience for many in the United States: nearly sixty thousand U.S. soldiers died, and the unpopular war left the country deeply divided.[9] After the U.S. military defeat in Vietnam, politicians and the public feared involvement in another intractable foreign war. Public aversion to U.S.-sponsored wars was framed in pseudo-medical language and given the rhetorical diagnosis of "Vietnam Syndrome."[10] This notion became embedded in U.S. political discourse and was invoked as a national malady by proponents of military involvement abroad. From the 1991 Operation Desert Storm—also known as the first Gulf War—to the present wars in Iraq and Afghanistan, the Vietnam War has been a constant historical referent in political rhetoric.[11] While the phrase "Vietnam Syndrome" originally implied congressional and popular aversion to U.S. involvement in foreign wars, it has since taken on an additional cultural resonance: Vietnam Syndrome now signals the idea that popular opposition to the Vietnam War systematically discouraged and demoralized U.S. combat troops, contributing to U.S. defeat.[12]

Myra Mendible describes the imprint of the Vietnam War on U.S. cultural memory as "a psychodrama of humiliation": "No longer signifying a nation, 'Vietnam' functions as metaphor for America's humiliation. This trope has served US presidents from Richard Nixon to George W. Bush, each of whom has relied on its compelling themes to garner support for military interventions and 'pre-emptive' strikes. It frames America's political rhetoric whenever leaders seek to stifle political dissent at home, 'harden' national borders, or rally nationalistic strains in the American character. Recalled in this way, the legacy of Vietnam becomes a story about 'our' humiliation, about the 'wrong' committed against *us*."[13]

Mendible argues that the "us" on whom this national humiliation was visited is embodied by Vietnam War veterans. Positioned in popular culture as human surrogates for the humiliation of a nation, the story of mistreatment of Vietnam War veterans provided the rationale and imperative to reassert military dominance:

> Stories about America's humiliation have circulated widely through popular lore and familiar images. They often play out through Hollywood film stereotypes of the Vietnam veteran, whose wounded body and psyche sign for the nation's crisis of honor. Spat upon by ungrateful anti-war protestors, lied to by their presidents, shackled by the policies of civilian whiz kids in Washington, America's protagonists in these tales form a sad cast of dishonored men, defeated warriors, forgotten sons and husbands. Vietnam veterans' memoirs further chronicle this emotional legacy, bearing witness to the dishonor that haunts warriors from a mighty nation defeated by small men in "black pajamas." These images and stereotypes have shaped the nation's popular memory over time and become fodder for its war machinery.[14]

While there is little actual evidence showing intentional harm to U.S. soldiers by antiwar protesters, the narrative of antiwar protesters mistreating troops still holds sway.[15] The trope of 1960s antiwar liberals and student activists invokes the narrative that the U.S. public actively renounced American soldiers in Vietnam and reviled them after they returned home as veterans. This narrative is accepted among many military supporters (including organizations such the American Legion and Veterans of Foreign Wars [VFW], and in some scholarship on higher education).[16] This narrative asserts an antagonistic and causal link between antiwar demonstrators and problems of veterans by implying that the peace activists of the 1960s are to blame for the problems experienced by many Vietnam veterans; not the war, or inadequate government attention to their needs, or public apathy. Thus the trope of civilian hostility toward veterans becomes a commonsense explanation for the historical reality of societal and governmental neglect of U.S. soldiers after they returned from Vietnam. It provides a tidy explanation for complex problems faced by veterans including homelessness, un- and underemployment, drug addiction, inadequate medical and psychological treatment, and feelings of alienation from civilian society.

As Rowe writes, the historical narrative implied in the charge that "we did not support our Troops refers less to isolated incidents of anti-war demonstrators 'spitting' on returning soldiers, chanting 'Murderers!' or otherwise condemning military personnel for the conduct of U.S. foreign policy than it refers to the aftermath of the Vietnam War, in which veterans were ignored or considered 'embarrassments' by their government and by the general population. The belated parades, monuments, and memorials often served only to remind veterans of the Vietnam War of the long silence that they met on their return."[17] In Rowe's symbolic retelling of history, the metaphorical act of spitting on Vietnam War veterans was really silence and ambivalence from U.S. society. Yet in the contemporary historical revision, passive neglect of Vietnam War veterans by civilian society has become a tale of intentional antagonism, and societal silence has been converted into a story of active enmity from civilian faculty and students.

Chilling Effects: The Myth of the Antimilitary Campus

Four decades after the Vietnam War, the specter of that conflict continues to haunt policies toward veterans on college campuses. Military supporters claim that liberal college faculty and students create a hostile environment for veterans and the institutional military.[18] These claims conflate support for student veterans with support for the institutional military. The characterization of college students as hostile toward veterans is constructed and advanced through the strategic deployment of what Burke calls "perfecting myths," or socially constructed narratives that provide justification for worldviews while reinforcing the relationship between individuals and the state.[19]

On contemporary college campuses, military advocates explicitly position Iraq and Afghanistan war veterans as modern-day equivalents of Vietnam War veterans. By symbolically fashioning and disseminating the story of the Vietnam veteran reviled by liberal civilian college students and professors, and by shifting the neglect of 1960s-era veterans onto Iraq or Afghanistan war veterans, an ostensible problem is created: contemporary college campuses are unfriendly to the U.S. military and to contemporary veterans. With this ostensible problem comes the need for a solution: to create more military-friendly campuses. Through these narratives, soldiers are positioned as both victims (rejected and discriminated against by antiwar college students and faculty) and heroes, separate from and superior to their civilian counterparts. This discursive positioning of veterans as deserving of unquestioning allegiance and support is then enacted as military support on college campuses, contributing to the production of militarized common sense.

The narrative of the reviled veteran relegates the student veteran to victimhood, but student veterans are also mythologized through the trope of heroism. Heroic military narratives have been promulgated throughout history to serve several purposes, including helping soldiers rationalize their participation in wars, helping surviving loved ones to grieve, allowing civilian societies to feel better about sending soldiers to war, and garnering popular support to wage war. Military and civilian societies celebrate the returning warrior-hero who fought on behalf of the nation's people and interests. This perspective has been taken up and amplified by civilian troop support organizations, and the heroic mythos is echoed in the rhetoric of campus veterans' support programs.

Roland Barthes described a myth as a type of speech. In examining ideologies hidden within the "decorative display of *what-goes-without-saying*," Barthes argued that heroic images should be studied "as mythical discourse" that imbues symbols of everyday life (gestures, clothing, and expressions) with archetypal material (love of nation, masculinity, social status) to predispose the interpreter to accept them as natural.[20] The discourse of care for veterans combines two mythologized figures: the warrior-hero and the spurned Vietnam veteran. The symbol of the archetypal soldier as defender of nation and freedom articulates with an equally mythologized twenty-first-century antimilitary college campus.[21] Some campus veteran support organizations frame student veterans as beleaguered heroes in an effort to remediate potential discrimination against the military; these understandings are naturalized, and form the basis of best practices for veteran support on college campuses.

My three years of ethnographic research on college campuses revealed no signs of active antipathy toward veterans; the majority of college students seemed indifferent to the presence of the veterans, and staff and faculty members showed supportive concern and a genuine desire to help student veterans succeed. Despite these manifestations of support, speakers at many of the veterans' support services meetings and classes I attended continued to invoke the image of the civilian college campus as hostile to military veterans.[22]

As described in the introduction, the antimilitary campus trope was evoked at Southwest University, when the VA representative described the Marine recruiter's professed fear of coming to the SU campus. Another example took place at SU, at an event to welcome new student veterans to campus in 2011. A featured speaker, an SU alumnus and Vietnam War veteran, opened his address by noting the warm welcome he received that day at SU, saying, "The reception I'm getting here today is a lot different than the one I got in 1973 when I came here to study," saying that as a student veteran he was unwelcome and vilified on the campus. This comment reinforces the trope of the beleaguered student veteran and negates the current reality. These are just two examples of a standard refrain on contemporary college campuses.

The narrative of antimilitary faculty was echoed by a Central College administrator who felt that it was necessary to strategically de-emphasize student veterans' military status when advocating for campus veteran support initiatives. She feared losing support from a faculty she believed was dominated by antiwar (and therefore, by extension, assumed to be antimilitary and antiveteran) professors. The administrator said that faculty might not want to support student veterans because they were veterans, so she emphasized their status as students: "Historically, faculty in education, as you may know, are very liberal oriented. And when it comes to the military, sometimes you have to have a conversation that focuses on *student* success (as opposed to veteran success) with this particular student population. I told [faculty] that we need to support *all* of our student populations, and this [veteran population] is a population of students with very specific needs that we need to support" (speaker's emphasis).

Though charges of antimilitary and antiveteran attitudes among faculty continue to circulate, I saw no negative bias against veterans at either SU or Central College. Nonetheless, reporting on a meeting of veterans' advocates in January 2013, the military newspaper *Stars and Stripes* published an article under the headline "Student Vets Say Anti-military Attitudes Persist on Campus." The article noted, "[Student] veterans said they still encounter professors and other faculty who blame them for the Iraq War, resent the generous GI Bill benefits, and assume the former troops aren't smart enough to make it to graduation. It's not the norm, they said, but it's something nearly every student veteran has had to deal with at least once in the last few years."[23]

The article's rhetorical strategy is worth noting: the first sentence asserts a problem resonant with the title, "Student Vets Say Anti-military Attitudes Persist on Campus," followed by a sentence contradicting this claim in its assertion that antimilitary attitudes are "not the norm." Despite this negation, the reader is left with an impression of persistent and pervasive antimilitary bias on college campuses.

Why is the accusation of antimilitary hostility invoked so often, despite a lack of documented proof of pervasively prejudicial attitudes against student veterans on college campuses? Loeb and Lembke argue that the image of the spitting antiwar protester of the 1960s was deployed as an icon of 1990s neoconservative ideology and used to intimidate potential present-day activists, while Cahill and Beukenhorst note that veterans' experience on civilian college campuses historically has been used to influence public opinion and stifle dissent about U.S. wars.[24]

The challenges veterans face in making the transition to college have been characterized as arising from college campuses being insufficiently military friendly. These claims become conventional wisdom when they are asserted in student services literature and resurface in popular and scholarly literature, where they become known as "best practices." These ideological formulations are the basis for college veterans' programs.[25] Much of the veteran support best-practice literature comes from a perspective that is openly supportive of the institutional military, and much of it is written by college faculty who are also veterans who received their college degrees after serving in the military.[26] While it is true that an insider's perspective can offer an important lens into veterans' issues on campuses, there is also a danger that this might result in a lack of critical scholarship. Indeed, there is a striking homogeneity in the problems presented by the student services literature. One common claim in particular is backed by little evidence: that civilian faculty and students are intentionally hostile to veterans.[27]

A different, yet also widely cited claim is that college faculty may unintentionally mistreat veterans in their classes when they hold discussions about or critique military policies or the wars.[28] This strand of argument cautions professors that expressing disagreement with military or government policy might make veterans feel uncomfortable and alienate them in class.[29] "Some professors make pejorative statements about the military during lectures, making veterans feel uncomfortable and setting them further apart from their classmates. Of course, most professors aren't trying to make veterans feel uncomfortable— *their objective is usually to voice disagreement with government policy or to stir up discussion in class*—but they should be mindful of the negative effects on veterans, and lead more-balanced discussions of the military and its role in society."[30]

The claim in the above passage conflates military veterans with military policies; the problem is not that professors are accused of making pejorative statements about veterans, but rather that they might make pejorative statements about the military as they voice disagreement with government or military policies. This passage implies that classroom debate about military campaigns—such as the current wars—could alienate student veterans from their classmates.

Implicit in this formulation is the assumption that all veterans actively and positively identify with their military service, with the institutional military, and with current military missions abroad.[31] By cautioning professors to lead "more balanced discussions of the military and its role in society" (which according to some literature means avoiding discussions about the current wars), the article conveys the message that expressing disagreement with government policy—even if only to spark discussion in class—is potentially damaging to veterans and should be avoided.[32]

The article's warning about unintentional slights by professors is immediately followed by a claim about intentional harassment of veterans by civilian classmates: "Further, students who vilify or harass veterans should be disciplined firmly; as they would for harassing any other student (veterans are occasionally singled out for verbal attacks on some campuses)."[33] The charge of antiveteran harassment supports the contemporary version of the Vietnam-era narrative of the student veteran bullied by civilian classmates and extends the conflation: critical remarks about the military by faculty are linked with antiveteran attacks and harassment, which are then used to support the charge that veterans are intentionally harassed by civilian classmates. Although I could find only sparse anecdotal mention of this alleged phenomenon and no documented examples of mistreatment in media reports (beyond the contested accounts in this chapter), the article offers an uncited parenthetical qualifier that "veterans are occasionally singled out for verbal attacks on some campuses." This requires acceptance on faith that verbal attacks against veterans by college students are so common as to warrant this stern preemptive admonition.[34]

In the course of my research, I found that many veterans came to college precisely to participate in critical debates about the wars, even when they had differences of opinion with civilian students or professors. Southwest University student and Navy veteran Ricardo said that he considered classroom discussions about military policies and war a good thing, and that the participation of student veterans in these discussions added important real-world experience that could augment the civilian students' education. He said that he did not mind sharing his opinions of the war and his military experience with civilian students, adding that veterans' experiential knowledge could provide context and depth to the abstract information found in textbooks. Ricardo said that having classroom discussions about military conflicts would be positive for the students, the veterans, and the professors. When asked whether he thought professors should avoid discussing war in class, Ricardo said,

> I think [avoiding talking about the war] is wrong. Joining the military when I did, everyone knew the war was wrong. I knew automatically that what I was going to do was something wrong. No, [students and professors] need to talk about it. Granted, information about the war is going to be in a textbook, but with veterans, what [students] are going to have in their class is solid gold. Those students will be able to say, "It says this in the book." Veterans bring more [lived experience] to that classroom. It's going to help the veteran to be able to talk. It's going to help the instructor to be able to learn more, to be able to project it to the rest of his classes. And the students in those classes, they're going to be able to take this material that they've read and the material that they are taking from the [veteran] next to them.

Ricardo felt that veterans represented a resource to civilian students, and characterized veterans' presence in college classrooms as "solid gold." However, he agreed with veterans' advocates who cautioned against vilifying student veterans. Ricardo said that he had once felt uncomfortable with a community college instructor's adamant stance against the war, but he added that classroom discussions about the military could and should be facilitated with respect for differing perspectives: "I think [having student veterans participate in discussions] is going to embellish [the classroom to become] a much broader learning experience. But it depends on how they present it. If it's the proper presentation, that's good. If it's 'Marine Corps baby killers,' then okay, that's something different."

The Rise of the Military-Friendly Campus

To remediate the ostensible problem of insufficient friendliness toward the military, educational initiatives designed to help returning veterans are developed and carried out by campus student affairs offices, nonprofit organizations, and veteran support consultants based on military-friendly best-practice literature.[35] A college may officially be designated a military-friendly campus.[36] This designation is generally determined by programmatic criteria, such as priority registration for classes, liaison staff to assist veterans, offering school credits for military training and certification, counseling services, tutoring, job placement services, and peer support programs.[37] The process of becoming a military-friendly campus also includes holding specific trainings for staff and veterans and campus-wide events honoring the institutional military and military service. In recent years, the student services literature has begun to shift from calling for military-friendly campuses to calling for veteran-friendly campuses. Articles in college student services publications stress the need to embed campus veteran services within a strategy to create campuses that are more military friendly or veteran friendly in response to a perceived legacy of disrespect and neglect for veterans on college campuses following the Vietnam War: "In the 1960s and 1970s, many veterans of the U.S. armed forces, on returning home from Vietnam, discovered that their service was not honored. The war effort had lost popular support, anti-war protests were common, and the country was divided. As a nation, we were unable or unwilling to separate an unpopular war from those who had been sent to fight it. College campuses, often places where the protests were held, did not respond well to the needs of the veterans who became students."[38]

This statement conceptualizes veteran services as necessary to counteract a presumed antipathy from civilian colleges toward military veterans. The quote above asserts that because colleges were the site of public opposition to the Vietnam War, military students' educational needs were neglected. While there is ample evidence of widespread campus demonstrations against the Vietnam War and against institutional military programs such as ROTC, there is little documented evidence of active opposition to military students (war veterans or ROTC students). In fact, there is evidence to the contrary. One documented example is from 1969, when Harvard University students occupied University Hall to protest Harvard's ROTC program.[39] Video footage shows a protester presenting demands, which included a statement of support for Harvard military students.[40] Yet a presumed link between campus protests against the Vietnam War and the neglect of veterans provides the rationale for military-friendly programming on contemporary campuses. Collectively, these claims promote the notion that opposition to U.S. wars and support for veterans are incompatible.

Books such as *Creating a Veteran-Friendly Campus: Strategies for Transition and Success* acknowledge that veterans generally enjoy a positive reception on contemporary college campuses. The authors state, "while popular support for these [contemporary] wars is also an issue, society, including campuses, is responding in mostly positive ways to veterans of the wars in Iraq and Afghanistan."[41] Yet the authors maintain that contemporary campuses are insufficiently friendly to the military, and thus to veterans.[42] The claim that contemporary U.S. soldiers who return home after fighting in unpopular wars face challenges similar to those of Vietnam veterans provides the rationale for creating veteran-friendly campuses. This claim fuses historical and contemporary tropes of soldiers as simultaneously reviled and heroic, conceiving of services for contemporary veterans as correctives to historic—though apocryphal—dishonor of student veterans during the Vietnam War.

According to Lokken et al., the term "veteran-friendly" "refers to marked efforts made by individual campuses to identify and remove barriers to the educational goals of veterans, to create smooth transitions from military life to college life, and to provide information about available benefits and services."[43] Yet proponents of military-friendly campuses promote interventions that reach far beyond streamlining administrative procedures and providing information to veterans. Ford, Northrup, and Wiley include in their list of Recommendations on How to Enhance the Success of Military Students the creation of student veterans' groups that coordinate with local military leaders and military advocacy groups such as the VFW.[44] This literature also calls for the development of campus programs designed "to show appreciation for military service to the country. Examples include annual appreciation programs and campus wide events on Memorial Day, September 11, and Veterans' Day."[45] Ford, Northrup, and Wiley conclude, "It is the responsibility of campus leaders, including those in student affairs, to first act locally and then partner with military leaders to meet the unique needs of the increasing population of students who are in the military. Without the determined leadership of student affairs officers, it is unlikely that campus efforts will be as successful as they need to be to help repay these students for their service."[46]

Some academics might disagree that repayment for military service should be the goal of college educators, arguing instead that their goal should be to provide an education for all students, civilians and military veterans alike.[47] Moreover, scholars like Jorge Mariscal and Christian Appy argue that a college education should never be contingent on fighting a war.[48] Nonetheless, Ford, Northrup, and Wiley have reframed the mission of educating military veterans as one of honoring military service and repaying veterans for their sacrifice in war. This argument implies that educators should support wartime military service and that colleges owe a debt to members of the military.

Searching for Evidence of Antimilitary Bias

In response to this contemporary literature, I looked for evidence of potential antiveteran bias on campus, but instead found the opposite. Believing it was important to be in places where observable antiveteran sentiment (if it existed) might likely arise, I attended some of the few war-related events on

FIGURE 5.1 Military-friendly campus logo from Appalachian State University.

FIGURE 5.2 Military-friendly campus advertisement, SUNY New Paltz.

the SU campus. One such event was a vigil marking a 2012 massacre in which an American soldier stationed near Kandahar entered two separate villages, fatally shot sixteen Afghan civilians in their homes, doused their bodies with a flammable liquid, and burned them. On the day of the shooting, the following e-mail message went out over campus electronic lists: "The Afghan Student Association will be participating in a worldwide vigil to mourn the recent civilian shootings in a village in Kandahar, Afghanistan tomorrow (March 12th) from 7pm-7:30pm on the [SU] Central Plaza. A U.S. soldier decided to leave his base and go to homes in the middle of night killing 16 civilians mostly women and children. We hope you can join us in a moment of silence to commemorate the victims and their families. Please wear all black tomorrow, and tape '16 Afghan Civilians Killed by a U.S. Soldier' on your shirts, to help raise awareness throughout the day."

The memorial took place on a cold, windy late winter evening. The event began as a group of women, dressed in black with their heads covered by scarves, gathered on the steps of SU's Central Plaza to distribute Styrofoam coffee cups to serve as windproof candle holders, along with candles to place inside. As requested by the organizers, most attendees (who appeared to be students) wore black clothing. Two local television stations covered the event, and reporters with cameras and microphones vied for photographic and audio angles. At precisely 7 PM, the organizers asked the forty people present to form a circle. The speaker, a representative of the SU Afghan Student Association, opened the vigil with some brief remarks:

> Good evening concerned citizens of the United States of America. Thank you for coming to show your respect and support for the innocent civilians who have lost their lives in the war in Afghanistan.
>
> There are vigils being held all over the world today in response to the tragic massacre that occurred yesterday, Sunday, March 11th at 3 am in Afghanistan. An armed U.S. soldier entered 3 homes, shooting and killing 16 civilians, of whom 9 were children, 3 women, and 4 men, all innocent. This occurred in a village that had been cleared of insurgents for 5 months. The soldier is said to have acted on his own. After shooting them, he dragged some of the bodies into one home where he set them on fire.[49]

The opening of this speech focused the vigil on two things: on the civilians killed and on the war in Afghanistan, followed by a neutral recounting of the facts of the massacre, framing the incident as a tragic, isolated, and individual act. The speaker went on to say that the war in Afghanistan had cost many lives without significantly advancing the cause of human development and human rights in that country. She then said something that may have seemed surprising to those anticipating statements of anger or disapproval toward the U.S. military: "While we respect and admire the bravery of and value all military service men and women throughout the world, the actions of this one soldier have left us shocked and hurt."

The speaker's expression of support and esteem for military service members (with implicit support for U.S. soldiers) may indicate the politics of the area's local Afghan community, many of whom publicly opposed the Taliban and left Afghanistan in response to Taliban ascendance. Some of the attendees may not have shared this respect and admiration for all military service members, but there were no public expressions of antimilitary sentiment at this event.[50] The feelings of shock and hurt expressed by the speaker indicated individual affective responses to death but portrayed neither anger nor antipathy toward either the U.S. military or soldiers. The event closed with a prayer for peace sung in Arabic. This was the only public su response to the killing of civilians by a U.S. soldier, indicating that the su campus is not a nexus of antimilitary sentiment.[51]

The topic of how student veterans are treated is part of the public discourse on college campuses, su and Central College included. In all of my formal interviews with student veterans at both su and Central College, as well as in numerous casual conversations over the course of my research, I asked veterans how they felt they were treated by civilian students and faculty. While some student veterans said that they felt uncomfortable being around civilian students, they attributed this feeling largely to differences in age, life experience, and the socioeconomic class privilege of the other students.

For example, in a student veterans' orientation class at su, the instructor distributed a questionnaire to class members to find out about their experiences on campus. In response to the question, "How do you feel the broader su community relates to veterans in comparison with other student communities on campus?," only one of the twenty-six students described feeling unsupported by civilian instructors and students. Other survey respondents in the veterans' class noted differential treatment given to veterans and feelings of distance from civilian students on campus, but they attributed this to differences in age and life experience. For example: "I feel that the broader su community relates differently to veterans in comparison with other student communities on campus. I say differently in so far as the community has a great deal of respect for veterans, however, they have a difficult time relating to us due to the age difference as well as overall maturity level."

While acknowledging social disconnections with civilian students, some veterans indicated that they wished they could develop closer relationships with their civilian classmates: "Indirectly, there are shared relationships, mostly academic ones between students; I would say however, since there is a significant age gap between most veterans and the 'average' su undergrad, forming direct community ties with the majority of su students isn't as common or present as I would like it to be. Also, since most, if not all, veterans are transfer students; there is a disconnection as well."

This student (like other participants in this research) identified commonalities with transfer students, who tended to be older than students who enrolled in su directly after high school. Like many other transfer students from community college, student veterans tended to come from less affluent circumstances and arrived at college with a diversity of life experiences, often having taken circuitous routes into higher education. The remainder of the survey respondents wrote that their treatment on the su campus had been positive to neutral. What follows are more written responses to the question about how they felt that the su community relates to them as veterans:

So far, it has been a very welcoming community here at su. From people I've met who I can compare with other student communities, all the communities are open to other perspectives and are not judgmental.

I think [su] is like most places. Most people do their own thing and achieve their own objectives and if their objectives cross, then there would be conflict. I have not experienced any negativity from others. Actually, people are surprised that I am a veteran.

I have received no backlash or implications from students that being a veteran is in some way a negative thing. I have however received gratitude and appreciation because of the fact that I am a veteran here at su.

I feel the su community relates to veterans fairly equal. There is a huge amount of respect for veterans from the entire su community, especially faculty.

When people find out that I'm a veteran I am often pleased with the reception. Just the other day I had a conversation where my veteran status came up and the whole conversation shifted to my service. I felt really proud.

[The broader su community] seems to be cautiously receptive. There seems to be a notion that we should be given our space, out of respect or uncertainty, I don't know, but on a personal level people seem polite, open and happy and willing to engage when you reach out.

In my opinion, SU does a good job of relating to veterans and providing help with benefits, priority registration, etc. However, I feel that in terms of visibility we are on the low end of the spectrum and that we need to change this.

While most of the veterans said they felt positively about the ways they were treated at SU, one respondent expressed ambivalence about the attention given to veterans on campus: "Sometimes I feel like the recognition we get as veterans is a mixed blessing. It's great to have a forum to discuss issues and also see that people are interested in vets. But sometimes I feel like a zoo animal."

It is hard to know which issues the above respondent enjoys discussing, but it would appear that he or she enjoys the atmosphere of open debate that can be found in some college classrooms. This respondent also seems to appreciate knowing that people on campus care about veterans, yet acknowledges that this attention can sometimes come with unpleasant side effects, such as having veteran status fetishized by civilians, or being treated as an exotic creature to be observed ("like a zoo animal").

Out of the twenty-six survey respondents, only one described a lack of support or animosity from civilian students. This student's response indicated that he felt invisible as a veteran on campus and that the meaning of his military status, service, and war-related disability were unknown and unappreciated on campus, particularly by younger civilian students.[52] This veteran wrote, "Most students don't know about veterans' service: what it entails, or means. Because [the U.S. military] is multi-ethnic, multi-major and multi-gender, it is not apparent that one is a veteran. A few junior students I've spoken with just don't care about what it *means* to be a disabled veteran [speaker's emphasis]. In my German class, I wear a hearing aid because I cannot understand the teacher's volume. I've told her, but she hasn't tried to speak louder. So I went to the VA for a hearing aid."

This respondent interpreted the low volume of the instructor's voice as a lack of regard for his/her hearing disability, and indicates that this respondent felt forced to wear a hearing aid because of the instructor's refusal to speak louder. For this veteran, the lack of recognition and acknowledgment of military service he perceived from fellow students intermingled with a lack of respect he perceived from the instructor. This response continued with a specific charge of antimilitary, antiveteran bias on the SU campus: "I do not want any special accommodation just for my service. I do, however, think that veterans have a negative stigma on campus. During the bake sale, for example, numerous students called me a murderer because I had my OEF [Operation Enduring Freedom] hat on as I walked through SU Central Plaza. It's the lack of education about veteran issues that perpetuates stereotypes like this. The campus, the entire nation needs to abandon the 1960s mentality and adopt a new, refreshed ideology about veterans."

Significantly, this student veteran invoked a "1960s [Vietnam War–era] mentality" in need of refreshing. It is also significant that the incident described took place at an affirmative action bake sale held on the Central Plaza of the SU campus, aimed at blocking the reinstatement of policies arising from another vestige of 1960s political movements: affirmative action. The bake sale event, one of many organized by conservative student clubs at college campuses across the United States, was staged as a protest against proposed legislation that would allow a return to the policies considering race and gender in college admissions. Student organizers sold baked goods at different prices to people based on race and gender; for example, white males were charged two dollars for cupcakes, while women and racial minority students could buy the same cupcakes at an "affirmative action discount" (black and Native American males were charged 75 cents and 25 cents, respectively; women received 25 cents off everything). The SU bake sale organizers acknowledged that the event was intended as a provocation, to protest what they considered preferential treatment of women and minority students, as well as a protest against what they saw as the dominance of liberal policies and attitudes at SU. Indeed, the event succeeded in provoking: shouting matches erupted as counter-protesters filled the plaza.[53] My interpretation of this incident is that the acrimonious tenor produced by the bake sale likely inflamed tensions and contributed to the animosity expressed against this student veteran.

Whether by design or simply effect, the discourse of care silences public discussions about veterans and the wars.[54] Military supporters advocating avoidance of classroom discussions of the wars depend on a critique of power (in this case the power wielded by an alleged majority of liberal, antiwar faculty) leveled on behalf of the injured (veterans and the alleged undervalorized military), based on politics of reproach and frustration. This politics of *ressentiment* denotes a specific site of blame for hypothetical suffering by positioning liberal college faculty, students, and historic events as responsible for the injury of insufficient valorization.[55]

An incident at Columbia University in 2011 serves as an example of this phenomenon. The incident took place during a period of heated discussions about whether the University Senate should vote to reinstate the ROTC program on campus. As part of a nationwide movement aimed at getting elite universities to rescind a Vietnam-era ban on ROTC programs, Columbia University opened the proposal to a campus-wide debate.[56] During a town hall meeting, one Columbia student, a disabled Iraq War veteran, spoke in favor of reinstating the ROTC program.

At one point in his speech, the veteran supported U.S. military intervention in Iraq, saying, "There are people who hate you and want to kill you." According to published reports, some Columbia students shouted disagreement from the audience.[57] They were quickly reprimanded by the moderator, and the heckling soon stopped. However, the incident was immediately taken up by the conservative media. Spearheaded by Fox News, the American Legion, and the VFW, the accusation of "spoiled university students disrespecting military heroes" spread quickly and widely. Columbia and other elite universities were branded as an unpatriotic and antimilitary. While this type of rhetorical attack has become a staple of conservative radio talk shows, what makes this case unusual is that the veteran at whom the heckling was directed, Staff Sergeant Anthony Maschek, felt compelled to publicly disagree with the depiction of Columbia as an antimilitary campus. In a series of public interviews, Maschek said that he did not experience that incident as inimical to him or to other student veterans; on the contrary, he said that he felt great support from fellow Columbia students and faculty, and he gave several media interviews contesting the VFW account. The following account, appearing on the military-interest website Military.com, describes the exchange:

"Heckled Vet Bucks Columbia Critics," Bryant Jordan
Military.com, February 25, 2011

It had all the makings of a classic clash of cultures: A disabled war veteran tried to speak in defense of the military and was drowned out by college students angered by the prospect of a reserve officer training corps program—long banished from the campus—returning to the school. As word spread about former Army Staff Sgt. Anthony Maschek's experience at Columbia University in New York last week, well-meaning supporters rushed to his defense, slamming the school's faculty and students for the "banal and juvenile" heckling. But there was less to the uncivil moment than met the eye, according to Maschek, the wounded and decorated Iraq war vet who endured the heckling. "I was on TV [Thursday] and told them how supportive Columbia is," he said in a telephone interview Feb. 24. "I didn't want people to think that the school has been anti-military at all. That is nowhere near true."

In a statement Feb. 22, the national commander of the Veterans of Foreign Wars hit the school and students for the "disrespect and shoddy treatment" they gave Maschek. "Their recent actions are representative of the University's overall long-standing anti-military environment that fosters contempt and condescension for the military services," the VFW's Richard Eubank said. Jimmie Foster, national commander of The American Legion, said that Columbia's students' time "would be better spent honoring this brave soldier for the wounds he sustained in honorable service, and acquiring an appreciation for the price others paid for the freedom they now enjoy."

But Maschek demurred. The news coverage "did get a little bit crazy there for a minute," he said. "I think I've gotten the message out that it's only a small group [of hecklers], and you can find those groups of people anywhere you go." . . .

Maschek said the negative response to his remarks was neither widespread nor directed at his support of ROTC. As he argued that keeping ROTC off campus was itself discriminatory, the audience listened politely. He believes the heckling was spurred by his saying that America has enemies in the world that "want to kill you."

It was then that some laughter and booing broke out; some reports claimed he was called a racist.

"I don't think the people were so far on the anti-ROTC side that they were willing to heckle me," he said. "When I made a response that was very personal, I think that brought them back to exactly why we are fighting a war." A moderator silenced the critics and Maschek continued for a few more minutes, though he says the heckling "threw me a little bit." It was an atypical experience, because Columbia has been a great place for veterans, he said. "Columbia University has an amazing veteran's benefit program," he said. "We have a pretty good veterans group there that I normally attend. The Columbia staff and faculty has been nothing but accommodating to us."

This incident shows an attempt by military advocacy groups to cast any statement or action by veterans as uncontestable, to label dissent against the war as unpatriotic, and to circumscribe public debate about the war. The American Legion commander asserted that the only acceptable posture that students should take toward their veteran classmate is that of praise and gratitude (the "students' time 'would be better spent honoring this brave soldier for the wounds he sustained in honorable service, and acquiring an appreciation for the price others paid for the freedom they now enjoy'").

The fact that Maschek publicly contradicted the military advocates' account mirrored something I found in the field: that it was often military advocates speaking on behalf of returning soldiers—and not the veterans themselves (with some notable exceptions, as shown in chapters 4 and 6)—who actively silenced or advised against campus debates about the wars. The Columbia incident illustrates the intent to circumscribe public debate by rendering one veteran's opinions uncontestable. In this incident, we can hear echoes of the iconic and apocryphal story of the U.S. soldier returning from Vietnam in the 1960s, who was said to be spat on by an antiwar protester on an airport tarmac—a story that has been at the heart of the contemporary veterans' support movement and that serves as both cautionary tale and disciplinary force in restricting public discussions about veterans and the wars.[58]

Mascheck's praise for Columbia did little to quell the Internet groundswell of charges that Columbia University is hostile to veterans. The narrative of the scorned veteran continues to be offered as proof that civilian college students and faculty are hostile toward the military. Despite Maschek's denial, the story of his mistreatment by civilian college students endures on weblogs and is animated by photos like one on the right-wing political satire site Politifake. The blog showed a picture of Maschek and the caption, "This student veteran has more balls than the entire Columbia University student/faculty population," which illustrates the narrative of the abused, yet virile and defiant veteran victimized by a hostile student body. Maschek is hailed as a masculine hero, possessing "more balls" than the feminized, antimilitary and antiveteran civilian student and faculty population. And despite (or perhaps because of) the tempest-in-a-teapot umbrage on Maschek's behalf, in April 2011—two months after this incident—Columbia students, Academic Senate, and administration voted to reinstate the ROTC program on campus.[59]

Remediation of a Manufactured Problem:
Militarized Common Sense

Creating Safe Spaces for Militarism

Given the charges of antimilitary bias and harassment, how should colleges fix this hypothetical problem? As a remedy, military advocates have developed specific interventions, which I group into two types. The first is the protective strategy, which claims to shield veterans against potential harassment from civilian students and faculty. This protective strategy lays the foundation for the second, celebratory or valorization strategy designed to elevate the profile of military members on campus by displays that purport to celebrate veterans but in fact celebrate military aesthetics, cultures, and missions. These two combined strategies rely on what Stuart Hall calls "articulation," or the process through which popular consent for dominant political projects is forged (in this case, when notions of veterans' interests and notions of military interests are conflated and articulate with notions of care and respect).[60] The concept of articulation helps explain how veterans, as representatives of the U.S. armed forces, one of the most powerfully hegemonic institutions in the world, can simultaneously be portrayed as victimized, underrepresented minorities and hailed as strong, masculine war heroes, superior in mind, body, and character to their civilian counterparts. Ideological discourses of discrimination that hold contemporary salience are deployed to position student veterans as victims and to call for programs that valorize and celebrate military projects on campuses in the name of shielding veterans from harm. By linking discourses of solidarity of historically oppressed populations (for example, LGBT groups and immigrants) with discourses of military support, military projects and logics become accepted on college campuses. In this way, articulation facilitates new forms of common sense or hegemony.

An example of the promotion of articulation through the combination of protective and valorizing strategies is the Vet Net Ally (VNA) program, designed to educate staff and faculty about the needs of military veterans in higher education. First developed and implemented in 2010 as a pilot study at a state university in California, the stated goal of the VNA program is to address barriers to veterans' success in college. The program is designed to "increase awareness and knowledge of, and sensitivity to, important issues affecting student veterans, faculty and staff" by providing training seminars for faculty, staff, and administrators focused on "pre- and post-military culture, personal identity issues, and the services available to veterans to assist them in achieving their personal, social, and educational goals."[61] The VNA program description below shows how the LGBT Safe Zone program is used as a template. The VNA program makes explicit this programmatic lineage in describing both programs as similarly voluntary and reliant on moral suasion, citing characteristics of campus LGBT Safe Zone programs on which the VNA program is based:

> While anti-discrimination training may be a part of an institution's orientation program, participation in Safe Zone training is most often vol-

untary. Participants who successfully complete the training are given an institutionally approved decal to display in their workspaces to indicate they are safe members of the campus community, who are often referred to as "allies." These allies are people with whom a student, staff, or faculty member may speak about issues regarding their status as an LGBT person without fear of prejudice or harassment. While not all participants choose to display the decal, those who do are advertising that they are allies to members of the LGBT community and those struggling with issues of sexual orientation.[62]

The VNA program discursively links discrimination faced by LGBT students and alleged discrimination against veterans on campuses:

> The training program for veterans has been modeled on the LGBT Safe Zone training, but instead addresses issues associated with students' status as veterans and the issues surrounding that status. Like LGBT Safe Zone programs, the veteran centered training intends to increase staff and faculty awareness of veterans' issues and increase sensitivity to veterans and their issues. Additionally, just as Safe Zone programs recognize the importance of including heterosexual allies in the creation of positive environments for LGBT students on campus (Bullard, 2004); the inclusion of non-veteran allies is a critical piece in the development of a Veterans Ally program.[63]

The program advocates for zones of safety, yet it ultimately turns the original protective objective into an objective of valorization and visibility. Wendy Brown (1995) writes that the struggle for inclusion in liberal political membership (in this case, as embodied in the student veteran) becomes a discursive battle to forge the politicized "we" from the unpoliticized "I."[64] Within veteran support discourse, the plight of the victimized, misunderstood individual student veteran is converted into a visible power bloc (the politicized "we") and results in a valorization of military identities and projects. Thus military veterans, ostensibly underrespected on civilian college campuses—who in their previous active military roles were by definition representatives of the U.S. state and its economic interests, political-military goals, and social formations—become symbols for a lack of respect for the U.S. state. Thus, the discourse of veteran inclusion simultaneously remilitarizes the veteran identity and positions it as a political interest.

The VNA program discursively positions veterans on campus as underrepresented minorities subject to discriminatory acts and harassment similar to

LGBT students. It was developed to address the following problem: that "veterans may be marginalized or even harassed about their service by other students, staff or faculty."[65] According to this claim, hypothetical discrimination against veterans might come from faculty members and students who are "significantly more politically liberal and are more likely to oppose military action than the public at large," and is informed by a "Vietnam and Post-Vietnam era academic tradition of opposition to armed conflict."[66] These two factors "may intersect to create barriers [to] the success of veterans pursuing higher education."[67] This problem statement lays the groundwork for a dual-pronged (protective and valorizing) corrective intervention: collegiate safe zones for veterans on campuses to protect from discrimination and harassment based on their status as military members combined with programs that make visible and celebrate the institutional military on college campuses.

The articulation here is between the apocryphal image of the veteran victim of discrimination blended with the well-documented contemporary reality of LGBT people as targets of hate crimes. The VNA program rationalizes adapting the LGBT Safe Zone training program because there was no previously existing educational model to sensitize faculty and staff to veterans' issues. However, the VNA program also asserts that the LGBT Safe Zone program offers an appropriate template because of ostensible parallels between the social oppression of LGBT students and student veterans; that is, according to the VNA rationale, both LGBT students and veterans are singled out for harassment because of their affiliation with a minority group. The VNA program description asserts explicit parity between veterans and LGBT campus members as targets of discrimination and harassment, and in terms of their status as an oppressed minority group facing discriminatory speech and actions: "Like veterans, the lesbian, gay, bisexual, and transgender (LGBT) population on college and university campuses is a numerical minority that has historically or periodically been the target of discrimination and harassment. . . . Unlike veterans, there is a robust training program available to educate and inform faculty and staff, and in some instances students, about LGBT issues on many college campuses."[68]

The VNA program argues that because veterans (like LGBT students) are a numerical minority on campus that has historically or periodically been victims of discrimination and harassment, veterans need visibly identifiable safe spaces on campus. However, this assertion of discrimination against veterans refers to historic instances rather than documented present-day events and is based on apocryphal accounts of discriminatory events alleged to have occurred during the Vietnam War era, and not contemporary incidents.

Moreover, the VNA program is professed to be needed because student veterans, unlike LGBT students, do not have visibility programs to raise campus consciousness about military issues, in contrast to programs calling for LGBT pride. In making the comparison, VNA asserts an equivalency of oppression, implying that veterans on contemporary college campuses face threats of physical and verbal attacks by civilians who are hostile and biased against them.[69] Calling for a remedy for a perceived historic social injury articulates with current civil and social rights movements, lending the VNA program the moral authority attached to these culturally and politically resonant social movements. The VNA program uses the language of marginalization and inclusion, invoking the image of an oppressed minority on college campuses—the symbolic site of historic struggles against oppression—which gives resonance to the idea that veterans must have an active and visible presence on campus to stay safe from civilian harassment. This facilitates the following process of articulation in the minds of students and faculty: because LGBT students advocate for campus gay pride movements, it is reasonable that veterans should likewise advocate for a military pride movement. My research questions the need for zones of physical safety for veterans and argues that the intention of the VNA program is primarily ideological, to increase valorization of the military on college campuses, which is part of the process of producing militarized common sense.

By modeling the veterans' program after the Safe Zone Ally program developed to protect LGBT students from homophobic speech and attacks on college campuses, the VNA program seeks to increase staff and faculty awareness of veterans' issues and increase sensitivity to veterans and their issues.[70] Also drawing from objectives of the LGBT Safe Zone Ally program, VNA seeks to foster civilian supporters for veterans on campus.[71] The content of this program departs significantly from the LGBT Safe Zone program, which focuses on raising consciousness about homophobia and violence and promoting campus inclusion of sexual minorities. Both Safe Zone and VNA programs include the centerpiece intervention: a sticker to be displayed in classrooms and offices of LGBT- and veteran-friendly staff and faculty. When displayed, this sticker both declares one an ally and marks campus offices as safe spaces where persecuted groups may seek, and expect, support and safety.

Both of the decals in figures 5.3 and 5.4 incorporate iconographic signifiers of their participants' respective social and political identities. In the LGBT Safe Zone sticker, the triangle icon and rainbow colors are used to signify that this project is part of the gay rights movement.[72] The words "SAFE ZONE" convey the primary goal of the project: to provide safety against homophobic attacks. The role of the Safe Zone ally is elaborated in the statement: "The person

FIGURE 5.3 Safe Zone logo, Radford University Facebook page.

FIGURE 5.4 Vet Net Ally logo, University of California, Irvine.

displaying this symbol is one who will be non-judgmental, trustworthy, and supportive."[73]

The VNA program decal privileges iconography over words; it includes only the public designation "ALLY" and thus gives no indication of the mission of the program beyond visible allegiance to the military members on campus. The decal uses imagery often associated with military service: "The black, olive-drab, and tan colors used have been used by military services as primary and secondary colors in uniform design both historically and in the modern era. The three colors are the most identifiable colors in modern camouflage utility uniforms worn by most services."[74] The five-pointed star, a common icon on military vehicles during the World War II and Vietnam eras, was chosen to signify the five branches of the U.S. armed forces, and the stencil font is used on this decal because it is common in the marking of military equipment. In casting veterans as marginalized and disfavored, this visibility strategy embraces the identity of the excluded minority. However, it may be difficult to see how this victimized narrative coincides with the image of military superiority upon which many veteran support programs are based, and a closer look at the program's mission statement shows that the purpose for which VNA program seeks to recruit allies is not protection but valorization. To demonstrate the valorizing intent of the VNA program, I compared mission statements from both Safe Zone and Vet Net interventions, beginning with mission statements of the Safe Zone Ally program to illustrate its protective aspects:

California State University, Chico

Safe Zone's purpose is to reduce homophobia and heterosexism on our campus and thereby make our campus a safer and freer environment for all members of our community. The Safe Zone project identifies individuals in the campus faculty, staff and student body to become safe zone allies. These people provide a safe haven, a listening ear, or an open accessibility for gay, lesbian, bisexual and transgender (GLBT) who are in need of advice or services from that individual. The Safe Zone program will provide the campus Allies with training, information, and community resource identification to those who express interest in becoming a Safe Zone Ally.[75]

The above statement addresses the need to provide emotional support for and ensure the physical safety of sexual minorities on college campuses. It links safety with the visibility of LGBT people on campus and seeks to build a campus climate of tolerance. The role of allies on campus is to provide a safe haven for LGBT people. It follows a social service orientation of campus intervention.

In comparison, the VNA mission statement, below, places more emphasis on visibility of veterans, rather than safety:

The mission of the VET NET Ally Program is to

- establish a network of visible Allies to provide support, information, and assistance for service members and veterans,
- provide service members and veterans with comfortable access to trustworthy, knowledgeable and sensitive people who can provide a safe and nondiscriminatory environment,
- provide an opportunity for faculty and staff to demonstrate support for service members and veterans,
- provide all students on campus an opportunity to respond to instances of discrimination or harassment based on perceived or self-reported status as a Service member or veteran,
- educate members of the university community about the needs and concerns of Service members and veterans,
- assist university personnel in understanding that discrimination based on status as a service member or veteran is harmful to the campus environment for all,
- foster a campus atmosphere that supports the academic freedom and professional, personal and social success of service members and veterans; and advance the university's progress towards a campus that discourages discrimination and openly celebrates diversity.[76]

There are similarities between the Safe Zone and VNA mission statements, but the VNA program focuses more on promoting networking and advancement of veterans on campus, and relies on undocumented assertions of discrimination. For example, the goal to "assist university personnel in understanding that discrimination based on status as a service member or veteran is harmful to the campus environment for all," implies that there is widespread discrimination based on status as a veteran or service member. Perhaps the most striking difference is the VNA program goal to "foster a campus atmosphere that supports the academic freedom and professional, personal and social success of service members and veterans." This goal carries a particular ideological valence, as it alludes to an alleged deprivation of academic freedom for military service members or supporters, which implies that military members are not only discriminated against but also censored. There is specific cultural resonance to this inference, as the statement implies that military members and their supporters are excluded from the tradition of academic freedom because of military status. This stated goal of safeguarding academic freedom in the VNA mission statement carries the implication that campuses typically deny military veterans academic freedom, hence the need for the VNA program. However, there is no mention of military service members' deprivation of academic freedom in the VNA programmatic rationale.[77]

This raises the question: what is the injury that the VNA program really seeks to remedy? It would appear that the injury to veterans on campus is invisibility, or a lack of sufficient military esteem. A review of the remaining elements of the VNA program indicates that consciousness-raising about military veterans is less about ensuring veteran safety and more about fostering civilian identification with the U.S. military mission. Thus, the remaining components of the VNA program rely on celebratory or valorization strategies.

The VNA program training includes a section in which faculty participants are invited to wear combat equipment, including body armor, Kevlar helmets, equipment harnesses, and CamelBak hydration systems, to create a sympathetic identification with soldiers. This intent is made explicit in the program description: "Participants were encouraged to handle and try on combat equipment borrowed for that purpose from a local National Guard unit. . . . Though heavy, participants were informed that the gear they were handling was less than half of the weight of the full combat load that service members in combat areas would commonly carry. Participants were further encouraged to imagine carrying such a load in the desert heat, which often hovers over one hundred degrees."[78]

It is easy to see how asking educators to imagine that they are carrying heavy combat gear through blistering desert heat can help foster civilian academics' positive identification with soldiers at war; less obvious is how this exercise addresses alleged discrimination against veterans on campus or infringement of academic freedom. It is also not clear how this exercise prepares faculty to teach student veterans.

Despite a lack of evidence of widespread antiveteran sentiment or actions in contemporary campus life, the assertion that veterans may potentially face antimilitary harassment is enough to bring programs such as the VNA onto campuses to remediate an ostensible antiveteran problem by encouraging educators to imagine themselves carrying combat gear through desert zones. The following sections explore another aspect of the valorization strategy used to combat the ostensible problem of discrimination against veterans. Valorization strategies call for campuses to publicly celebrate the military and the symbols of war, if not war itself, by promoting military displays and military-valorizing discourse.

There is fairly consistent consensus about what state-of-the-art veterans' programs on campus should entail: priority registration and designated staff to assist veterans with financial aid and disability services, tutoring, counseling, and classes.[79] These accommodations can provide important support to veterans in college, and my research argues that they should be made available to student veterans. Yet many of the recommendations for the creation of veteran- or military-friendly campuses extend beyond providing administrative support services. For example, an article on veteran support service best practices states, "Policies and procedures that recognize and honor service members and veterans must reach into the business office, administration, classroom, advising, transfer, and credit awarding policies."[80] The call for this far-reaching valorization of the military throughout the campus far exceeds the provision of direct services to veterans; in calling administration, students, faculty, staff, and campus policy makers to recognize and honor service members and veterans for their military service, it confers upon military members a status above that of other students. Thus, this mandate both produces and is produced by militarized common sense.

Campus military sensitivity and inclusion programs incorporating both protective and valorization strategies highlight the tension between the victimized and heroic positions into which student veterans are placed. This tension becomes visible when campuses institute initiatives like the VNA program on their campuses and reconcile the two positions. As noted earlier, when the problem for veterans in college is framed as campuses not being sufficiently friendly toward the military, then part of the solution is to teach faculty and staff to become friendlier through sensitivity training. As the online publication *Inside Higher Education* notes in its special issue, "Creating a Veteran-Friendly Campus":

> In Minnesota, colleges and universities have heard a need for a support team and an infrastructure that facilitates a [veteran] friendly environment. . . . Foremost is a need for faculty and staff awareness and sensitivity training. All employees at a college or university can say or do things that could be insulting, and sometimes this happens. Yet almost all of those offending words or deeds are said or done without malice, intent or without knowledge. Over the past several years, hundreds of hours of employee training sessions have been conducted, most in partnership with a veterans affairs and/or a military staff person. Training

sessions on campus can help to bring an awareness of possible concerns and is a base level step.[81]

The language of military-friendly best practices travels and is reproduced in campus veteran support programs around the country. A Minnesota Office of Education publication asserts the need for Safe Zone stickers and sensitivity training, and a recommendation to curb potentially offensive (antimilitary or antiwar) speech is clearly informed by warnings from educational journal articles regarding classroom critiques of military policy.[82] Also taking the lead from military-supportive best-practice literature, the following article applauds Minnesota campuses for implementing the VNA program, involving "a veteran-friendly sticker, modeled after the 'Safe Space' sticker denoting support for gay and lesbian students. 'Just to let the veterans know all through the campus that these are places that are veteran-friendly. . . . Although veterans don't necessarily need safe zones, they do need to know that they're welcome here. It's a vet-friendly environment and it's all through campus.'"[83]

The victim-hero tension surfaces within the above program description, where the image of the heroic warrior is at odds with that of the harassed veteran in need of safety, and thus the narrative shifts from protection of individual veterans to celebrating and promoting the institutional military. While the VNA program is intentionally crafted around public identification with marginalized groups ("employees at a college or university can say or do things that could be insulting"), veteran support programs like the above seek to garner support for hypothetical victims of discrimination without portraying the veterans as weak or needy. Unlike gays and lesbians, the above-quoted veteran advocate states, "veterans don't necessarily need safe zones," yet it would appear that veterans need to be publicly welcomed on campuses with displays of the military mission, icons, and culture, blurring the distinction between the veteran friendly and the military friendly.

The program referenced above configures veteran support as military support by holding campus-wide veterans' appreciation events celebrating not only veterans themselves but military weapons and iconography: T-shirts, marching bands with F-16 fighter jets flying overhead.[84] Thus, the strategy to create veteran-friendly campuses becomes one of creating military-celebrating campuses, and militarized common sense is produced by the support of veterans by nationalist displays of militarized patriotism.

In the name of easing transitions from military life to civilian student life, initiatives such as Warriors to Work, Combat to Community, Boots to Books, and Combat to the Classroom demonstrate the discursive power of framing demilitarized student veterans.[85] These initiatives simultaneously reify military status and superiority while attempting to help veterans reintegrate into non-militarized civilian life, which has the effect of discursively re-militarizing the veterans while celebrating military cultures in civilian academic spaces.

Veterans Day

Every year on Veterans Day since 2006, Los Olmos Community College has hosted a daylong event honoring veterans and military service; in 2012, the celebration featured a Vietnam War theme. The program featured talks by a retired U.S. Army helicopter pilot who had completed two tours of duty in Vietnam, a former CIA agent, and a pilot for Air America in Southeast Asia. In this context there was no ambiguity about the significance of the Vietnam War and no rancor associated with it; this was a celebration of that conflict and of those who fought in it.

Sidewalks flanking the school's courtyard were adorned with dozens of U.S. flags, and displayed a type of spatial before-and-after tableau: to the left of the courtyard where the color guard stood, Army and Air Force recruitment tables provided convenient access to Los Olmos students interested in enlisting.

On the opposite side of the courtyard, to the right of the color guard, representatives from local veterans' services groups offered support to soldiers after they returned home from war: housing, medical, and mental health services. Civilian therapists encouraged student veterans who served in Iraq and Afghanistan to sign up for no-cost trauma therapy offered by licensed volunteer civilian therapists. Staff from the local Vet Center also offered individual therapy and peer support groups for former combat soldiers. Volunteers handed out informational brochures about PTSD, military sexual trauma, and suicide prevention with the crisis line phone numbers and warning signs of suicide.

The parking lot adjacent to the recruiting tables hosted a display of military aircraft and ground vehicles and equipment; college students and family members could take turns sitting in the vehicles and imagine driving or flying them. Children climbed into the cockpit of a decommissioned helicopter and pretended to fly it into faraway battles.

Alongside the recruiters, an American Legion table displayed World War II–era rifles and military medals, establishing a connection with more distant military conflicts and veterans. There was also a table promoting Operation Postcard, a project of the Blue Star Mothers—mothers of active-duty service members—to collect messages of support from civilians, which would be included in care packages compiled by mothers and military supporters.[86] Post-

FIGURE 5.5 Army recruitment table, Los Olmos College. Photo by author.

FIGURE 5.6 Military aircraft display, Los Olmos College. Photo by author.

FIGURE 5.7 Blue Star Mothers' table, Veterans Day celebration, Los Olmos College.
Photo by author.

cards came with instructions to ensure that the personalized notes conformed to the U.S. military mission: "1. Keep the messages positive. 2. Teachers please edit cards and letters from your students," and "Ideas for beginning your message: 'Dear U.S. protector . . .'" The two women staffing the table took care in their mission to gather messages of gratitude: when I asked permission to take a photograph of the Operation Postcard table, I was told that I would be allowed to do so only if I wrote a postcard thanking service members for their military service.

Blue Star Mothers are held in great esteem at community events like this one. On an emotional level, there is something unassailable about soldiers' mothers collecting messages of support and hope for their sons and daughters deployed in war zones. At civilian meetings of veteran support service providers, the moral authority afforded to Blue Star Mothers is unequivocal and palpable. When a Blue Star Mother is identified during opening introductions, a sense of reverence can be felt in the room, which renders these mothers the embodiment of wartime military sacrifice. The representational juncture of mothers, children, danger, love, fear, hope, and nation provokes an inchoate emotional response, so that it feels unseemly to critically analyze their efforts on behalf of their children and, symbolically, on behalf of the nation's children. I do not gainsay these mothers' commitment or their sacrifice, much less the sacrifice of their children. And yet, at the table at Los Olmos Community College, as I filled out my postcard wishing the unknown recipient a safe journey home, I felt unhappily coerced.

This event was a special occasion—an annual event specifically designed to celebrate veterans. This commemorative event shows how military discourse is introduced, reproduced, and enforced on campuses such as Los Olmos through institutional participation in special celebrations. For example, community college students have the opportunity to learn crowd control techniques while celebrating past and present soldiers and wars. While this Veterans Day celebration offers one example of the valorizing strategy that conflates veterans with the military mission, it tells us little about how affinities for military perspectives are produced outside of Veterans Day. More subtle and pervasive examples of the inculcation of military discourse can be seen in the sensitivity training that college faculty, staff, and administrators are encouraged to attend as a matter of mandated and voluntary professional development.

I attended one such sensitivity training that appeared to have incorporated elements of the VNA program. It took place on an urban community college campus in California. It was billed as a cultural competence training to prepare community college instructors to teach veterans in their classrooms.

The trainers, one former marine and one civilian clinical psychologist, told the assembled community college instructors that to become culturally competent to teach veterans, they needed to be able to identify weaponry (rocket-propelled grenade launchers and M-16 automatic rifles) and to differentiate between the battle cries of the Army and the Marines. The trainers divided the room into two groups to competitively perform those battle cries. In doing so, the trainers reconfigured the discursive space such that civilian trainers became proxy drill instructors and community college instructors acted as recruits. In this process of creating identification with the military, support for the veteran was embodied and enacted as support for the military.

The session's training materials included a handout titled: "Questions to Avoid Asking Veterans." The list contained a range of questions, including some that I considered appropriate to refrain from asking a new acquaintance as a matter of simple human sensitivity, for example: "Did you kill someone?" and "What is it like to kill?"[87] The list also contained questions that were absurdly provocative (e.g., "Are you crazy like the Vietnam vets?"). Finally, the list also included a question that at least some veterans explicitly wanted to discuss in their college classrooms: "What do you think of the war?" Rendering this question off-limits forecloses discussions about the war and conflates support for veterans with silent quiescence to the war. In this way, militarism becomes part of the hidden curriculum of community college instruction, and training like this helps produce another form of militarized common sense.

In this training, college instructors were told that military veterans do not consider themselves political and that discussing the politics of the current wars would alienate student veterans. This training promoted an essentialized veteran identity that eschews thinking or talking about politics, diminishing the rich diversity of veterans' opinions. Thus, efforts intended to welcome veterans to campus can produce silence about or tacit support for the wars in which veterans fought, and promote the position that to criticize or dissent from the Iraq and Afghanistan wars is tantamount to criticizing veterans.

The training packet also included the following sample script, with the suggestion that it be printed in all course syllabi and recited to each class by instructors at the beginning of each semester: "Welcome home returning veterans! We are honored to have you on campus and look forward to your continued success here. For some returning veterans, going back to school can present unique challenges. If that is true for you, remember that you do not have to face these challenges on your own. We are here to help. Please feel free to discuss any questions or concerns you may have about the curriculum, the assignments, or your academic program with me in person. Thank you for your service, and welcome home!"[88] This message was very welcoming, and some instructors with whom I spoke felt comfortable with the idea of publicly welcoming student veterans into their classes; one instructor thought the scripted message was "nice." Yet the suggestion that all class syllabi should carry this message honoring veterans reproduces the discourse of military superiority.

Instructors on diverse contemporary college campuses were not similarly encouraged to give such an explicit appreciation and welcome to any other group, and no one suggested that they read scripts expressing gratitude and honoring, for example, immigrant students, or African American students, gay and lesbian students, or older, reentry students. Thus, veterans' status was elevated solely based on their association with the military. Trainings like this one conveyed the message that to be culturally competent to teach veterans, they must publicly thank veterans for their military service and avoid talking about the wars.

By advising instructors to thank veterans for their military service, the training suggested that they publicly express gratitude for military projects. Doing so would implicitly endorse military missions that instructors might disagree

FIGURE 5.8 Southwestern University basketball halftime salute to veterans.
Photo by Yeji Mun Fitzgerald.

with. The performance of public endorsement—despite the possibility of private disagreement—forecloses discussion of the wars, promotes discourses of military superiority, and reinforces heroic narratives about soldiers, producing a militarized common sense.

At the time, this newly developed training had not been widely implemented in colleges, but even without prescriptive curriculum guidelines, some faculty and teaching assistants told me that they self-monitored their speech in class to ensure that they were being supportive to veterans. One student veteran at SU said that his teaching assistant asked him to review her syllabus and lecture notes, to make sure that she wasn't saying anything offensive or wrong because she did not want to offend student veterans. This practice made veterans the medium for the production of militarized common sense.

Along with sensitivity training, manifestations of nationalism and militarism were increasingly incorporated into the everyday life of college campuses. In addition to the overtly militarized campus helicopter landings, everyday rituals at collegiate sports events demonstrated military amity. For example, on Veterans Day 2011, the SU athletic department put on a show honoring the military during the half-time break of a men's basketball game. The show concluded with a patriotic tribute, during which student veterans unfurled a gigantic U.S. flag across the court. While the flag was unfurled, a reverent silence descended on the crowd as all the spectators rose to salute: some stood silently, some stood with hands over hearts, and some gave a hand-to-forehead military salute.

This particular flag ritual has become increasingly common—perhaps to the point of being unremarkable—at major sporting events, but until recently, it was unusual at su. This moment illustrated a conjuncture of what Michael Billig calls banal nationalism (or the attachment of nationalist symbols to popular cultural icons) and what he calls the hot nationalism, of overt assertions of national supremacy. The articulation of banal and hot nationalisms at su is one example of how militarist symbolism is sutured to a nationalist narrative in what is generally considered to be a non-militarist, non-nationalist university.

Militarized common sense, and the accompanying silencing of campus debate about war, is produced by preemptively declaring civilian college faculty and students hostile to the military and, by extension, to veterans. Advocates of military-valorizing veteran support programs are not required to prove that civilian campuses are actually hostile to veterans: by articulating a revised cultural remembrance of Vietnam veterans with the current reality for veterans of the Iraq and Afghanistan wars, the problem of the antimilitary campus is produced. This provides the rationale to enlist faculty, administrators, and students in a social project that aims to ameliorate an apocryphal history of antiveteran abuse. This strategic narrative engenders support for the military and its projects not through overt coercion, but through a discourse of care for veterans, who are positioned simultaneously as underrepresented minorities, victims of harassment by students and faculty, and heroic figures. In the name of helping U.S. war veterans succeed in college, campuses become militarized in quotidian ways, often unseen or considered unremarkable.

· 6 ·

"THANK YOU FOR YOUR SERVICE"

Gratitude and Its Discontents

A true war story is never moral. It does not instruct, nor encourage virtue, nor
suggest models of proper human behavior, nor restrain men from doing things men have
always done. If a story seems moral, do not believe it. If at the end of a war story you feel
uplifted, or if you feel that some small bit of rectitude has been salvaged from the
larger waste, then you have been made the victim of a very old and terrible lie.
TIM O'BRIEN, *The Things They Carried*

As freedom is both negated and realized by choice,
so is silence convened, broken, and organized by speech.
WENDY BROWN, "Freedom's Silences"

There is widespread and justified concern among educators about war veterans'
process of transition into college, and an array of supportive interventions have
been designed to ease this transition. As the previous chapters show, these interventions include sensitivity training for faculty and students, military celebrations on campuses, and admonitions against classroom discussions of the
wars. Support programs have been built around the assumption that all veterans
actively and positively identify with their military service, the institutional military, and the mission of the current wars. Yet because war veterans had complex
and contradictory feelings about the U.S. military, about their military service,
and about the wars in which they fought, support programs predicated on an uncritical celebration of the military mission did not effectively serve all veterans.

Militarized common sense has negative consequences not just for open
campus debate and dissent, but also for veterans. This chapter examines some

effects of militarized common sense on student veterans by providing veterans' views on military-valorizing programs on their college campuses.

Within civilian society and particularly in colleges, veterans' public identities and interests are cast as political-military identities and interests. Support programs developed based on a claimed unity of interests between veterans and the U.S. military have been hailed as best-practice templates for veteran support. Yet when programs glorify a particular military mission, they can alienate veterans who have conflicted or negative feelings about that mission.

Military veterans described needing diverse forms of support that depended on their own diversity of opinions and experiences. Veterans had varied views of their role in the campus community and of how they wanted to be understood by their civilian teachers and classmates. While the participants in this research cannot speak for all veterans, it is nevertheless important to understand their reactions to veteran support. In the course of my discussions with student veterans, a complex picture emerged involving societal reverence, silence, denial, and patriotic gratitude. This diversity contrasted with a best-practices literature that presented a unitary picture of how veterans see themselves within their college communities and how they view their military service and the wars.

This chapter begins with a discussion of student veterans' experiences within their college communities followed by an examination of student veterans' views about their military service and their participation in the wars. The later parts of this chapter offer examples of veterans' complex relationship with societal silence about the wars and public gratitude for fighting in them. My intention in using lengthy quotes is to offer a fuller contextual understanding of the issues and to allow—within the confines of my role as interlocutor and interpreter—the participants to speak for themselves.

Veterans' Perspectives

To understand student veterans' experience on campuses, I return to the survey taken in the veterans' class at Southwest University discussed in chapter 5. Veterans provided varied responses to the question of what they would like people on the SU campus to know about their military service. Three general themes emerged in these responses, reflecting three distinct self-perceptions of their position as student veterans. Of the twenty-six respondents, three expressed pride in their service and wanted to be honored publicly for having served in the military; three characterized themselves as being no different from civilian students and wanted to be treated as such; and the remaining twenty wrote that it was important to recognize that their experiences in the military and in the wars had shaped them in important ways, though they resisted public categorization on the basis of their status as veterans.[1] Within these groupings, responses revealed a complex mix of self-identifications, at various times incorporating elements of all three self-perceptions.

In response to the question, "What do you want people on the SU campus to understand about your service or being an SU veteran?," the following three responses expressed that veterans should be treated as different from civilian students:

- That the freedom they enjoy was paid for by our service.
- I want them to understand that I served in the Army for them. Our sacrifice was done to protect all of their freedom under the Constitution.
- The only thing I feel is important for the people on the *su* campus to understand about my military service is that I am proud to have served honorably, I am honored to have worked alongside the people I had the opportunity to serve with, and that I am who I am today because of the sense of responsibility I learned from the military.

The three veteran responses above express pride in their military service. The first two portray a narrative of military sacrifice for the common good and conceptualize the mission of the current wars as protecting civil liberties in the United States. The third expresses pride in personal growth and accomplishments and in the relationships formed during military service. Implicit in the first two responses is the idea that veterans are owed a debt of gratitude from civilians for their sacrifice.

The next group of responses expressed the theme of wanting to minimize differences between veterans and their fellow (civilian) students. These veterans considered themselves students first and foremost, and they did not want to be treated differently from the general student body.

Question: "What do you want people on the SU Campus to understand about your service or being an SU veteran?"

- Nothing. I like the positive efforts, but personally I don't want to be in any spotlight. If my professors and classmates don't know, then I'm just a student.

This respondent reflected a position that I heard from other interview participants: that the easiest way to transition back to civilian society and school was to blend in with the rest of the campus and to be seen as "just a student." Others did not want to stand out as veterans because they felt that other students might view them as representatives of a particular political stance. For example:

- Being a veteran doesn't define my politics. I had a conversation awhile back about our political system and when I revealed that I was a veteran, it seemed as if I had confirmed some underlying assumptions. We are just another group of students trying to make it at SU.

In the comment above, the student veteran asserted that his or her views may align with political support for the military, but that other civilian students used that veteran status to invalidate her or his ability to freely form those views. A third respondent (below) seemed to be reacting against stereotyped portrayals of those who enlist in the military as intellectually inferior to their college peers:

- Veterans are not stupid. Aside from that, I don't "expect" anything nor desire any special recognition.

The remaining survey responses reflected a mix of opinions, motivations, and identities. The respondents asserted an independence of thought; some expressed commonalities with civilians and the desire not to be seen as exceptional, and others indicated some desire that instructors and teaching assistants recognize their military service, and suggested that veterans may need academic or medical accommodations. For example:

- I want them to understand that we are adults and have the same general concerns as other transfer students. Some of us have mortgages, families, full time jobs, commute, [and] go to more than one school. Some of us are dealing with the latent pressures and stresses of deployments, including ongoing medical problems. I do wish instructors and teaching assistants were told, or it was shown on the roster somehow, which students are veterans. Priority registration is amazing, but even smaller acknowledgement and understanding (and hopefully slight accommodation) would be awesome.
- A lot of misconceptions surround the veteran community. Most of what people see on television is a gross dramatization of military service. While some aspects ring true, it is better to ask a veteran an open-ended question than to approach with a biased one. We also have our own opinions and political beliefs that we may share in common with you, we are not mindless drones programmed with preconceived notions.

The above responses signal a desire for communication with civilians and for civilians to approach veterans with open minds and open-ended questions. The themes of commonality with civilians, and a clear separation between soldiers and the wars in which they fought, surfaced in many of the responses. For example:

- I would like the SU campus to know that we are people just like them. Our experiences have changed our perceptions of the world, and changed who we are, but this shouldn't be held against us. Regardless of how you feel about the wars do not reflect those feelings onto veterans themselves.
- First and foremost—[I want people on the SU campus to understand] that student veterans still belong to the general community of students. There should be, however, a subtle respect set aside for the veterans on behalf of their life experiences and willingness to be active—as opposed to passive.
- As far as being an SU veteran goes, I think that we bring experiences to the table that no other group can offer in terms of cooperation, organization, or just life outside academics. But personally I'm not looking for accolades or recognition.
- What I want people to understand about my service is that it was something that I did for myself. Not for love of country, though I do have that, or to go to war—a violent thought—but so that I could prove me to myself and grow as a person. And the G.I. Bill helps too.
- SU veterans have unique experiences and skills as a result of military service that are not necessarily taught in the classroom but still impact the veteran and those around him/her (leadership, maturity, teamwork and many others).
- Many people assume that veterans are pro-war. This is not true. We don't condone war. We have learned a lot from our experience and have a lot to share.

In a simple statement, one respondent painted a picture of an unbridgeable divide:

- Unfortunately, the things I would like the student body to know, I feel they will never understand.

These responses reflect the diversity of views held by veterans about the wars, and in the course of my research, I found that some war veterans were more tolerant of discussions with civilians about the wars than some of their civilian supporters. War veterans' complex positions are often informed by what is referred to in military slang as the "ground truth," or the lived reality of combat and military occupation. The closer that one's lived experience is to the reality of war, the more difficult it is to reduce that experience to simplistic heroic or vilifying narratives and iconography. Military supporters who have not experienced war may rely on purely philosophical arguments, abstracted from complications of physical and emotional trauma of being both victims and perpetrators of violence. For some, uncritical valorization of military projects reflects this lack of embodied knowledge combined with social pressure to avoid mistreating veterans (as it is believed that Vietnam War veterans were mistreated); this facilitates the idealization of both war and warrior.

Many veteran participants in this research chose to study philosophy, history, political science, linguistics, or Middle Eastern studies to gain a greater understanding of their combat experiences. While many veterans, including some participants in this research, choose to study within science, technology, engineering, and mathematics (STEM) fields, others studied the humanities because they were actively seeking out different perspectives than the ones taught in their military service. The majority of veterans with whom I spoke showed a more nuanced understanding of the effects of war, and greater understanding of the complexities involved, than are evident in celebratory displays of military prowess.

Previous chapters explored competing narratives about soldiers and wars: the celebratory narrative of the warrior-hero who fought at great personal sacrifice in defense of the nation alongside societal silence and apathy about the wars. There is no real debate about the fact that in war, combat soldiers endure extreme danger and sacrifice, yet the rationale behind this sacrifice is contested within U.S. society, within veterans' communities, and within the minds of individual veterans. The following case of su student Connor, introduced in previous chapters, represents an example of someone who actively grapples with contradictory feelings about his military experience.

While deployed in Afghanistan, Connor worked as a turret gunner on a weapons-mounted armored security vehicle. The job of the then twenty-year-old recruit from rural Northern California was to support military operations by discharging suppressive machine gun fire into suspected hostile areas, to "destroy, neutralize or suppress insurgent forces."[2] When I asked Connor to tell me about his job in Afghanistan, he said that his first sergeant told him his job was to "kill hajji." In the first of three two-hour formal interviews, Connor spoke at length about the emotional and spiritual crises he faced after returning from Afghanistan to the United States, where he had the time, physical safety, and psychological distance to reflect on his combat experience. Connor said that he realized his participation in combat created a rupture with his previous worldview and caused him to lose his Christian faith. His remorse turned to fantasies aimed against the U.S. military:

> None of the stuff we did when we were deployed really hit me at the time. I just did it. And after I got back, [the feelings] starting building, about what we did and what we are doing, all the killing. It built into a really festering feeling inside me. So I became very angry toward the Army as an institution. I used to think if I could just destroy this entire military infrastructure, I would be wiping out a parasite in this world. That's what I felt like we are: we're parasitic. We're killing other people, so many other people, and Fort Bragg is one of the epicenters of American military might. And I thought, "If I could just kill it all"—not the people, but all the equipment and the buildings [pauses]. I used to fantasize about that.

Connor remained connected to military life and combat even as he rejected the mission of the wars. He returned from war angry and alienated from the institution and mission of the Army, yet he also felt estranged from what he saw as the superficiality and privilege of civilian life: the emphasis on material accumulation and mindless media diversions. Connor missed the asceticism, discipline, and sacrifice he felt in Afghanistan, saying that he was drawn to the austerity that characterized his life as a soldier: "It's a monasticism to be deployed. You can only have so many possessions that you can fit in a duffle bag. You don't have all these distractions. You can't go out and party with women, drinking, all those sorts of things. For most people, it just drives them crazy, but people handle it in different ways. Say I'd gone [directly] into college instead of going into the military. I don't think I would've had that [ascetic] experience at all."

Connor's comments demonstrate ambivalence about his wartime experience that I heard from other veterans. On one hand, Connor thought of himself as a violent "parasite" killing enemy combatants and participating in a military occupation of Afghanistan. On the other hand, military deployments brought intensity and focus to his life and offered him the opportunity to participate in new experiences. In combat, Connor challenged himself, tested the outer limits of his endurance, and overcame fears. Connor said that he felt more vital and alive when he was in stationed in Afghanistan. Like other combat veterans, he said that the combat environment felt more real to him: "I hated being back Stateside. I saw no purpose in being at the base. Not that there was any purpose in what we were doing in Afghanistan, but at least it was more real. . . .

I volunteered to go to Iraq immediately when I got back, I guess because I felt like it was more intense overseas, and I kind of liked that." Despite recognizing that he participated in what he called acts of "inhumanity," Connor identifies his overall military experience as positive in his life, saying that he gained invaluable maturity through his military training and experience. Connor said that although he rejected the U.S. military mission in Afghanistan, he said he is happy to have had the experience:

> Now, people ask me, "If you could do it again, would you join the Army?" And I say definitely, I'd do it all again. I never believed politically in the mission, or had any reason like that. It was just the experience, the living of life. And my life's been all the richer for me because of it. Richer in experience, richer in places I've gone, people I've met, attitudes I've held that I had to break down and challenge. Things that I know and I've learned that are not academic, that there's no way that you can learn except by experiencing them.

Psychologists note that part of the process of healing from trauma requires coming to terms with the contradictory nature of thoughts and feelings produced by the traumatic experience.[3] Connor began to reflect on his contradictory thoughts, feelings, motivations, and impulses through talking with other veterans, with community college teachers, and with students and staff at su. Connor's reintegration process included dealing with conflicting feelings about his service, about the military mission, and about the human consequences of war. The fact that these ambivalent thoughts resurfaced later in the conversation indicates that he still actively grapples with these contradictions. When asked how he was changed by his military experience and training, Connor said, "The personal changes are both positive and negative. Positively, I feel pretty self-confident and physically capable of doing things." But Connor also acknowledged that his experience in combat had changed him in what he characterized as negative ways: "Well, I feel like [pauses], well, you know, there is a stereotype of veterans being like on edge [pauses], and I don't know. I'm coming to be more complete in understanding myself and realizing that yes, I am a bit more on edge than most people."

In the second of three interviews, having reflected on our previous conversation, Connor returned to the topic of how he had been changed through his military experience. He realized that he had held back in his previous response, and he wanted to give a more complete answer about the changes he had undergone during his combat experience.

There was something I wasn't really saying that I was conscious of, but I didn't voice it out. I saw that I wasn't saying it. I think it's [about] my ability to do violence. As I was telling you about how I would go back in the pool [reenlist] and do the same thing again, that's an acknowledgment of myself and my own capability to do violence, to be psychopathic, as it were. To do killing that makes no sense in an arbitrary fashion. That's what I wanted to say. I'm pretty aware of my ability to kill, and that is something that's with me all the time. It's kind of a strange thing to live with, I guess.

Having participated in what he called "psychopathic" organized and arbitrary violence, Connor found the power he felt as a soldier to be disturbing. He continued, "It's a freedom, a power to know that I could take a life. I've already done it, so afterwards it's not as big of a leap. But it makes me fearful of myself and what I'm capable of. That I'm capable of killing for arbitrary reasons in the military, and being aware of how arbitrary the killing was in general. It's really frightening." Connor returned to this topic because he felt it represented an important aspect of his experience of war and because it informed his life after the Army. This kind of reflection was facilitated by talking openly about the different facets of his wartime experience, and all of his reactions to it, whether positive, negative, or ambivalent.

Connor's lived experience caused him to reject the dichotomous military tropes of good versus evil deployed in war. Rather than learning hatred of a wholly evil enemy, his combat experiences taught him that good and evil are socially constructed; not fixed, but malleable and perspectival. The reintegration into college of veterans like Connor would not be served by ignoring or attempting to deny their ambivalent feelings toward their military service by avoiding the topic of war, or by glorifying or vilifying the institutional military.

In Connor's view, civilian life facilitated the dichotomous portrayal of soldier and enemy as good and evil through war-themed video games. He was dismayed by their popularity among civilians, who imagined they knew what it was like to participate in combat. For Connor, the (largely male) civilian preoccupation with simulated combat games obfuscates real war experiences:

I see people in video games acting that out as a fantasy: here you've got these macho heroes going in, killing bad guys and stuff. But I've come to the place where I don't think there are any bad guys anymore. I feel like the people who fought against us in Afghanistan were just doing what they had to do. Because we're an invading army going in and killing people. I feel like I would want to do the same thing if they were here invading my country and killing my family and friends. I empathize with [the Afghan insurgents'] situation—we're the ones who deployed to go there and kill.

Soldiers live with ambivalence and contradictions. Connor emerged from his combat experience with a nuanced understanding of what it meant to be publicly praised for actions that he felt were wrong: "It's just kind of the dual nature, the dark side of human nature, what you're capable of, what you're doing, and you know that it's wrong. But you're also condoned by your country to do what you're doing, going over there and fighting a war, and your whole country says, 'Oh yeah—it's good that you're doing that.'" The glorification of a mission from which some veterans feel estranged can alienate those veterans and distort their experiences of fighting a war. Heroic narratives can foster cognitive dissonance for soldiers who do not feel always or only like heroes. For some veterans, this estrangement negatively influences their ability to integrate into college.

Army veteran Bridget, age twenty-four, was raised outside of Denver, Colorado, in a white working-class family. Her father was an Army veteran and her mother was a homemaker. Bridget's early home life was unhappy, and she spent her teenage years trying to build an alternative family among her friends. After getting married at age sixteen, she realized that the horizons for her future had become constricted, and she dropped out of her high school and enrolled in an alternative high school, where she excelled.

I had a really unstable childhood, so I didn't go to high school for the first two years, and I didn't really care about anything but socializing and just building a base of support or a base that wasn't my family. And then I realized that all of my female friends, all of them like [at age] fourteen, fifteen, they were all pregnant. And a lot of the guys were going to juvenile hall, just getting so wrapped up in drugs or gangs that they couldn't function in school. I didn't see them anymore and I realized that I had to leave that school. And I wasn't going to succeed in any way, so I went to this alternative high school, and I did pretty well there. I went to school every day, which was huge for me, and I tried really hard.

Bridget's teachers at her new school supported her love of learning and encouraged her to go to college. Bridget enrolled in her local community college but needed to find a job to support herself.

I was looking for a job while I was going to school. I had just started school, and nobody was hiring but the Army at the time, and I couldn't afford both eating and college so I joined. I wanted to get my life started, and I wanted to have a way to support myself. I was married. I got married very very young with my mother's consent. So I sort of wanted to give [my husband] some time to grow up and I wanted to support myself and give us a starting point in our lives, and [enlisting in the Army] just seemed like a good way to go about it and a fast way to go about it, and I would be able to afford college when I was done, and that was really important to me.

Bridget said that her experience in the Army helped her to develop her leadership skills. However, she also said that while stationed in Iraq, she developed a political critique of the U.S. military mission there and expressed remorse at what she was required to do to support that mission. In Iraq, Bridget was an Army intelligence specialist whose job was to intercept messages and identify "target packages" of Iraqis to be arrested or killed. After discharge and back in the United States, Bridget said that she did not identify as a hero, and she suspected ulterior motives behind that label. She said, "People want to make us icons. They want heroes. We're not icons. We can't all be heroes for them." For Bridget, this heroic narrative acted as a social erasure of her conflicted feelings about her experience, but it also spurred her to be an advocate for veterans' issues on her community college campus.[4]

For some veterans, feelings of disconnection from civilian society that result from public glorification of their combat experience can cause them to isolate and intensify the feeling that no civilian can ever understand them. Southwest University student and former U.S. Marine Jordan experienced this disconnect. As noted earlier, during Jordan's two tours of Iraq as a cryptological linguist, he listened to intercepted messages, and, like Bridget, he determined who would be targeted for arrest or assassination. As with many of the veterans I interviewed, when I asked Jordan about his military job, his response conveyed feelings of regret and remorse about Iraqi deaths. He said, "I listened to people all the time. In a sense, I lived in this alternate universe where I didn't see this person, but in a way I was following them around, [listening to] everything they said, everything I could hear in the background, who they were talking to, their tone of voice, how they were breathing. That was my job: to have an intimate relationship with people. But it wasn't a desired or a two-way relationship—I felt like a hunter."

Jordan had a difficult return to civilian life, and especially to college. Despite having enlisted in the military for college funding, Jordan ended up dropping out of SU the first time he enrolled, because he couldn't reconcile his combat experience with his life as a college student. He found it hard to relate to civilians whose only exposure to war was mediated through movies and popular culture, where the imperative for war is portrayed as clear, where the U.S. side always wins and is always heroic, and where nobody really gets hurt or dies. He said, "People here think 'sergeant' and they think John Wayne. I was a sergeant. I was twenty years old. And these twenty-year-olds, they are the corporals and sergeants, the noncommissioned officers that are running shit on the ground. People here don't have any sense of what's really going on."

When I asked if he planned on attending a campus Veterans Day celebration, Jordan said that he avoided such events, because he felt disconnected from the laudatory atmosphere surrounding talk about wartime military service. He said that hearing jingoistic speeches about the military and the wars left him feeling disaffected and angry rather than honored and supported: "I don't want to have to sit through something that's going to infuriate me. I'm not very good at keeping my mouth shut, but I don't want to speak up and smash someone else's point of view. . . . But if we're really going to talk about this you can't just toe the party line and have these fucking talking points like politicians." For student veterans like Jordan, Connor, Bridget, and others, reintegration into civilian society and college involves conflicting feelings about having participated in war. But some campus support organizations leave little room for veterans to address those mixed feelings. Some groups emphasize unconditional support for the troops that precludes ambiguity or dissent from the wars or the general military mission. Thus many campus veterans' groups are fashioned as no-politics zones, where critical examination of the military is prohibited in the name of supporting veterans.

An SU Veterans Club meeting that occurred in 2010 illustrates this. The meeting took place three days after an SU veteran died of a self-inflicted gunshot wound in his off-campus dorm room. The veterans' group met in a small classroom. The president of the club began by addressing the packed room: "It's good to see people here tonight. I'm sure you all know what happened to our brother. This is a big loss for our community. After a moment of silence, we'll open the floor for comments, but I want to remind people that we are a nonpartisan group; we are not here to talk about politics or to debate the wars." This Veterans Club meeting typically began with an admonition against partisan politics; in that respect, the president's reminder was not unusual. It was also neither unusual nor unreasonable that the group leader would want to focus comments on remembering the deceased rather than engaging in policy debates. However, during the period of open comment, former combat marine Adam spoke up. Adam had arrived late to the meeting, and he carried a military rucksack filled with ceramic cups to give to members of the club as a gesture of support and solidarity. Because he came in late, Adam missed the president's instructions about public comments. When the president opened the floor, Adam said, "I had to come here tonight to be with my brothers. But I want to know—when are we going to stop these fucking wars that continue to take the lives of the best of us?" The president gently reminded Adam about the group's no-politics rule, and that was the end of the discussion. No one else said anything about the deceased veteran or about why this young man might have taken his own life. The meeting quickly moved on to administrative announcements.

This meeting created a double silencing for Adam: he was not allowed to fully express his grief at the loss of his fellow veteran, and he was not allowed to talk about what he saw as the force that caused his comrade's death. This exchange also taught the rest of the attendees that silence would be enforced. But beyond dictating what is and is not publicly grieveable, the act of rendering off-limits discussions about the war narrowed the task of veteran peer support to dealing with the so-called apolitical social and psychological effects of military service, prohibiting discussion of the cause of the trauma that contributed to this act of a veteran taking his own life. This apolitical approach reflected the position that to support veterans one had to be, at least implicitly, part of a greater, unified war effort. Veteran support services that created ostensibly apolitical spaces foreclosed discussions that some veterans need to make sense of their combat experience and denied veterans the chance to express the full complexity of their relationship to war.

Yet this prohibition on political speech was enforced selectively. Within campus veteran support discourse, politics was coded to mean talk that challenged or critiqued the military or the war. In Veterans Club meetings, when participants made a laudatory comment about the war (for example, when someone celebrated news of a successful battle, or announced the death of an insurgent leader), there was no similar admonition to silence. This reflected an environment in which the naturalized politics of militarism was taken for granted and considered an expression of patriotism rather than politics. This tacitly advanced the position that to support the troops, one must support the war.

Whereas some veterans were frustrated by the cautionary avoidance of discussing the wars, social spaces where veterans could openly express their ambivalent feelings about the military and the wars helped some to work through their contradictory feelings. In my research, interviews that began with veterans talking about classroom experiences would often, guided by the veterans, end with conversations about their deployments in Iraq or Afghanistan. The following lengthy interview excerpt with Central College student Mitchell illustrates this veteran's desire to talk about difficult yet important military experiences. The excerpt includes my responses to Mitchell; including my response is intended to illustrate the ways that Mitchell guided the conversation to talk about his experience in Iraq. This interview took place in a conference room on a far corner of the Central College campus. As in all of the individual interviews with veterans, Mitchell and I were the only ones present.

Friends and administrative staff identified Mitchell as someone who had been having difficulty in his transition to college. He was the student who once pantomimed locking and loading an imaginary rifle at a faculty meeting out of frustration. Mitchell was studying in the administration of justice program, intending to apply to the police academy after completing his associate's degree at Central College, but he had begun to have second thoughts about a career in law enforcement. Mitchell had experienced difficulties adjusting to Central College and had struggled with periods of deep depression and isolation. I asked Mitchell what had been helpful to him, in or out of the classroom, in his transition to Central College. He replied that he appreciated the way his English composition instructor led class discussions; she had invited veterans' contributions in class without appointing individual veterans as spokespersons and without singling them out by requiring them to comment, especially during classroom conversations about military conflicts. As an example, Mitchell recalled a writing assignment he chose to base on the short story collection *The Things They Carried* by Vietnam War veteran Tim O'Brien: "English 1B is creative-style English. [You have] to understand why authors do this or do that, and then you have to write your own creative story at the end. And I chose to use Tim O'Brien's format for my short story as a model, because [O'Brien's book] is bouncing all over the place, which is pretty much the way he wrote it, in the fog-of-war style because everything about the war is [a] fog. You don't understand what's going to happen."

Mitchell said that he was drawn not just to the format of O'Brien's book—the stream of consciousness, fog-of-war style that reflected combat soldiers' confusion—but also to the content and description of the chaos of battle. For Mitchell, writing about his combat experience in the contained environment of his English class allowed him to express his conflicted feelings about the war and his participation in it. Privately communicating with his instructor through his essay allowed Mitchell to express his thoughts on this difficult topic. He described the experience as "cathartic":

MITCHELL: It was very, very cathartic for me. Don't get me wrong—I still deal with my demons—but it helped to get out a really, really hard incident that I had to go through. [Writing the essay] helped me deal with it a little bit easier.

EM: I'm wondering how it is to read that book, and also how it is to be writing an essay about it in the context of a civilian classroom. Do you think it would have felt any different for you if you had been in a veterans-only class?

MITCHELL: Well, Alex was in the class with me. Him and I, we both did not want to talk. [The instructor] didn't probe us but she would ask generalistic questions: "What do you guys think about this?" Not asking just Alex and me, but "you guys," meaning the class.

In addressing questions to the entire class, Mitchell felt that his English instructor was protecting the two student veterans by keeping their writing private and treating their compositions as a vehicle for them to express themselves. Mitchell continued, "She didn't have anybody else read our writing or anything like that, but if she did have a chance to read [out loud to the class], she would read a paragraph or so from somebody's writing, but she never read anything from ours. She knew [not to do] that. Alex and I both went through very, very hard, hard experiences." Mitchell said that while he appreciated that the instructor wanted to know about their experience, he added that it was helpful that she also respected their privacy. He said he felt more understood and less isolated because the instructor expressed compassion for the difficulties he and Alex faced in having to recount their combat experiences: "And she would write on our essays, 'I don't know what that's like. But I can imagine. But even my imagining is not enough.' She just [pauses], she wanted to know. She wanted to understand, but she knew she couldn't. So it was nice. I didn't feel as if I was the only person in the class."

While it was important for Mitchell to begin to identify his thoughts and feelings privately, in the process of sharing his essay with his instructor, he came to believe that it was important for him talk about the war with his civilian classmates. He wanted to educate them about an issue he considered vitally important and to make his combat experience visible and comprehensible:

MITCHELL: But me and Alex came to this consensus that we need these people [civilian students] to understand [about the war]. We have to [tell them]. But there's no way in the world that these people are going to understand. I'm not saying we live in a dumb society, but if they aren't told, they can't understand. Actually, we spoke up a lot in the class, but the fact of the matter is that we didn't talk a lot [about combat]. But when we did, you could tell that the class was very, very intently listening to us. Very, very intently. They were zoned in. They wanted to know, and that's something that I think was really good.

EM: It seems to me that this English class presents a kind of a dilemma: you're coming back to a civilian classroom with—as one veteran called it—a wealth of knowledge about war. But you're coming back full of experience that other people don't know anything about, and this experience might be hard to talk about.

MITCHELL: It seems that with this, well, in my personal experience, the knowledge, this "wealth of knowledge" as you call it, is not needed.

EM: What do you mean?

MITCHELL: Like [pauses] I don't regret [my service]. The only thing that I wish is that I would have taken something from my actual craft and been able to use it. And unfortunately, no one, no one, *no one's* hiring someone who can go kill someone [speaker's emphasis].

EM: So you're saying that knowledge of how to kill is not needed in the civilian world.

MITCHELL: No, it's not, and that's why it's kind of hard for me to even think about being a cop. Because I want to help other people. I really do. But it's just, the first thing that I see, if someone's going to go shoot somebody, I'm going to take them down. And you can't do that. You can't do that all the time. And that's what I'm kind of worried about.

EM: Okay.

MITCHELL: And my wealth of experience is, is that I've already lost one friend. So I don't want to lose any more [becomes tearful].

EM: So it's experience that you can't use, or don't want to use, right now.

MITCHELL: Right.

At this point Mitchell became increasingly tearful. Because we were in a conference room on the outskirts of campus, and unlikely to be interrupted by anyone, we sat in silence for few minutes, after which time Mitchell indicated that he wanted to continue the conversation:

EM: You were saying that in civilian classrooms, people don't know what you've gone through. But you said that you think it's important that they know [about the experience of war].

MITCHELL: [Yes,] that they know, but they're still not going to understand. But it's, I think, I think, them knowing is half the battle. Just like everything, knowing is half the battle. And I think they need to know.

This moment highlights a dilemma veterans face in trying to bridge the experiential divide between civilians and military: many veterans felt the need to educate civilians, to make them understand the human costs of war, but this effort to educate came at an emotional cost. Moreover, Mitchell was not optimistic that even with education from combat veterans, civilians would be able to understand the human consequences of war. This echoes the words of the anonymous SU student who wrote, "Unfortunately, the things I would like the student body to know, I feel they will never understand." Mitchell added that because the human consequences of current wars are invisible to most in the United States, Americans are able to live in a constructed state of denial:

MITCHELL: In [the war in] Vietnam, when the war was televised, it was a huge problem. [People said,] "Oh my God, this is what they're doing?" Yeah, war's not freaking pretty. It's not some kind of dog and pony show. This is no joke. This is people dying. And [it would be better] if people could really understand that war is not so trivial.

EM: Do you think civilians at Central College understand that it's not trivial, or do you think they don't understand?

MITCHELL: I don't know. I don't think that anybody wants to get it. Everybody wants to live in their own little virtual home world now, with all these video games, and all these kids think that they understand what war is when they play Modern Warfare and all these dumb-ass video games. I mean, don't get me wrong—I play them. But it's not like I play them just to get my, my killer high on or anything like that. I play them with friends because it's fun. I don't care about my kill-to-death ratio. I don't care about how many people I kill in these games. But these kids do. And it's getting closer and closer. That virtual reality is finally going to give them what they want.

EM: What do you mean by that?

MITCHELL: Carnage. They're going to give it to them. It's already almost there. I mean, even the military is incorporating [electronic simulation] games [into infantry training].

EM: So you're saying that people trick themselves or delude themselves into thinking that they know what war is like because they—

MITCHELL: Yes.

EM:—Have a high kill ratio in video games?

MITCHELL: Yeah. They have a kill-to-death ratio. Or they know all the weapons. They've studied them. But half of them have never shot them, or even been anywhere near somebody who's shot them.

Though Mitchell played combat-themed video games with other veterans, he objected to the vicarious nature of the games for civilians because he felt that these games facilitate a societal denial: they allow people to fool themselves into thinking that they have an understanding of war.[5] The process of rendering vicarious that which has been intimately embodied and indelibly inscribed in Mitchell's consciousness served to widen the separation Mitchell felt between himself and other civilians. This type of war fantasy speaks directly to the kind of teaching strategies used in campus sensitivity trainings, where in the name of becoming culturally competent, college instructors learn to identify the superficial accoutrements of war.

However, as Mitchell's comments show, simply knowing about military gear, weapons, and battle cries does not make one an expert on soldiers' needs, nor on the less laudable and more troubling aspects of war. For Mitchell, the simplistic equation that familiarity with weaponry equals cultural competence was precisely what rendered civilians incompetent to engage with him in an authentic way about his experiences. Vicarious thrill-seeking from simulated war games trivialized real injury and death of the kind that produced Mitchell's very real and still-present grief response. The process of erasure by pseudo-familiarity increased Mitchell's sense of distance from civilians and ultimately impeded his ability to function in civilian social spaces.

This extended excerpt offers one counterexample to the contention that silencing discussion about the wars is helpful to or desired by veterans. I included this interview excerpt not only for its content but also because the process of the interview informed my argument. This transcript excerpt (edited only for punctuation) shows that Mitchell guided the interview to talk about his experience in war. The interview began with a question about classroom practice, and Mitchell went from talking about sharing his difficult combat experiences, privately, with his instructor, to expressing an urgent need to educate civilians about the reality of war as a means of shaking his classmates out of their denial about the wars. The fact that Mitchell brought the conversation around to these topics indicates that he wanted to or perhaps needed to talk about these issues. The support that Mitchell said he was looking for—understanding, explanation, and education, as well as compassion—could be achieved through more open and honest communication between veterans and civilians.

Processes of silencing are not only produced though large-scale public displays of military prowess and patriotism; they are also produced in small, everyday classroom practices and through affiliative speech acts. For example, as a civilian doing research about military veterans, I was counseled by civilians working with the military to refer to "our soldiers" and "our veterans" instead of "the soldiers" or "the veterans." These performative utterances produce military affiliations that facilitate the militarization of civilian subjectivities.[6] The narrowing of public debate through public denial of the wars and the linguistic enlistment of civilian subjects into a unified military family illustrate what Foucault would call the "productive power" of veteran support talk.

In this contemporary period of prolonged undeclared wars, where lethal-force conflicts are waged not against designated nation-states but against rhetorical abstractions (Terror) in the name of other rhetorical abstractions (Freedom), speech and language are a locus of power. I did not set out in this research to study the discursive power of silence and praise, but the themes of praiseful gratitude and respectful silence surfaced again and again in veteran support organizations, in trainings, and in classrooms. These words and themes became, in the words of Comaroff and Comaroff, "the animating vernacular around which the discursive flow is organized."[7] I noticed two principal pathways of this discursive flow: silence about the wars and mandated gratitude expressed in the phrase "thank you for your service." These flows of silence and gratitude extended ubiquitously within and beyond classrooms and campuses, demonstrating their salience as a social force.

"Thank You for Your Service"

In the summer of 2012, I stopped in a drug store in rural Northern California. As I stood in the checkout line, another customer complimented me on the new Army-issue combat boots I wore. In preparation for a forthcoming research trip to Fort Knox, I had been issued a complete Army combat uniform to wear on base. I'd been advised to wear the new boots to break them in before my trip, or risk blisters when I would have to wear them on a daily basis. The commenting observer—a white man who appeared to be in his forties and who was wearing a camouflage-print fishing hat and vest—seemed to be signaling some kind of mutual identification, and I wondered if he was a veteran. When I asked if the boots looked familiar to him, he hastened to say that he had never served in the military, but that he shopped at the Army surplus store and recognized the boots. I replied that I was also not in the military, but that the boots had been issued to me as a researcher studying military training and veterans. As I picked up my purchases and prepared to leave the store, he looked me in the eye and said sincerely: "Thank you for your service."

This stranger's public expression of gratitude was prompted by my boots, which signified "military" to those familiar with the gear. That I was wearing these boots caught his attention, and that my work was associated with the U.S. military led him—without knowing the theoretical orientation nor the findings of my research—to thank me for my service. Walking out of the store, I tried to figure out why I felt jolted by his seemingly sincere thanks, and why it made me feel uncomfortable and vaguely guilty. I tried to imagine what he thought he was thanking me for. Perhaps he assumed—correctly—that I cared deeply about the fates of war veterans. Or perhaps he assumed—incorrectly—that I was a military enthusiast, and that my research was intended to improve the training of combatants, or to support a unifying national project, or to support U.S. war efforts. In any case, I experienced the phrase as disconnected from the reality of my actual work and therefore undeserved.

William Deresiewicz writes about a contemporary "cult of the uniform," in which U.S. civilians with no personal connection to the military treat uniformed soldiers with "ritualistic piety." Deresiewicz argues that when people glorify soldiers without understanding what they do, their piety makes it more difficult to have an honest debate about empire, wars, and the defense budget.[8] In the years since 2001, the phrase "thank you for your service" has become a central feature of that ritualistic piety that is routinely enacted in airports, schools, shopping centers, and movie theaters; it can take place wherever identifiable military veterans or active-duty service members come into contact with civilians. Veteran support meetings on campuses routinely began with civilian speakers thanking the student veterans for their service. At the beginning of this research, I was advised by a civilian contractor working for the U.S. Army that I should introduce myself to veterans by thanking them for their service because it would facilitate communication. For some potential interview subjects, this may have indeed been the case, but because the phrase was so ubiquitous, instead of repeating it, I chose to ask veterans to describe how they feel when they heard the phrase "thank you for your service." Answers ranged from casual appreciation to active dislike, but many said that the phrase, coming from strangers who knew nothing about them beside their military status, seemed like a platitude; it seemed like something civilians thought they were supposed to say. Central College student Mitchell said,

> I've had people tell me, "Thank you for your service" or whatnot. I think it's more of a passing nod now these days. "Thank you for your service." I mean, don't get me wrong, there are people that actually mean it. And you can tell—at least I can tell—that people mean it when they say it. But there are some people that come and say, "Thank you for your service. Thank you for your service." It kind of makes me want to puke sometimes. "Thank you for your service"—it makes me want to puke.

I asked him to explain further, and Mitchell said that it felt like an insult when the phrase was spoken out of apparent obligation. Without intention or irony, Mitchell evoked the apocryphal image of the spitting 1960s antiwar protester, turning that trope on its head:

MITCHELL: It's almost like a spit in the face. It's like because they, it's, because they need to, or they should do it. Oh, because everybody else is doing it, they should do it. No. No. If you don't mean it, I don't want it.

EM: So it trivializes . . . ?

MITCHELL: Yeah. Don't get me wrong. Our soldiers have done some very, very messed-up things. We're young. We were brought [to war] too young. We're forged to be killers. It's not something that a seventeen-year-old kid should go through. It's not something a twenty-one-year-old kid should go through. It's not something a twenty-four-year-old man should go through. When they say that there is wisdom in age, and they're not kidding. I always have older friends. Alex is thirty-two. My friend Tommy is twenty-nine. I'm twenty-four. I can't get along with people my age. They scare me because they're so dumb. Don't get me wrong—I've made my mistakes—but I just wish [pauses]. That's why I want to be a psychologist because I wish if I could help some people understand that life is something.

Mitchell was adamant that he did not want his painful experience in the war—and the wisdom that he had acquired at such a high price—to be trivialized by a formulaic response from strangers. Mitchell's desire to understand, respond to, and heal from his combat experience led him to change his career plans mid-semester. Instead of applying to the police academy, Mitchell changed his major to psychology. He hoped that as a psychologist, he could help civilians and veterans move beyond clichés to learn about the "messed-up" realities of war and "help some people understand that life is something."

Gardiner notes that veteran clichés are "formulas that offer escape from the silence that pervades war experience or any experience lacking in a rich and familiar descriptive vocabulary" and that common expressions about war tend to be less believable coming from those who have never experienced combat.[9] Thus, who was speaking the phrase mattered to the recipient and helped veterans determine whether it was heartfelt appreciation or compulsory cliché. Conventional expressions of gratitude and respect coming from other veterans were generally received more kindly than those coming from unknown civilians. For example, when I asked Jordan what he thought when someone thanked him for his military service, he said, "It depends on who it is. Like when a Vietnam vet thanks me, it's real and it's legit and they understand all of the pieces of it. It's one of the most moving experiences, honestly, because they understand so much of it. But other times people just really don't know. And they just know that that this is one of the things that we're supposed to do—we're supposed to thank people."

In contrast to the Vietnam War veteran who understands the pain, fear, and anguish of combat, Jordan suspected that civilians thanked him for their own benefit:

> When I hear that [phrase] from certain people, I think, "Okay. Do you think you're *done* now? Do you think you're done with your side of this bargain?" It's not fair, because the people are fighting these wars—they don't come from all walks of life—they come from poor and working-class families, and more often than not, rural areas. These are the people who are carrying the burden. I would say to people who want to thank me: if you want to be thankful and appreciative, write to Congress and ask for a draft, because you're *not* done. If you want my appreciation for that thanks, put your money where your mouth is and make everyone pay attention. [speaker's emphasis]

The theme of feeling insulted by superficial expressions of gratitude surfaced in other conversations with veterans. For Jordan, when the phrase came from civilians with no relationship to the military, it signified a quick and easy way to expiate their guilt at having poorer people's sons and daughters fight U.S. wars. Rather than thanking him for something he deeply regrets doing, Jordan said he would ask that people demand a return to mandatory conscription so that the burden of fighting wars would fall on the nation as a whole. Only then, he believed, would people "pay attention."

It is important to note that not all veterans objected to this phrase. Some liked being thanked for their service and hailed as heroes, and some felt indifferent to it. Southwest University student Mack said that he was not bothered by what he saw as a pro forma expression of thanks, but that it too often represented a prelude to unwelcome conversations with civilians about his combat experience: "I never liked it when people would be like, 'Oh, thank you for your service.' I just felt uneasy about that. I don't like a lot of attention like that. It's nice if people would wave and say hi. That's nice, but it turns into a discussion, and there's an interview of me, every time I'd meet someone. 'So, you went to Iraq?' and this and that. I'm supposed to tell my whole life story to these people. It's like, I was just going to go get some pizza."

Amid the silence, praise, and public gratitude, what I found missing in veteran support discourse was the understanding that veterans have highly variable and often contradictory feelings and needs. Most of the veterans I spoke with felt pride in aspects of their military service, but they also experienced a lot of pain and conflict about their actions in war. Some veterans described their military service as producing what one called "the best self I ever was" and wanted to celebrate this personal transformation. But when this particular wartime experience was the only one given voice in military recruitment efforts, popular media, and veteran support discourse, veterans with more conflicted stories were silenced. When soldiers' individual stories of triumph over adversity substitute for public debate or provide justification for military policies, conversations about war are removed from the political-analytic realm and relegated to the affective realm. Jordan's fantasized rebuke of the guilt-ridden civilian remained simply a fantasy; his resentment of disconnected civilians was drowned out by a chorus of public gratitude and deafening silence about the wars.

Asked what he wanted civilians to know about his military service, Jordan said that he wanted U.S. civilians to understand the consequences of sending young people to war. Jordan felt that young people should be sent to war only after careful public consideration of the rationale and as a result of a national consensus. For Jordan, true support and gratitude could come only from a citizenry informed about why the country is at war and about what going to war means for the soldiers sent to fight:

> Essentially, what we have to do is understand that this is what we ask of the young men and women who put uniforms on and go do what they do. We should collectively understand that this is what we're asking them

to do. If we understand it and we still are going to request this of people, okay. But then that means by understanding it, we also know that there are going to be ramifications and that we need to undo this warrior-making process and doing of warrior acts. We need to keep all of that in mind and realize, unless we're going to have an entire population that is a standing army and never unwarrior our warrior class. If that's what we're going to do, then that's the decision we need to make collectively.

The lack of conscious collective political debate about the lived reality of war made it difficult for Jordan to accept or even tolerate expressions of gratitude from civilians. If strangers wanted to thank him for his service, he reasoned, they should at least be willing to understand what they believed they were grateful for: "For me the biggest problem is that the people of this country don't understand what we're asking. They don't understand what we're doing. They want to be appreciative. They want to understand. I really believe that. They want to be thankful. They want to be supportive. But all of these things require being informed, being knowledgeable and not burying our heads in the sand when we get to the ugly truth." For Jordan, a lack of public debate about military conflicts allowed kind, caring, sincere people to avoid dealing with the "ugly truth" about war: that the human costs to both perpetrators and victims of war violence are profound and enduring. The power held by abstractions of silence and gratitude is rooted in the distance between U.S. civilian society, the current wars, and those who fight in the wars. This distance is made possible and maintained in part because only about one-half of 1 percent of Americans serve in the military, so most Americans live their lives untouched by the current wars. Few civilians ever gain intimate knowledge of returning soldiers' wartime experiences. A fractured narrative celebrating the warrior while obscuring the war heightens veterans' feelings of disconnection from civilian society.

Narratives of gratitude and praise engendered support for military projects though a discourse of care that supported some viewpoints but silenced others. This discourse of care links notions of respect and disrespect toward contemporary veterans with allegiance to military projects. Yet—as noted by Jordan and Mitchell—beyond simply promulgating military ideologies, reflexive mandated gratitude also absolves U.S. civilians from engaging in public debates about wars carried out on their behalf.

Conclusion

> If militarization took on myriad and often unnoticed forms,
> then demilitarization would start only when the invisible
> became visible, when the naturalized was made problematic.
> **CYNTHIA ENLOE**, *Globalization and Militarism*

So what's wrong with campuses becoming more veteran friendly? My answer is, absolutely nothing, if that designation means that veterans—like all other students—would receive educational services that will help them succeed in college. Veterans' experiences detailed in this book indicate the need for supportive services to ease the transition to college. However, some campus programs that are designed to support student veterans reproduce military social relations and are based on an ideology of military superiority, which can have the effect of both further distancing veterans from their civilian classmates and serving as a forum for military valorization on college campuses. On the campus level, equating veteran support with military support exerts a disciplinary power by exhorting faculty to actively declare alliance with veterans by celebrating veterans' military status while avoiding discussions of the military mission abroad. When "veteran friendly" automatically comes to mean "military friendly," critical examination of the wars will be suppressed, and some veterans will be excluded. Moreover, suppression of critical examination of the current wars risks naturalizing and tacitly accepting the practice of waging unexamined and potentially permanent wars.

The story told in this book about what happens to veterans in college is also a story about the United States at war. Campus veteran support efforts and relationships between campus and non-campus actors shape discourse about the military on campus and about the wars. This happens through the diffusion of a militarized common sense that glorifies the military mission while obscuring the reality of war and venerates veterans while demanding silence about the war. Militarized training is not limited to soldiers; civilians also receive training about how to perceive and relate to military projects within colleges and other civilian institutions.

This concluding chapter returns to my original question: what causes difficulties for war veterans returning to college? A partial answer to this question is that veterans must learn to navigate conflicts between the practices and norms learned through military training and those required in civilian colleges. Through embodied practices, recruits learned to shed their previous identification as civilians and to identify as members of a military corpus. When they left military service and enrolled in college, many veterans responded to their environments in militarily structured ways, carrying certain practices, assumptions, beliefs, and expectations (sometimes consciously, but more often unconsciously) with them into college classrooms. For some, this led to conflicts between military and civilian academic styles of teaching and learning. In addition, effects of combat trauma exacerbated pedagogical and cultural differences, impeding veterans' abilities to function in the classroom. Thus, significant disconnects and inconsistencies in the processes of making and unmaking the soldier, coupled with combat trauma, complicated veterans' ability to redeem the educational promises offered at recruitment.

During the three years I spent talking with veterans, professors, and staff, I learned that the primary obstacles veterans faced in college arose from problems stemming from military/civilian cultural and pedagogical disjunctions and the effects of combat trauma. Despite claims by some veterans' advocates that civilian students and faculty create a hostile environment for military members, I saw no evidence that veterans were treated poorly by civilian students, faculty, and staff on college campuses. Instead, I found that veterans' struggles to connect socially and emotionally to the college milieu were rooted in a culture of denial about the war and its effects on those who fight. In other words, veterans had trouble returning to a society that ostensibly supports warriors while ignoring the wars.

Military recruits learned to identify with the military institution, military mission, and fellow soldiers in basic training. The pedagogical techniques and embodied rituals and practices taught recruits to shed their previous self-definition as civilians to identify as members of a military corpus. When veterans left the military and entered college, these highly situated military lessons were transposed onto civilian academic settings. Veterans experienced the military environment and civilian college as spaces of difference and contestation, and conflicting pedagogical and cultural expectations and practices created a disjointed experience for student veterans that interfered with veterans' ability to succeed in college.

Some veteran support initiatives were marked by military-inflected relations, and some promoted an exceptionalist view of veteran students as more disciplined, dedicated, and serious than their civilian counterparts, creating barriers to interaction with nonveteran classmates. Some campus veteran support programs engendered diverse forms of militarism that tended to preclude debate and discussion of current wars. When veteran support programs contained ideologies that some veterans disagreed with, they produced the unintended effect of alienating those veterans. However, student veterans employed diverse strategies to adapt to post-military life in college. For some, this included creating peer support networks that sustained and re-created military bonds; for others, this involved distancing themselves from military relationships and ideologies.

The push to create military-friendly campuses involves celebrating soldiers and avoiding critical discussions about the wars. This approach can damage free and open campus debate and impede veterans' attempts to integrate into campus. Programs that promote a sanitized or glorified version of war can feel superficial to veterans who have conflicted feelings about their military service, about the current wars, and about their actions in combat. Heroic narratives may alienate some student veterans from the resources intended to help them.

I found that militarized common sense was a disciplining force on college campuses, but it was not totalizing. The experience of Erica, a student veteran who joined the off-campus group Iraq Veterans against the War, illustrated moments of contestation from and among student veterans. Yet political organizing against the Iraq and Afghanistan wars was not common among campus veterans. Few veterans on the Central and su campuses took a public stand against the wars, though many privately expressed their differences with official U.S. military policies and the wars. These veterans expressed their opposition to military policies in private conversations and at informal gatherings and enacted disagreement through passive means, by avoiding military-valorizing spaces.

In 2012, more than three hundred veterans were enrolled on the su campus, yet about twenty-five regularly attended Veterans Club meetings. At Central College, it was difficult to get eight out of the 119 enrolled student veterans to come to a meeting. There may be many reasons why students would choose not to be part of their campus veterans' clubs, including the need to prioritize studying, families, and part-time jobs, but some veterans told me they chose not to affiliate because they felt estranged from the military mission and did not identify with the militarized culture promoted in the campus clubs. For some veterans, this refusal to be part of a patriotic imaginary was a form of resistance. The veterans in this study were not passive military subjects but active social, political, and cultural agents. Most veterans considered deeply the implications and effects of their experiences and actively grappled with their personal, political, educational, and moral commitments. Some publicly resisted the role of proxy for the U.S. wars. Jordan, Mitchell, Connor, Adam, Cody, Erica, Bridget, and Kevin all found ways to support fellow veterans while holding critiques of the wars, with or without the support of official campus veterans' clubs. And building on the strong ties developed through their shared military experiences, some veterans participated in organized and individual efforts to bring the reality of contemporary wars into public consciousness. Groups like Iraq Veterans against the War and the Civilian-Soldier Alliance offered veterans spaces to critically examine their experience; for some veterans this entailed pushing back against the idealized heroic discourse surrounding war. These new alliances provided veterans with what Holland et al. call "spaces of authoring" that allow veterans to sustain their military identities while reworking their positionality through political action.[1]

This brings us back to the importance of understanding the diversity and difference in veterans' needs: some veterans wanted to be acknowledged for their service while others just wanted to blend in on campus and be seen as ordinary students. Some veterans wanted to engage civilians about the wars while others wanted to avoid discussions they feared would lead to unwelcome interrogations. This diversity of needs highlights the need for more complex and targeted supports for student veterans. It also raises the question of how to provide room for conversations involving political difference within student veteran support settings.

As the Iraq and Afghanistan wars end, veterans enter civilian colleges in increasing numbers. The VA reports that in 2009, approximately 500,000 student veterans and beneficiaries were receiving education benefits. By 2013, there were over one million.[2] According to one VA report, student veterans are enrolled at most institutions of higher learning, as 96 percent of all postsecondary institutions enroll student veterans.[3] Student veterans are adapting their military learning styles, skills, and identities to fit civilian institutions. These increasing numbers point to the need for research that can inform policy decisions that will support veterans' reentry into civilian society and participation in postsecondary education.

My research found that many veterans on campus were not able to fully engage with civilian students and faculty. They felt that they stood apart from civilians by virtue of age or experience. Veterans' clubs provided crucial support, but they also reinforced social distance from civilian students. This separation was exacerbated by enforced silences about the wars. Public veneration of veterans on campus masked some veterans' complex wartime experience, relegating this experience to the margins of campus discourse: distant, unspoken, and ill understood. Military cultural competence training promoted the idea that college instructors should avoid mentioning the military or the wars in anything but a flattering light to avoid insulting veterans, but this silence produced an erasure of veterans' experience.

In the previous chapters we saw that military valorization was engendered by initiatives that responded to an ostensible claim that civilian college faculty and students were hostile toward the military and toward veterans. Societal silence about and denial of the wars, maintained ostensibly to protect veterans from public displays of disrespect, created feelings of distance and alienation between student veterans and civilians. This divide formed yet another obstacle to veterans' success in college, impeding the creation of supportive alliances that might have been helpful to civilian and military students.

Militarized common sense arises from assumptions embedded in the collective popular consciousness; it is not handed down through edicts from ideologues. Commonsense understandings about who veterans are and what veterans need are taken up by a diverse range of civilians and military personnel: service providers and students, teachers, social workers, and clergy. Though many veterans' service providers neither professed nor believed in ideologies of military superiority, they nevertheless delivered services shaped by that discourse. Campus support initiatives reproduced military social relations, often as a result of college instructors' sincere desire to help war veterans adjust to civilian classrooms. College programs that required veterans, faculty, students, and support personnel to adopt an uncomplicated view of military service and the wars inhibited important discussions that some veterans wanted and needed for their own benefit and for the benefit of their classmates. For many veterans, enforced silences and heroic narratives about the wars increased cognitive and emotional dissonance between their lived military experience and their campus lives. The problem was not that college campuses were hostile, nor that they were overly friendly. Rather, by adopting a military-friendly discourse that promoted uncritical discussions of the institutional military and of the wars, colleges showed themselves to be unfriendly to many veterans.

Methods Revisited

The veterans in this study are a fairly representative demographic cross-section of recent veterans attempting college, but they are also a subset of a subset: a group of veterans who were enrolled in college. My study represents a small slice of veterans in college. Those who wish to quarrel with my analysis and findings will doubtless point to what they will call my small sample. Yet in this current epistemological era of large-scale data sets, which holds that reliable social truths can only be discovered through a large N and algorithmic patterns, there is a danger of losing sight of the individuals in whose names these studies are conducted. As social scientists such as danah boyd and Kate Crawford have warned, an "epistemological blindness" can result when researchers rely on patterns detected in the behaviors of the faceless masses over the individual stories of those whose thoughts and feelings cannot be explained by algorithms.[4]

I began this study with an interest in student veteran support programs. By immersing myself in the experience of student veterans and their supporters, I also found protective veneration, selective exclusion, and cautionary silences. This led me to focus on exclusions and absences from the observable. An investigation of silence and denial does not lend itself to a quantitative lens, which is why I rely on veterans' expressed feelings and perspectives.

The experiences of fifty veterans at two colleges are not intended to stand in for the experiences of one million current recipients of GI Bill education benefits.[5] Military veterans are represented in media campaigns and news stories and in the multiplicity of commercial ad campaigns featuring uniformed soldiers to sell beer, real estate, dating services, and even dog food.[6] But while these images present one picture of soldiering, highlighting heroism, loyalty to country, and sacrifice, there are few public representations of the ambivalence and conflict that were prominent in so many veterans' stories. Given this great divide between public and private representation, I chose to give voice to the stories that tend not to make it into the public narrative.

My interview group was small, but it was marked by diversity in views and needs. For many student veterans, campus veterans' clubs helped them feel visible, less isolated, less alienated, and more affiliated. Some experienced the veneration of their military identification as beneficial because it reinforced an identity they valued. But veterans' clubs and the overt veneration of military allegiance did not work equally well for everyone and served to exclude some who did not fit in. This diversity signals the need for further studies of veterans with different backgrounds who attend different institutions of higher education in different locations.

The majority of veterans I interviewed worked hard to succeed in higher education. Most came from working-class families, and many, as first-generation college students, entered college with a keen appreciation for the analytic intellectual work demanded of them. As an instructor, I found many veterans in my undergraduate classes to be deeply engaged in the process of learning; most took assignments and classroom discussions very seriously, sometimes more so than their civilian counterparts. Perhaps this was because they did not take for granted their place in the college classroom or because they were acutely aware of the costs they incurred to get there. While participants in this study encountered difficulties adjusting to college, many were successful and, at this writing, most had graduated or finished their programs. Many, including Connor, Mack, and Brandon, went on to graduate programs.[7] Yet in addition to the strengths student veterans bring to college campuses, it is important to recognize the obstacles many face in the transition from soldier to civilian student, and how these obstacles are framed in a broader national political conversation.

Moving beyond Obstacles

The issue of veteran reintegration into civilian life is not just confined to higher education. Veterans return from war to reenter civilian society; they return to families, communities, workplaces, and schools. As educational institutions, colleges and universities do not and should not bear full responsibility for veterans' post-military transition. The Department of Defense offers specialized reentry programs for military members returning from overseas deployments, where recently returned soldiers attend seminars on gun safety awareness, domestic violence, drug and alcohol abuse, and suicide prevention, and attend workshops about their medical and disability benefits. These are intended as broadly preventive mental health and social service interventions. While these programs may or may not ameliorate social difficulties faced by returning soldiers, they do not speak to the specific academic needs of student veterans.

When I began this project in 2009, there were veteran support services on individual college campuses, but no national initiatives dealing with support for student veterans beyond the economic affordances of the GI Bill. When I asked student veterans what they thought would help them succeed in college, many said that they needed academic tutoring and writing coaching, while others wanted help with registration and veterans' benefits. Others were just looking for a supportive learning environment for veterans. College and university faculty were teaching veterans who clearly needed academic and psychological support, but faculty didn't know how to help them. They wanted to be able to consult with people knowledgeable about issues affecting student veterans' performance and academic success. Individual campus initiatives and local non-profit organizations were addressing these needs.

In 2010, the VA began a pilot program called Veterans Integration to Academic Leadership (VITAL) designed to support veterans in college.[8] This program incorporates many of the services that coincided with my findings about veterans' academic needs. The VITAL program offers tutoring and peer mentoring, VA work-study jobs, counseling, and ongoing treatment for stress, anger, depression, anxiety, sleep problems, and other readjustment issues. Veterans Affairs staff members can request that colleges and universities provide academic accommodations on behalf of student veterans, and offer veterans coping strategies when they experience trauma symptoms in the classroom. Program staff assist student veterans to enroll in the VA health care system and to obtain resources and vocational rehabilitation services from the Veterans Benefits Administration. On some campuses, VITAL programs also offer free-weight training, yoga, tai chi, and distress tolerance groups.

The VITAL program offers consultation to faculty and staff about issues affecting student veterans' classroom performance and academic progress, and consultation to counseling staff about mental health issues. It promises direct communication between the VA health care system and college and university staff about veterans' concerns, resources, and needs. And finally, in what sounds like an iteration of the military cultural competence trainings found in previous chapters, the VITAL program offers training for college and university staff on "military culture, deployment 101, post-deployment adjustment, and common concerns."[9]

While the success of this program is as yet undemonstrated, its comprehensive nature addresses many of the specific needs voiced by veterans, faculty, and staff with whom I spoke. Moreover, the VA appears to have made a commitment to this model of veteran support: in 2011, the VITAL program was at five colleges and universities; it is currently at twenty-three sites around the country, with plans for more in the near future. With this program the VA has begun to offer services to remediate veterans' challenges in college. Colleges and universities that do not have access to on-site VA programmatic support can serve veterans by continuing to offer priority registration, priority hours for financial aid appointments, disability accommodations (such as authorization for reduced course loads, increased time to take exams, and adaptive equipment), tutoring, support staff knowledgeable about veterans' needs and issues, support and space for veterans' club meetings.

Importantly, I found that veteran success was not aided by constraining campus conversations about military service and the wars. A crucial task of veteran support is opening up honest dialogue among veterans and between civilians and veterans about what it means to go to war. Without this kind of open dialogue, veteran support interventions will continue to rely on ideological mystification, failing to meet the needs of many student veterans. Within and even beyond college campuses, to serve the needs of veterans, we must broaden our national discussion about the role of the military and war by promoting environments that foster dialogue with combat veterans.

These kinds of discussions will not happen if talk about war is made off-limits in college classrooms. Mitchell's experience provides evidence for one argument of this book: silencing talk about the wars does not help veterans make the transition to college in a way that promotes their mental and intellectual health. The words of Mitchell, Connor, Bridget, and Jordan offer a window into war veterans' contradictory feelings by and about their actions in combat. It is important for civilians to be aware of these feelings as soldiers return to schools, families, and communities after discharge. While many, and perhaps most, veterans successfully make the adjustment to civilian life, some seek to calm these conflicted feelings with drugs and alcohol, and unprecedented numbers of soldiers commit suicide. This represents a serious challenge for post-secondary educators who are charged with addressing the needs of recently returned student veterans.

This book has argued that it is not possible to fully unmake the soldier and remake the civilian if society will not honestly address the rationale of the current wars and their consequences. While there are some designated therapeutic spaces for veterans to deal with their internal conflicts, most notably Vet Centers and VA mental health treatment programs, these are segregated spaces that generally do not involve conversations with non–military affiliated civilians, and they do not involve conversations with the broader civilian society.[10] Discussions with and among veterans usually take place behind closed doors. At Vet Centers, the psychological treatment model is based on the philosophy that veterans can best be helped by military peers. The implication of this model is that it is counter-therapeutic to have conversations with civilians about the realities of war. Yet enforcing a separation and silencing dialogue with civilians maintains the gap between civilians and veterans, and makes it more difficult for veterans to return to civilian schools, where intergroup communication and interaction is integral to a successful academic experience.

But what kind of spaces should we open up? What kind of conversations should we be having? These are questions we should be asking veterans. The veterans with whom I spoke felt that there is a need not only for more meaningful dialogue around the wars in general but also about their military experiences in particular. Their comments foregrounded not just issues about the relationship between the military and education, but also about relationships between U.S. society, U.S. wars, and the soldiers who fight in them. And the question posed so emphatically by Jordan still requires an answer: If war is truly a national priority, why is the burden of fighting not shared by the entire nation? How will the nation discern if war is a national priority without open debates, not just in the chambers of Congress or the highest levels of government, but in workplaces, union halls, and college classrooms? These are crucial questions to raise in national political discourse, and recently returned war veterans are well positioned to ask them.

These questions ultimately raise more issues about the relationship between the military and education. In our society, the problem of social inequality and surplus labor maps onto a military solution. Because military service is consistently proposed as an honorable and heroic route to college, and going to college is proposed as a route to social and economic success, it is important to look at the social practices involved in the making and unmaking of soldiers and how these practices then serve or do not serve veterans once they leave military service.

On one level, this research clearly signals a need for supportive services to facilitate a smooth transition for veterans as they utilize their earned education benefits. But the underlying cause of student veterans' distress is not located on college campuses. Rather, the underlying cause of veteran distress is located in the aftereffects of war and in the repercussions of a national policy that compels young people go to war in order to go to college.

Many civilians recognize that for soldiers, wartime military experience demands great physical and emotional sacrifice, and they feel a desire to ameliorate soldiers' postwar suffering. But when a sincere impulse to ameliorate suffering becomes attached to a mandate to support specific military missions, this impedes critical examination of the wars. Militarized common sense subsumes the diversity of political sentiments, motivations, values, and beliefs that exist in the United States about war under a national narrative that frames support for veterans as either unquestioning allegiance or silence.

In doing so, it serves to naturalize a state of permanent war. This book has attempted to draw attention to the remarkable yet unremarked-upon ways that militarization in our daily lives has expanded in recent years. It has argued that the banality of militarized common sense allows us to avoid seeing the ways that military priorities have become embedded in our daily lives, as it encourages silence about the wars that have caused so much destruction. But perhaps the greatest danger of increasingly banal militarization is that it risks making wars easier to wage. As Cynthia Enloe notes, drawing attention to the militarization of society offers us the possibility of working toward alternative visions. Critical examination of the everyday assumptions offers us the vocabulary, the historical knowledge, and the opportunity to begin the demilitarization of our world.

Notes

Introduction

1   Color guard is the ceremonial display of flags representing different military branches, regiments, campaigns, and military support organizations (for example, VFW and American Legion). Color guard flag bearers are flanked by armed soldiers.

2   Becker and Schulz, "Cops Ready for War."

3   Price, *Weaponizing Anthropology*. Moreover, Mariana Mazzucato (2011) writes that technologies originally developed for military use such as drones, robotics, and biometrics are increasingly being used on campuses and commercially in the private sector: "The role of government in the Defense Advanced Research Projects Agency (DARPA) model goes far beyond simply funding basic science. It is about targeting resourcing in specific areas and directions; opening new windows of opportunities; brokering the interactions between public and private agents involved in technological development, including private and public venture capital; and facilitating commercialization" (76). Mazzucato adds that the U.S. Department of Defense has funded the formation of entire disciplines on university campuses: "Going way beyond simply funding research, DARPA funded the formation of computer science departments, provided start-up firms with early research support, contributed to semiconductor research and support to human computer interface research, and oversaw the early stages of the internet" (77–78).

4   Jorgenson and Wolf, "A Special Supplement"; Foster, "The Truth and Reconciliation Commission and Understanding Perpetrators"; Price, *Anthropological Intelligence*; González, *Militarizing Culture*; Noble, *America by Design*; Noble, *Forces of Production*; Cahill, "Fighting the Vietnam Syndrome"; Enloe, *Maneuvers*; Franklin, *Vietnam and Other American Fantasies*; Price, *Weaponizing Anthropology*; Kraska, *Militarizing the American Criminal Justice System*; Stavrianakis and Selby, *Militarism and International Relations: Political Economy, Security, Theory.*

5   Mazzucato, writing about the Cold War period in the United States, notes that "DARPA officers engaged in business and technological brokering—linking university

researchers to entrepreneurs interested in starting a new firm; connecting start-up firms with venture capitalists; finding a larger company to commercialise the technology; or assisting in procuring a government contract to support the commercialisation process. Pursuing this brokering function, DARPA officers not only developed links among those involved in the network system but also engaged in efforts to expand the pool of scientists and engineers working in specific areas. An example of this is the role DARPA played in the 1960s by funding the establishment of new computer science departments at various universities in the USA" (Mazzucato, *The Entrepreneurial State*, 79). See also Noble, *Forces of Production*; Price, *Anthropological Intelligence*; Price, "Cloak and Trowel"; Price, *Weaponizing Anthropology*.

6   See Jungk, *Brighter Than a Thousand Suns*.

7   Bogart, *Unwarranted Influence*.

8   Department of Veterans Affairs, "Department of Veterans Affairs Education Program Beneficiaries: FY 2000 to FY 2012," 2013, http://www.va.gov/vetdata/docs/Utilization/EducNation_2012.xls; Fain, "Follow the Money"; Cate, *Million Records Project*.

9   Shepherd and Shepherd, "War and Dissent"; Shepherd and Shepherd, "War Attitudes and Ideological Orientations of Honors Directors"; Herrmann et al., *Educating Veterans in the 21st Century*; Herrmann, Raybeck, and Wilson, "College Is for Veterans, Too."

10 See Williamson's Iraq and Afghanistan Veterans of America report, "A New GI Bill." That report found that 30 percent of veterans made no use of their educational benefits.

11 Accurate data on the postsecondary academic enrollment and outcomes of contemporary student veterans are difficult to find. Critics of this statistic, including the advocacy group Student Veterans of America, note that inconsistent methods of data collection create confusion about the higher education enrollment and completion rates of student veterans. More recent data are both more comprehensive and more encouraging. A 2014 joint study by Student Veterans of America and U.S. Veterans Affairs indicates that in 2009–2013, 51.7 percent of veterans of the Iraq and Afghanistan wars completed college; a more comprehensive post-9/11 iteration of the GI Bill was in effect at that time (Cate, *Million Records Project*). Despite the problems with the methodologies of earlier studies, more student veterans took advantage of GI Bill benefits and graduated higher education institutions after 2008. This is because the post-9/11 GI Bill offers more money for housing, books, and tuition than the previous post-Vietnam Montgomery GI Bill, making college a more attractive option for veterans. In addition, during the prerecession period of 2001–2007, civilian jobs for returning veterans were relatively plentiful, making paid employment a more attractive option for veterans. Finally, concern about low rates of veteran success encouraged colleges to provide support services that increased student veteran retention and graduation rates (Cate, *Million Records Project*). Improved education benefits and depressed civilian employment opportunities increased enrollment while campus veteran support services improved retention and completion. The VA is expected to publish graduation rate metrics for four-year

institutions of higher learning after six-year and eight-year outcome studies. See U.S. Department of Veterans Affairs, "Education and Training," http://www.benefits .va.gov/gibill.

12 Berdahl, "Voices at the Wall," 113. While returning war veterans may individually challenge and resist unified versions of American identity and government, public representation of soldiers' sacrifice has served historically to bind national interests with military interests. For example, after the Civil War, the zeal for honoring dead soldiers was leveraged to consolidate federal authority, as private lands were annexed for war memorials. These memorials were intended as object lessons to promote patriotism and to venerate not only war casualties but also a unifying and newly remilitarized national project. Battlefield monuments were created to manifest the power of the federal government and to link inextricably the good of the nation with its military: "Can [the federal government] not erect the monuments provided for by these acts of Congress, or even take possession of the field of battle in the name and for the benefit of all the citizens of the country for the present and for the future? Such a use seems necessarily not only a public use, but one so closely connected with the welfare of the republic itself as to be within the powers granted Congress by the Constitution for the purpose of protecting and preserving the whole country. It would be a great object lesson to all who looked upon the land thus cared for, and it would show a proper recognition of the great things that were done there on those momentous days. By this use, the government manifests for the benefit of all its citizens the value put upon the services and exertions of the citizen soldiers of that period. . . . Such action on the part of Congress touches the heart and comes home to the imagination of every citizen, and greatly tends to enhance his love and respect for those institutions for which these heroic sacrifices were made. The greater the love of the citizen for the institutions of his country, the greater is the dependence properly to be placed upon him for their defense in time of necessity, and it is to such men that the country must look for its safety. The institutions of our country, which were saved at this enormous expenditure of life and property, ought to and will be regarded with proportionate affection. Here upon this battlefield is one of the proofs of that expenditure, and the sacrifices are rendered more obvious and more easily appreciated when such a battlefield is preserved by the government." *United States v. Gettysburg Elec. Ry. Co.*, 160 U.S. 668 (1896): 682.

13 For example, George Washington instituted the first U.S. system of military bonuses for soldiers after mass desertions at the Battle of Valley Forge.

14 In the summer of 1932, 43,000 World War I veterans and their families and supporters (called the "Bonus Army" in press accounts) marched in Washington, DC, demanding immediate cash redemption of service bonuses that had been issued to them as bonds that could not be redeemed until 1945.

15 This belief in veteran exceptionalism continues even in the current era of public rejection of redistributive programs. Current recipients of the GI Bill are still spared the stigma of accepting government welfare. Frydl, *The GI Bill*, 24, 37.

16 Frydl calls the original GI Bill "social welfare in the superpower state, a program of redistribution designed under and made possible by the most powerful federal

government the U.S. had yet known" (*The GI Bill*, 10). Benefits included low-cost home mortgages, low-interest business loans, one year of unemployment compensation, and tuition and living expenses to attend universities, vocational schools, or high schools. Frydl notes that this wealth redistribution initiative, though massive, was uneven because nonwhite and female veterans were excluded from many benefits. For example, the federal government guaranteed low-cost home and business loans to all veterans, but banks could and did selectively refuse to provide loans to African American and single female veterans.

17 Statement of President Franklin D. Roosevelt on enacting the original GI Bill, June 22, 1944. Available at U.S. Department of Veterans Affairs, "Education and Training" section, "History and Timeline": http://www.benefits.va.gov/gibill/history.asp.

18 Altschuler and Blumin write that the original GI Bill was seen by some as a Marshall Plan for returning soldiers. Some critics of the Marshall Plan claimed that it was wrong to allocate money to rebuild Japan and Germany unless the United States also invested in its own soldiers (*The GI Bill*, 4).

19 Many scholars, including Bennett (*When Dreams Came True*), Mettler (*Soldiers to Citizens*), and Humes (*Over Here*), give uncritical accounts of the legislation, arguing that the GI Bill had a lasting positive effect on the social and economic landscape of the United States. For a critical discussion of the GI Bill's affordances, see Frydl, *The GI Bill*. A good example of scholarship that actively constructs this hegemonic narrative is the U.S. Department of Defense publication *When Dreams Came True: The GI Bill and the Making of Modern America*, Michael J. Bennett. For a more critical assertion of this argument, see Bouffard, "The Military as a Bridging Environment in Criminal Careers."

20 Military entitlements—which for political ends are often exempted from being framed as government entitlements—were among the few government benefit programs to survive the proscriptions against government welfare spending resulting from neoliberal economic reforms of the 1970s to the present day.

21 Frydl, *The GI Bill*; Bennett, *When Dreams Came True*; Pérez, *Citizen, Student, Soldier*; Guttman and Lutz, *Breaking Ranks*; Mariscal, "The Poverty Draft."

22 Frydl, *The GI Bill*; Altschuler and Blumin, *The GI Bill*. After the Iraq War, 45,000 troops returned to recession and high unemployment in the U.S. economy. With the anticipated end of the war in Afghanistan, many more are expected to leave the military and enter college. Because military recruiters aggressively target poor and working-class high school students, promising that military training and experience will pay for and prepare them to go to college, many recruits enlist for education funding.

23 Bouffard, "The Military as a Bridging Environment in Criminal Careers"; and Grubb, Badway, and Bell, "Community Colleges and the Equity Agenda" discuss problems of lack of academic preparation as an impediment to working-class students' success in higher education. Bouffard's work engages military members more directly, arguing that military service creates a "bridging environment" that allows low-income participants in criminal activities to learn skills that

improve their social and economic circumstances. Amy Lutz published a study in the *Journal of Military and Political Sociology* showing that lower family income was an important predictor of military service. She writes, "the military may indeed be a career option for those for whom there are few better opportunities" (2008:184).

24   Cantrell and Dean, *Once a Warrior*; Armstrong, Best, and Domenici, *Courage after Fire*; Tick, *War and the Soul*; Hoge et al., "Combat Duty in Iraq and Afghanistan."

25   Herrmann, Raybeck, and Wilson, "College Is for Veterans, Too"; Herrmann, Hopkins, Wilson, and Allen, *Educating Veterans in the 21st Century*; Thomas, "Safe Zone for Veterans"; Briggs, "Stray Anti-military Vibes Reverberate"; Holloway, "Understanding Reentry of the Modern-Day Student-Veteran"; Lederman, "Preparing for an Influx"; Lewis, "Serving Returning Vets"; DiRamio, Ackerman, and Mitchell, "From Combat to Campus"; Boulton, "A Price on Freedom"; Byman, "Veterans and Colleges Have a Lot to Offer"; Bunting, "Class Warfare"; Roth-Douquet and Shaeffer, AWOL: *The Unexcused Absence of America's Upper Classes from Military Service—and How It Hurts Our Country*.

26   Cantrell and Dean, *Once a Warrior*; Armstrong, Best, and Domenici, *Courage after Fire*; Tick, *War and the Soul*; Hoge et al., "Combat Duty in Iraq and Afghanistan."

27   Humes, *Over Here: How The GI Bill Transformed the American Dream*; Bennett, *When Dreams Came True*.

28   For example, see the news stories: Briggs, "Stray Anti-military Vibes Reverberate"; Shane, "Student Vets Say Anti-military Attitudes Persist on Campus"; and Petrovic, "Anti-military Sentiments on an Elite American College Campus."

29   There are many contemporary examples of domestic militarization; one of the most notable occurred in Ferguson, Missouri, in the summer of 2014.

30   Merryfinch, "Militarization/Civilization," 9, cited in Cock, "Rethinking Militarism in Post-Apartheid South Africa," 2.

31   Mann, Incoherent Empire, 16–17, cited in Shaw *Post-Military Society: Militarism, Demilitarism and War at the End of the Twentieth Century*, 7.

32   Mann, "The Roots and Contradictions of Modern Militarism," 35–36.

33   Thompson argues against the position of Dwight D. Eisenhower, who decried the spiritual and moral effects of the military-industrial complex ("Exterminism," 21–22).

34   Thompson, "Exterminism," cited in Cock, "Rethinking Militarism in Post-apartheid South Africa," 2.

35   Enloe, *Maneuvers*, 3.

36   Kraska, *Militarizing the American Criminal Justice System*, 15.

37   Sherry, *In the Shadow of War*.

38   Excluding instances when the U.S. government gave only aid with no military personnel involvement, and excluding Central Intelligence Agency operations.

39   The following categories of conflict are outlined in Grimmett, "Instances of Use of United States Armed Forced Abroad, 1798–2009" and Axelrod, *America's Wars*. Conflicts considered major U.S. wars include the American Revolutionary War (1775–1783), the War of 1812, the Mexican-American War (1846–1848), the American Civil War (1861–1865), the Spanish-American War (1898), the

Philippine-American War (1899–1913), World War I (1917–1918), World War II (1941–1945), the Korean War (1950–1953), the Vietnam War (1959–1975), the Gulf War (1990–1991), the war in Afghanistan (2001–2014), and the war in Iraq (2003–present). Examples of military-enforced territorial expansion include the so-called Indian Wars (1776–1777, 1785–1795, 1816–1880, 1890) and the annexation of Hawaii (1893), Samoa (1898–1899), and South Pacific territories. Examples of U.S. military occupation include the following countries: Nicaragua (1867, 1910), Haiti (1915–1934), Dominican Republic (1916–1924), China (1932), Philippines (1944–1946), South Korea (1945–1949), Germany (1945–1948), Austria (1945–1955), and Japan (1945–52). Instances of military troops being sent in to protect U.S. business interests are too numerous to list here, but examples include China (1854, 1856, 1859), Uruguay (1855–1858), Egypt (1882), Panama (1856, 1865, 1885, 1925, 1990), Korea (1888,1894–1896), Hawaii (1889), Haiti (1891), Nicaragua (1857, 1896, 1898, 1899, 1926, 1933), Honduras (1903, 1911, 1912, 1925), Cuba (1912), Turkey (1912), and Dominican Republic (1965).

40 Quoted in Tom Lasseter, "Officers: Military Can't End Insurgency," *Philadelphia Enquirer*, June 13, 2005, cited in Bacevich, *The New American Militarism*, 227.

41 Bacevich, *The New American Militarism*, 227.

42 Veterans for Common Sense, "Iraq and Afghanistan War Impact Report," December 2, 2011. Updated figures from Crawford, "War-Related Death, Injury, and Displacement."

43 Crawford, "War-Related Death, Injury, and Displacement." Moreover, official Pentagon statistics do not include the many troops who return home and kill themselves as a result of psychological wounds such as PTSD, nor does DoD report suicides among non–active duty reservists.

44 Crawford, "War-Related Death, Injury, and Displacement."

45 Shaw, *Post-Military Society* .

46 Sparke, "Critical Geographies of the Global South."

47 Social practice theory helps us understand how individuals and institutions shape and are shaped by the cultural environment in which they operate by examining the interactions between individual agency, social practices, and cultural norms.

48 Gramsci, *Selections from the Prison Notebooks*, 323n1.

49 Binder and Wood, *Becoming Right*.

50 Gramsci, *Selections from the Prison Notebooks*, 118.

51 Billig, *Banal Nationalism*.

52 See Klein, "The New Greatest Generation."

53 See Lifton, *Home from the War*; Grossman, *On Killing*; Sherman, *The Untold War*; Gutmann and Lutz, *Breaking Ranks*.

54 Litz et al., "Moral Injury and Moral Repair in War Veterans"; see also Shay, *Odysseus in America*; Maguen and Litz, "Moral Injury in Veterans of War." Treatment programs in the VA are increasingly adopting Shay's (*Odysseus in America*) framing of moral injury. These programs tend to limit the scope of moral injury to psychological conflicts soldiers feel when the demands of combat require that they violate their personal ethical or religious moral codes—they do not relate moral injury to

broader issues such as the rationale for specific wars or the overall military mission. I argue that this individually focused definition of moral injury does not allow veterans to heal from war trauma from a position of active opposition to war.

55 Hautzinger and Scandlyn, *Beyond Post-Traumatic Stress*; Maguen & Litz, "Moral Injury in Veterans of War." U.S. Department of Veterans Affairs data show that veterans of the Iraq and Afghanistan wars are two and a half times as likely to commit suicide as people the same age with no military experience. Cited in Aaron Glantz, "After Service, Veteran Deaths Surge," *New York Times*, October 17, 2010, 29A.

56 Feldman, "Difficult Distinctions"; Artexaga, "Engendering Violence"; Feldman, "The Actuarial Gaze"; Feldman, *Formations of Violence*.

57 Brison, "Trauma Narratives and the Re-making of the Self." Brison explores the role of trauma narratives, which she labels "speech acts of memory," in remaking the self. She argues that remastering traumatic memory involves a shift from viewing one's self as the object of another's speech to being the subject of one's own. The act of bearing witness to the trauma facilitates this shift, not only by transforming traumatic memory into a coherent narrative that can be integrated into the survivor's sense of self and worldview but also by reintegrating the survivor into a community. Brison writes that trauma research supports a view of the self as fundamentally relational and notes the multiform and fluctuating nature of memory. Memories of trauma are experienced by the survivor as inflicted, not chosen. In contrast, narrative memory, or narrating memories to others, is a chosen act that enables survivors to gain more control over the subjective experience of the trauma. "Narrative memory is not passively endured," she writes. "Rather it is an act on the part of the narrator, a speech act that diffuses traumatic memory, giving shape and a temporal order to the events recalled, establishing more control over their recalling, and helping the survivor to remake the self."

58 Enloe, *Does Khaki Become You?*; Bederman, *Manliness and Civilization*; Sue, "Whiteness and Ethnocentric Monoculturalism"; Madriaga, "The Star-Spangled Banner"; Belkin, *Bring Me Men*.

59 The U.S. military claims to offer the template for a colorblind deracialized America (for a prime example of this claim, see Moskos and Butler, *All That We Can Be*). However, Sue, "Whiteness and Ethnocentric Monoculturalism"; and Madriaga, "The Star-Spangled Banner" point out that the U.S. military as an institution is in fact thoroughly constituted in discourses of whiteness (Roediger, *The Wages of Whiteness*; Blatt and Roediger, *The Meaning of Slavery in the North*; Ignatiev, *How the Irish Became White*) and ethnocentric monoculturalism (Sue, "Whiteness and Ethnocentric Monoculturalism").

60 Contemporary scholarship in the fields of sociology, anthropology, and human geography clarify that gender is multivariate and not fully encompassed in a male-female binary. For this study, I consciously adopt the static and reified typologies of the U.S. military by using the dichotomous categories of male and female for gender.

61 For more on this, see Kirk and Okazawa-Rey, *Women's Lives*; Nagel, "Masculinity and Nationalism"; Acker, "Hierarchies, Jobs, and Bodies"; Enloe, *Bananas, Beaches and Bases*; Enloe, *Does Khaki Become You?*; Enloe, *Globalization and Militarism*;

Oliver, *Women as Weapons of War*; Belkin, *Bring Me Men*; and Gardiner, "The Warrior Ethos."

62 Enloe, *Bananas, Beaches and Bases*, 45. See also Kirk and Okazawa-Rey, *Women's Lives*; and Lutz, "Living Room Terrorists." Writing about the U.S. military, Lutz notes that "there is no workplace more supportive of a masculine identity centered on power, control, and violence" ("Living Room Terrorists," 17–18).

63 Nader, "Controlling Processes."

64 Generally, I find dichotomizing structure/agency frameworks reductive and unhelpful, as they tend to reify idealized poles while eliding the complex, mutually constitutive, and shifting subjective relations within social and ideological structures.

65 Lutz, "Empire Is in the Details."

66 The website gijobs.com maintains and promotes a list of schools designated as military friendly. The criteria by which campuses qualify for this designation varies, but it generally means that there are staff, funding, and supportive services dedicated to military veterans on campus, and that there is a difficult-to-quantify atmosphere of respect for former service members. Every year since 2009, GI Jobs.com has named SU one of the "Top 50 Military Friendly Schools."

67 All formal interviews were conducted using research protocol from the Institutional Review Board for the Protection of Human Subjects.

68 The additional campus research sites are identified in the text as Los Santos Community College, Mountain Community College, Inland Community College, Fulton Community College, Coastal University, and Urban State College.

69 As a public university, SU has a mandate to accept qualified students transferring from community colleges. In 2014, 17 percent of the SU incoming class was transfer students.

70 Programs benefitting veterans have been a source of some conflict. For example, many of these benefits (such as reduced course loads, priority course registration, and increased time for exams) began as an accommodation to disabled students, and veterans previously accessed them through the campus Disabled Students Services (DSS). But many veterans and veteran advocates objected to the fact that these benefits were routed through DSS. They particularly objected to the "disabled" designation, a qualifier that was anathema to veterans who were not, or did not consider themselves, disabled. They advocated for the decoupling of veteran services from DSS (interviews JD, FL, October 9, 2011). Today, many campuses have programs that explicitly offer this service to student veterans without being associated with DSS.

71 I discuss differences in support services at the respective campuses in chapter 3.

72 A 2014 report by the Student Veterans of America states that 89.7 percent of Iraq and Afghanistan war veterans begin their postsecondary, postservice education at community colleges. Cate, *Million Records Project*.

73 National Priorities Project (2001–2010); Kleycamp, "College, Jobs, or the Military?"; Kleycamp, "Military Service and Minority Opportunity"; Asch, Heaton, and Savych, *Recruiting Minorities*.

74 According to the 2010 U.S. Census, Latinos constituted 58 percent of Orchard Valley's population.

75 Southwest University promotional materials, retrieved September 30, 2011.

76 I used a modified chain sampling method to identify participants at each site. I began by presenting my research proposal in classes, campus veterans' clubs, and veterans' community meetings, after which I distributed my contact information with a request for participants. I followed up with the veterans who contacted me. While I did not ask veterans to refer me to other potential participants, I did ask some to vouch for me with potential interviewees who expressed skepticism about talking to a civilian researcher. In some cases, instructors gave my name to veterans who might be interested in participating.

77 For example, one participant, having grown up in conditions of community violence, said that he enlisted (in December 2003, well after the Iraq War was underway) to help provide for his family. He explained his decision to go to war through a cost-benefit lens, saying that if he died as a result of street violence in California his family would be left with nothing, whereas if he died in combat, his mother would be entitled to death benefits.

78 E-1 is the first and lowest rank and pay grade for the U.S. Army. E signifies enlisted, and E-1 is the most entry-level private rank; E-2 signifies private second class (E-3 is private first class, etc.). Many of the SU veteran participants left the military with the rank of E-5 (sergeant) or E-6 (staff sergeant). The Navy and Air Force rank designations have different names, but participants in this research enlisted in similar entry-level ranks.

79 Studying cultural practices from the outside presents particular challenges, but as anthropologist and army captain Alexandra Jaffee ("The Limits of Detachment") notes, there are also challenges involved in attempting to produce ethnography while positioned within a "total system" (Goffman, *Asylums*) like the military. Jaffee was unable to write an ethnography of her military experience because she was unable to separate her civilian and military identities inside the totalizing discourse of her military environment.

80 See, for example, DuBois, "Passionate Scholarship"; Abu-Lughod, "Do Muslim Women Really Need Saving?"; Abu-Lughod, *Writing Women's Worlds*; Jaffee, "The Limits of Detachment."

81 Lykes, "Activist Participatory Research."

82 I fully answered all questions from participants about the process of this research, but I was unable to provide a full account of my findings because my analysis was still being developed.

83 No student veteran who served in the Coast Guard was interviewed.

84 *The American Heritage Dictionary of the English Language, Fourth Edition.*

85 For example, the Marines ("The Few, the Proud, the Marines") are promoted as the most elite fighting force—tougher, more committed, and braver than other military members. Members of the Army have a reputation as workhorses (perceived by members of the Air Force and Navy to "work harder, not smarter"). Members of the Navy and Air Force have a reputation as more intellectually rigorous and technologically skilled than members of other branches.

86　One convention of academic ethnographies is to place theoretical chapters in the front of the book, followed by chapters informed by ethnographic observation. This book follows a different roadmap. I have chosen to invite the reader to follow a process of discovery similar to mine as I researched this book. I began my research exploring the hypothesis that veterans might encounter difficulties in college due to differences in military and academic training methods, and so the study began by looking at veterans' experience during their military training and in college. However, through observation on college campuses I came to identify contradictions between public discourse about antimilitary campuses and the fact that even campuses said to be hostile toward military veterans were actually quite welcoming to them. This finding raised questions about this divergence between public image and lived reality, which I examine in later chapters. For these reasons, the placement of the chapters is intended to represent my method as well as my findings.

87　Hall, "Gramsci's Relevance for the Study of Race and Ethnicity."

Chapter 1. Basic Training

1　This study began with focus on the lived effects of lessons learned through structured institutional practice. I did not set out to study the educative aspects of living through wartime combat, which takes place in highly diverse and situationally specific sites. This important topic is aptly explored in academic literature such as Hautzinger and Scandlyn's *Beyond Post-Traumatic Stress*, and in fiction and nonfiction memoirs by war veterans, for example: Boudreau, *Packing Inferno*; O'Brien, *The Things They Carried*; and Williams and Staub, *Love My Rifle More Than You*.

2　I think of basic training as forming part of what Mary Louise Pratt calls a "contact zone" or "social spaces where disparate cultures meet, clash, and grapple with each other, often as highly asymmetrical relations of domination and subordination" (1991:34).

3　Goffman, *Asylums*.

4　Foucault, *Discipline and Punish*; Lande, "Breathing Like a Soldier."

5　Bourdieu, *Distinction*; Bourdieu, *In Other Words*; Bourdieu, *Practical Reason*. Bourdieu describes "a socialized body, a structured body which has incorporated the immanent structures of a world, or a particular sector of that world—a field—and which structures the perception of that world, as well as action in that world" (*Practical Reason*, 81).

6　All active-duty Army soldiers and officers must go through this process, with the exception of certain specialty branch officers (MDS in the Army Medical Dept., legal, judge advocates, and religious): "Chaplain Corps officers do not participate in BT due to the extensive rifle marksmanship, weapons familiarization, and combatives training conducted in the course. The mission of the Chaplain Corps as noncombatants is considerably different than the mission of other officers thus requiring a different training philosophy." United States (TRADOC) Army Regulations AR 350–1 Section 3–24, 65.

7 "Initial Military Training and Warrior Transition Course," AR 350–1, sec. 3–24. The Warrior Ethos: "I will always place the mission first. I will never accept defeat. I will never quit. I will never leave a fallen comrade." It is contained within the Soldier's Creed, an oath that soldiers recite daily in training. The Soldier's Creed and Warrior Ethos are fundamental to Army values as outlined in military doctrine. Basic training for each branch of service—Army, Navy, Air Force, Marines, and Coast Guard— is carried out slightly differently, but this chapter concentrates on basic training as carried out by the Army as a prototypical basic training experience. The Army is the largest branch of the military and the branch in which the majority of my interview respondents served.

8 Scholars such as Grossman, *On Killing*; Franke, "Women in the Military"; Herbert, *Camouflage Isn't Only for Combat*; and Sasson Levy, "Constructing Identities at the Margins" explore sociological implications of gendered military training practice. The rigors and lessons of basic training prove to be a perennial topic in Hollywood films, as depictions of basic training (e.g., *An Officer and a Gentleman*, *Heartbreak Ridge*, *Full Metal Jacket*, *G.I. Jane*, *Tigerland*, and *Jarhead*) reify the ritualized physical and emotional trials of basic training.

9 Belkin, *Bring Me Men*, 3.

10 Belkin writes, "The ideal of military masculinity seems to depend on situating the practiced annihilation of the feminine as central to what it takes to avert the annihilation of the nation. Femininity is coded as an arbitrary, fictional construction which represents weakness, subordination, emotionalism, dependency and disloyalty. These traits are framed as dangerous aspects of the unmasculine that warriors must reject at all costs if they are to acquire the strength necessary to defend national security" (*Bring Me Men*, 26). However, Belkin calls into question any essentialized, unidimensional version of military masculinity or monolithic concept of manhood. He argues instead that the discourse of military masculinity performs deeper political and ideological work, and that the "complex relationship between the masculine and the unmasculine, in particular those parts of the unmasculine designated as abject" serves to stabilize masculinity as well as empire (30).

11 Goffman, *Asylums*.

12 It is official policy to refer to recruits by last name and rank, but drill instructors also routinely bestow on recruits derogatory nicknames based on perceived physical, characterological, or performance flaws. For example, SU student and Navy veteran Mark recounted that he got his nickname in basic training as punishment for smiling in the lunch line: "You always had to have a blank look on your face, but when I was going through the [dining hall] line, the lunch ladies would be like, 'Hey honey, how you doing? You want some grits today?' So I'd just give her a little smile and go, 'Yes, ma'am,' and for that little smile, the drill instructor slapped my tray from out of my hand and yelled, 'What the hell you doing smiling? Is this a joke to you?!' And you just had to stand at attention, take all this stuff. He nicknamed me Smiley—he'd be like, 'Hey Smiley, come over here and do this.' You could never smile or do anything."

13 Lande, "Breathing Like a Soldier," 96.

14 In their book *Situated Learning*, Lave and Wenger theorize that this kind of learning, which employs pedagogies designed to help newcomers master new skills, increases participation in communities of practice.

15 Erica distinguished between the training of enlisted ranks and commissioned officers. She stressed that commissioned officers, unlike enlisted recruits, were indeed taught to think, in that in military academies officer candidates receive academic training concurrently with military training.

16 The characterization of high- and low-context communication within cultural groups, introduced by anthropologist Edward T. Hall (1976) has been embraced by business management and marketing professionals. Low-context learning is characterized by (1) a single source of information; (2) inductive thinking proceeding from specific to general; (3) focus on detail rather than the big picture; (4) following explicit directions and explanations; and (5) speed. Efficiency is emphasized in low-context learning (Guffey, *Essentials of Business Communication*).

17 "Hooah!" is the Army battle cry, used interchangeably as a greeting or farewell, to signal consent, hostility, or enthusiasm, or to assert a challenge.

18 The phrase "flying under the radar" was often mentioned in interviews when subjects spoke about their military experience, particularly in basic training, where the ability to get by unnoticed was a highly prized skill. For example, Army veteran Erica described the difficulty of managing the physical challenge of fitness training alongside the psychological challenge of name calling: "Of course, the physical challenge became enough that I wasn't focusing on the psychological challenge. My main thing was I just always wanted to stay under the radar. I wasn't that good at [basic training], because there were a lot of the physical challenges that I wasn't that good at. I wasn't a really fast runner, I couldn't do a hundred push-ups in a minute, and I kept getting injured—fell off the monkey bars, or horizontal cross-fitness bars, and sprained my ankle. But of course I felt like I had to keep going."

19 In the Army's basic training, this practice of forced physical activity as group punishment is known colloquially as getting smoked. It is a typical punishment for infractions committed by an individual member of the group.

20 Foucault, *Discipline and Punish*, 177.

21 Belkin, *Bring Me Men*, 5.

22 In subsequent chapters I show how this self-governing reluctance to challenge authority is also present on college campuses in veterans' clubs and organizations. For some veterans, this learned behavior has the effect of maintaining military discipline and its mind-set. For other student veterans, these military behaviors and ways of thinking are transformed by contact with civilian students and faculty.

23 Army Training Manual AR 350 1–19 (9).

24 According to Grossman (*On Killing*), infantry soldiers in World Wars I and II intentionally missed shots aimed at enemy combatants in whom they could recognize humanity. Thus, Grossman argues, the science of military training became devoted to developing rifle drills that would disconnect the act of shooting from conscious cognition of humanity in the targets.

25 Bourdieu, *Outline of a Theory of Practice*; Bourdieu, *The Logic of Practice*.

26 Several veterans spoke about the job assignment of raking rocks in which they had to rake the area around their combat base—terrain consisting of sand and rocks—for no apparent reason. This was not necessarily a punitive assignment but rather a make-work task designed to maintain discipline and prevent boredom in times of low activity.

27 Other scholars have written about the role of military uniforms in identity formation. For example, in her study of Latino/a high school students in the Junior Reserve Officer Training Corps (JROTC), Gina Pérez notes that for JROTC members, the military uniform signifies "visibility, respect, and dignity for students seeking to do well in school, find employment and develop the skills, relationships and financial security necessary to succeed once they graduate from high school" (*Citizen, Student, Soldier*, 61).

28 Authoritative discourse entails communication that has power to exert control and support the dominant order (Bakhtin, "Discourse in the Novel"; Bakhtin, "Heteroglossia"). While authoritative discourse is ideological, it depends on social structures to introduce, reproduce, and enforce it, such as media outlets, government, schools, churches, and military institutions. Rituals of speech and gesture serve to reify authoritative discourses, as power is transmitted in the performance of particular speech and actions. Within this paradigm, as Connor and Erica show us, it is more important to repeat words than to believe them.

29 Foucault, *Discipline and Punish*, 178.

30 Group punishment for individual infractions, or what Goffman (*Asylums*, 35), calls the "disruption of the usual relationship between an individual actor and his acts," is yet another feature of disciplinary practices within the total institution.

31 Belkin, *Bring Me Men*.

32 Bourdieu, *In Other Words*.

33 Bourdieu, *Practical Reason*; Lande, "Breathing Like a Soldier."

34 The set program of basic training allowed for patterns to emerge, without falling into schematics: veteran participants recalled intensely and complexly personal reactions to their military initiation in basic training.

Chapter 2. What They Bring with Them

1 Contrary to popular belief, medical care through VA facilities is not an entitlement available to all veterans. Combat veterans who have a service-connected disability rating are allowed to receive long-term care through the VA, while noncombat veterans without service-related disabilities may enroll in a medical benefits system, an HMO contracted by the DoD to provide medical care to veterans and their families. The process of enrolling in this multitiered system is complex, and workshops to explain the different programs and levels of care are an integral part of the TAP process.

2 I observed one military-to-civilian transitional weekend encounter for National Guard soldiers returning from deployment in Iraq and Afghanistan, called Yellow

Ribbon events. National Guard members and their families attended workshops, panel discussions, and theatrical presentations intended to ease the transition back into civilian life, and put particular focus on the effects of combat on mental health. Attendees were given information on the warning signs of PTSD and advised against engaging in problematic behaviors associated with soldiers returning from combat: domestic violence, self-medication with drugs and alcohol, and carrying firearms in daily civilian life. Yet these encounters were available only to soldiers of the Army National Guard, or about 28 percent of U.S. soldiers who fought in Iraq and Afghanistan.

3   From "A Review of the Transition Assistance Program TAP," American Legion, January 27, 2015, http://www.legion.org/legislative/testimony/225815/review-transition-assistance-program-tap.

4   From the DoD guide to transition support services: "Transition Resources: Making the Connection," U.S. National Guard and Reserve, 6, http://download.militaryonesource.mil/12038/Project%20Documents/DoD%20Transportal/TAP_booklet.pdf.

5   Many veterans, particularly those attending community college, traveled long distances to school because of housing costs. Veterans enrolled in a college located in a county with a relatively high cost of living received a higher VA housing stipend, but many chose to spend this stipend in surrounding counties with a lower cost of living. This provided extra income, but for some it also meant commuting several hours a day.

6   The civilian academy is commonly perceived as a space of free, unrestricted intellectual activity, but in reality, colleges are similarly regulated, albeit less overtly and to a lesser degree. Jaffee writes that, as in the institutional military, academic disciplinary practices are inculcated, enacted, and enforced by a hierarchical ranking system and gendered practices of privilege and expectation. Also as in the military, success or failure in college is determined by performance and adherence to traditions, conventions, and rank (Jaffee, "The Limits of Detachment"). Thus, when veterans attend civilian campuses, they move from one regulated social space to another. But the rules of the academy are much less explicit, and the norms of these two institutions are in some cases diametrically opposed.

7   While Brett's military-inflected approach to homework may have helped him to feel more conscientious and secure and ensured that he completed his assignments, it may also have undermined his academic performance. Some professors at SU and Central College noted that submitting homework well in advance of the deadline can deprive students of development of ideas presented in class by the teacher.

8   This military adage was invoked and regularly enacted by participants in this research. In contrast to the accepted SU practice of starting classes and campus meetings at ten minutes past the designated hour, veterans would routinely show up early for scheduled interviews.

9   Jack did this through the Army's delayed-entry program, which allows recruits to enter a pre-enlistment program prior to their eighteenth birthday in which they receive physical training and military mentorship to prepare for basic training.

10 Keilani's description of having a new disciplined reality "slapped" into her was meant both figuratively and literally (see her discussion of military hazing in chapter 1).

11 Evie reenlisted in the Army Reserve, but she also made a second, successful attempt at college when she enrolled in Central Community College. Evie graduated from Central and was accepted into a physician's assistant program at a highly competitive university, which she entered at the end of her military contract.

12 The VA requires students using the post-9/11 GI Bill to provide mitigating circumstances when they withdraw from or drop a course after the drop/add period and receive a nonpunitive grade (a grade that does not count as earned credit and that does not affect a student's progress standards for graduation, like a grade for an audited class). If mitigating circumstances are not accepted, any benefits paid from the beginning date of the term are considered an overpayment, and the student may be responsible for repayment. Veterans are not required to graduate from any institution and are only responsible to repay the VA for tuition costs if they withdraw from classes after the official withdrawal date. It is unclear from Julio's statements whether he understood that graduation was not a requirement for GI Bill education benefits.

13 The GI Bill "kicker" (officially known as the Army, Navy, or Marine Corps College Funds) is offered by the DoD through each service branch as part of an enlistment or reenlistment bonus. It is additional money that increases a veteran's basic monthly GI Bill education stipend by as much as $950 a month, offered as an alternative to a cash signing bonus. Recruits who opt for the kicker and pay into this "buy-up" program (as Grant did) demonstrate the intention of attending college with enhanced GI Bill education funding.

14 This sense of nostalgia is by no means exclusive to military combat veterans. I documented similar responses among veterans of U.S. social movements, particularly civil rights and anti–Vietnam War activists and activists who participated in national liberation solidarity movements of the 1960s, '70s, and '80s. In all cases, this nostalgia is connected to the loss of a feeling that one's participation was of consequence to global or national events, a feeling that one's life was in service of a greater cause, and the intensity of participating in confrontations (Moore, "Art, Politics and Education").

15 In interviews, community college instructors said that outbursts like Mack's can have a destabilizing effect on the class. They said that these outbursts are unnerving to class members and instructors, and are more disruptive than the precipitating circumstance of students talking during lectures. (Reported in observed instructor trainings and interviews with instructors LH, LD, FL and RW.) These classroom eruptions are often interpreted by instructors and class members as military behavior when they actually arise from frustration with civilian manners.

16 As a typical disciplinary response in the military, a soldier who is found to be not sufficiently attentive is made to stand in the front or the back of the room as a form of public punishment.

17 A commonly stated goal of postsecondary education is to teach students to critically examine opinions and data from multiple points of view. Morson argues that this is

a critical function of schools: "We live in a world of enormous cultural diversity, and the various languages and points of view of students have become a fact that cannot be ignored. Teachers need to enter in dialogue with those points of view and to help students do the same. For difference may best be understood not as an obstacle but as an opportunity" ("The Process of Ideological Becoming," 317). However, few community college campuses utilize formal curricula designed to foster teamwork and appreciation for cultural diversity. And even at su, curricula designed to teach respect for and understanding of cultural differences were concentrated in a single course requirement.

18 Yesenia alludes to the slogan "Be All You Can Be," the official Army recruitment slogan in 2000, when she enlisted.

19 Yesenia was drawing on benefits from the Montgomery GI Bill, the previous iteration of the GI Bill in effect from 1984 to 2008. The current post-9/11 GI Bill took effect in 2009. This bill provides expanded benefits, including a fifteen-year window for veterans to use their education stipend.

20 Janowitz and Moskos, "Racial Composition in the All-Volunteer Force"; Appy, *Working Class War*; Mariscal, "Chicano and Chicana Experiences of the War"; Kleycamp, "College, Jobs, or the Military?"; National Priorities Project, 2011.

21 A U.S. Department of Defense report notes that since 2000, black enlistments in the Army have fallen precipitously while Hispanic representation has increased. Kleycamp, "College, Jobs, or the Military?," argues that this decline results from the fact that during wars, the social and economic advantages of a career in the military are outweighed by the risk of death, and that in general, black Americans are less likely to enlist to fight in contested wars. Mariscal, "Chicano and Chicana Experiences of the War," argues that the rise in Latino/a enlistment in the same time period has to do with the social and economic incentives offered, which are especially attractive to recent immigrants. In addition to signing bonuses and death benefits, some immigrants are given expedited paths to citizenship.

22 Like other veteran participants who were once treated as not college material, Oscar has been successful at su and received the support of staff and faculty. He has held internships in Washington, DC, and won a competitive summer session fellowship to an Ivy League college.

23 American Psychiatric Association, *Diagnostic and Statistical Manual*, 467.

24 American Psychiatric Association, *Diagnostic and Statistical Manual*.

25 Cantrell and Dean, *Once a Warrior*, 33.

26 Recruits are prohibited from working in a medical, nuclear, or any high-security job in the Navy if they have a history of drug or alcohol-related offenses within three years.

27 Because roadside bombs are the weapons most commonly used in contemporary combat zones, tinnitus is one of the most common and enduring physical symptoms of combat trauma experienced by veterans of the wars in Iraq and Afghanistan.

28 This sentiment was reflected by civilian students, graduate teaching assistants, and some professors.

29 "The Death of the Ball Turret Gunner," Randall Jarrell, 1945:

From my mother's sleep I fell into the State,
And I hunched in its belly till my wet fur froze.
Six miles from earth, loosed from the dream of life,
I woke to black flak and the nightmare fighters.
When I died they washed me out of the turret with a hose.

30 Like many other veterans, Jordan later returned to college, attending a state college near his hometown before ultimately graduating from Southwest University. Chapter 3 discusses programs designed to address issues of veteran attrition and retention in college.

Chapter 3. Campus Veteran Support Initiatives

1   Kraines, "The Veteran and Postwar Education," 290.

2   Sander, "Out of Uniform."

3   It is difficult to quantify and correlate rates of GI Bill usage with successful completion. The VA tracks how much money is spent on GI Bill payments but not graduation rates. Therefore, we lack a full picture of how many veterans are currently in college and how many graduate. In addition, many veterans, if not the majority, face interruptions after beginning college. No statistics exist on veterans who drop out at some point but ultimately return to graduate.

4   Hedges, *War Is a Force That Gives Us Meaning*.

5   González, *Militarizing Culture*, 22.

6   Belkin, *Bring Me Men*, 38.

7   On population decline, see National Center for Veterans Analysis and Statistics 2010; "The Military-Civilian Gap: War and Sacrifice in the Post-9/11 Era" (Pew Research Center 2011) cited in Gardiner, "In the Shadow of Service," 70–71.

8   Kraska, *Militarizing the American Criminal Justice System*, 15.

9   Gardiner, "In the Shadow of Service."

10 Gardiner, "In the Shadow of Service."

11 Gardiner, "In the Shadow of Service," 69.

12 Mike McCullum, *Insight into Student Services* (Spring 2010).

13 Current evidence of the deleterious psychological effects of combat-associated violence is the heartbreaking statistic that more soldiers have taken their own lives than have died in combat (see Glantz, "The Truth about Veteran Suicides"). Moreover, DoD suicide statistics are cited in Cunningham, "A Sign of Empire Pathology"; and in Altman, "Military Suicide Rates Surge." For more discussion about the effects of posttraumatic combat stress, see Shay, *Odysseus in America*; Hoge et al., "Combat Duty in Iraq and Afghanistan"; Tick, *War and the Soul*; Grossman, *On Killing*; Lifton, *Home from the War*.

14 Global War on Terrorism (GWOT) is the name given to the constellation of current wars currently being waged by the U.S. military. (This is a pseudonym for the event.)

15   According to the Horses and Humans Research Foundation, more than thirty Depart-
     ment of Veterans Affairs medical centers participate in equine-assisted activity pro-
     grams throughout the United States (source: Horses & Humans Research Foundation,
     "Facts: Veterans rehabilitation and Equine Assisted Activities/Therapies," http://www
     .horsesandhumans.org/Veterans_Fact_Sheet_HHRF.pdf) Hippotherapy is shown to
     improve muscle symmetry in people with cerebral palsy (Benda, McGibbon, and
     Grant 2004). "Improvements in Muscle Symmetry in Children with Cerebral Palsy
     after Equine-Assisted Therapy (Hippotherapy)," *The Journal of Alternative and Com-
     plementary Medicine.* July 2004, 9 (6): 817–25. DOI:10.1089/107555303771952163.
     Hippotherapy also helps people with some types of autism to engage in social
     relations (Bass et al. 2009). "The Effect of Therapeutic Horseback Riding on Social
     Functioning in Children with Autism," *Journal of Autism and Developmental Disorders*
     39, no. 9 (Sept. 2009): 1261–68.

16   Horses began to be used as an adjunct to physical therapy in the 1960s and '70s, as
     therapeutic riding centers were established by physical and occupational therapists
     in Europe, Canada, and the United States. Koca and Ataseven, "History, and Hip-
     potherapy in the World," 2015, DOI: 10.14744/nci.2016.71601.

17   Slotkin, *Gunfighter Nation: The Myth of the Frontier in Twentieth-Century America.*
     Norman: University of Oklahoma Press.

18   Slotkin, *Gunfighter Nation*

19   Bederman, *Manliness and Civilization.*

20   Vietnam Veterans of America, Southwest Montana Chapter 788, accessed May 15,
     2017, http://vva788.org/resource_center/heroes__horses.

21   Belkin, *Bring Me Men*; Gardiner, "Heroic Masochism," 6.

22   Gardiner "Heroic Masochism," 5–6, emphasis in the original.

23   Dowd, *The Man Question*, 64.

24   Including transgender, as Shane Ortega, Kristen Beck, Chelsea Manning, and others
     have shown.

25   The oft-used but ill-defined term "best practice" refers to practices that are believed
     to be most effective and efficient. The term is commonly used in evaluation of
     evidence-based programs. The term is very popular in business management, yet
     its subjective nature makes it highly problematic. I use the term "best-practice lit-
     erature" as a descriptor of a particular genre of literature, not as a descriptor of the
     value of the actual practices.

26   DiRamio, Ackerman, and Mitchell, "From Combat to Campus"; Ackerman, R., D.
     DiRamio, and R. L. Garza Mitchell, "Transitions: Combat Veterans as College Stu-
     dents"; Herrmann, Raybeck, and Wilson, "College Is for Veterans, Too"; Armstrong
     et al., *Courage After Fire.*

27   This literature includes strategies for welcoming veterans by creating military-
     friendly campuses, which include raising the public profile of military service mem-
     bers and military institutions through events such as military-themed barbecues,
     sports competitions, and armament displays. DiRamio, Ackerman, and Mitchell,
     "From Combat to Campus" ; Ackerman and DiRamio, "Creating a Veteran-Friendly
     Campus"; Herrmann, Raybeck, and Wilson, "College Is for Veterans, Too"; Arm-

strong et al., *Courage After Fire* ; Shenk, "Veterans Returning to College"; see also Clarke and Coyner, "From Access to Accommodation."

28 Clarke and Coyner, "From Access to Accommodation"; DiRamio, Ackerman, and Mitchell, "From Combat to Campus"; Armstrong et al., *Courage After Fire*; Thomas, "Safe Zone for Veterans."

29 The group included representatives of long-standing nonprofit organizations including the Salvation Army, the VA, and public mental health agencies, but also more recent members of the burgeoning (and alliterative) sector of veteran-specific support programs such as Warriors to Work, Combat to Community, Boots to Books, and Horses for Heroes.

30 I observed this ritual of allegiance enacted in various ways at meetings of different civilian support networks. For example, at another support network meeting, after spoken introductions, meeting facilitators broadcast a musical "Tribute to the Troops" video in which heavy metal band Kiss sang a medley of military anthems. We were instructed to rise and sing along when the medley reached the anthem of our stated affiliation: Navy affiliates sang "Anchors Aweigh"; Army affiliates sang "When the Caissons Go Rolling Along"; Air Force affiliates sang "Off We Go, into the Wild Blue Yonder"; and Marine supporters sang the "Marine Corps Hymn." The Coast Guard's less well-known "Semper Paretus (Always Ready)" was not included in the video medley. Following that ritual, the leaders asked the group as a whole to stand and sing "God Bless America."

31 The mobile clinic was in a van the size of a tractor-trailer. Inside, the health clinic had a reception and triage area for filling out enrollment forms and performing blood pressure tests and an exam room where a nurse practitioner conducted physical examinations. The van was staffed by male military veterans who acted as intake workers and informal counselors, enrolling students into the VA medical system and scheduling their appointments. A nurse practitioner hired by the Veterans Clinic performed basic medical tests such as taking vital signs (blood pressure and oxygen level monitoring). The clinic offered referrals for physician visits, blood tests, X-rays, and prescription refills. These basic services, while useful to some veterans on campus, did not take the place of comprehensive medical care; the main objective of these campus visits was health education and outreach to engage student veterans in treatment.

32 Veteran services at Central College continued to increase and evolve with time. As of May 2014, veterans and veterans' services had a much higher profile on campus: a photo of the mobile clinic was featured on the home page of the college website along with links to myriad of campus veterans' services, including the mobile clinic, the campus veterans' club, counseling services, VA forms, and the Veterans' Council (an advisory body that advocates on behalf of veterans to the school administration). There is also a link that provides answers to an array of frequently asked questions about enrolling in community colleges and transferring to four-year institutions.

33 The EOPS program is intended to increase the number of underrepresented (by race, socioeconomic status, or involvement in the foster care system) students in

community colleges by providing counseling services, tutoring, workshops on stress management, nutrition, parenting, and transfer assistance to four-year colleges. Veterans were less likely to avail themselves of EOPS training and tutoring programs, perhaps because they were seen as remedial service programs historically tied to a discourse of affirmative action. Thus, these programs were at odds with the identity of the competent, self-sufficient military student.

34 One of the difficulties in trying to describe programs within public educational institutions is that constant funding shifts result in programs that are provisional and contingent. This was especially true of veterans' services at Central College. Services at SU were much more stable and tended to grow, rather than shrink.

35 The center offers services to students transferring from community colleges, reentry students (a classification meaning students who are twenty-five years old or older), and students who are parents.

36 When California's Master Plan for Education established a tiered universal-access system, it mandated public universities (California State Universities and Universities of California) to set aside upper-division admission placements and give priority in the admissions process to eligible California Community College transfer students.

37 A professor was considered veteran friendly if she or he actively demonstrated support for veterans on campus. Some, but not all, professors known as veteran friendly talked about their own military experience or that of their family members.

38 For example, the day after a fire destroyed an apartment house next to the university, a VFW member arrived at the SU veterans' office, saying that he had heard that one of the displaced residents of the apartment was an SU veteran. He said that his local VFW group wanted to donate the funds this student needed to help him relocate.

39 Brint, "Few Remaining Dreams."

40 By way of contrast, two days earlier, I began the semester teaching a similar orientation class for nonmilitary transfer students. The class was held in the same room, with the same furniture configuration. I made the same request that the civilian students rearrange the chairs in a circle. A few students made half-hearted attempts to move some chairs individually, but they did not collaborate on the task, and the ultimate outcome after five minutes of shuffling around was a jumble of chairs and tables scattered throughout the room.

41 In counterinsurgency wars, enemies are not even given the title of soldiers: Enemies of the U.S. forces are formally known as insurgents or terrorists and colloquially known as "bad guys" or other racialized epithets, such as "hajji" or "rag heads."

Chapter 4. Veteran Self-Help

1 "Military sexual trauma" is the term used by the military to describe any sexual harassment or sexual assault that occurs in the military by other military members.

2 Within military contexts, communal ties are gendered masculine and enforced through ritualized practice (Herbert, *Camouflage Isn't Only for Combat*); they are conceptualized and instilled as duty to country, mission, and fellow soldiers (Moskos, "The Military"); as logistical imperative; as the necessity of coordinated movement; as culture and tradition; or as the need to create a group identity for social and ideological unity (Francke, "Women in the Military"). Social scientists have different names for this type of mutually dependent relationship: Erikson (*Everything in Its Path*) called it communality; Tönnies (*Community and Society*) called it Gemeinshaft; Cooley (*Human Nature and the Social Order*) called it primary group formation, and Durkheim (*The Division of Labor in Society*) called it mechanical solidarity. All of these terms describe interdependent communities that animate and depend upon intense familial connections of brotherhood, sisterhood, and comradeship felt by military members.

3 Gardiner, "The Warrior Ethos"; Gardiner, "In the Shadow of Service."

4 Erikson, *Everything in Its Path*, 196. Erikson theorized social bonds in his study of survivors of a devastating flood in a West Virginia coal mining region.

5 Erikson, *Everything in Its Path*, 196.

6 For more discussion of military masculinity, see Belkin, *Bring Me Men*; Gardiner, "The Warrior Ethos"; Gardiner, "In the Shadow of Service"; Francke "Women in the Military"; Enloe, *Does Khaki Become You?*; and Herbert, *Camouflage Isn't Only for Combat*.

7 Belkin, *Bring Me Men*, 26.

8 Gardiner, "In the Shadow of Service," 70.

9 Herbert, *Camouflage Isn't Only for Combat*; and Benedict, *The Lonely Soldier* both provide excellent discussions of female social bonds within the male-dominated military. See also Francke, "Women in the Military"; and Belkin, *Bring Me Men* for analysis about perceptions of transgressive gender role behavior in the U.S. military.

10 Enloe, *Does Khaki Become You?* This assertion is supported by virtually all critical gender studies of the U.S. military, and the only contestations to this assertion I could find were in the U.S. armed forces recruitment material and military policy documents.

11 Belkin, *Bring Me Men*, 38.

12 Goffman, *Asylums*, 23.

13 Herbert, *Camouflage Isn't Only for Combat*, 17.

14 Literature has documented the perception in the masculinist U.S. military that female soldiers are physically deficient (see Enloe, *Does Khaki Become You?*; Herbert, *Camouflage Isn't Only for Combat*; Nelson, *For Love of Country*; Benedict, *The Lonely Soldier*; and Belkin, *Bring Me Men*). Most male and female veterans I interviewed also described this perception.

15 Jessica's drill instructors believed that her vision impairment, which would have excluded her from enlisting had it been discovered during her initial medical screening, was a temporary psychological reaction to the stress of basic training. An Army ophthalmologist formally diagnosed the condition immediately prior to her scheduled deployment to Iraq, which meant that she could not deploy with her

training unit. To Jessica's great dismay, she had to separate from her unit and was assigned to laundry and custodial duties at her base at Fort Jackson, South Carolina, until her contract ended. Jessica was honorably discharged with full benefits, yet she continues to feel that she was not able to fulfill her duty because she could not deploy with her fellow soldiers. A ruck march is a long training hike over rugged terrain with a heavy backpack (a rucksack or ruck).

16 Herbert, *Camouflage Isn't Only for Combat*, 13.

17 It is unclear from her words whether the category into which she feared being placed meant that other soldiers would think that she was a lesbian. The potential for that perception was certainly a possibility, as I heard from other military women who reported having to manage their appearance (by keeping their hair long, shaving their legs, and wearing cosmetics) and friendships (by avoiding the appearance of intimate relationships with identified lesbian soldiers) to avoid being perceived as lesbians. The theme of not wanting to appear too masculine or too feminine repeatedly surfaced in interviews with military women. The perceived threat of the masculinized military woman has endured through the history of women's involvement in military conflicts. Referring to female U.S. Army soldiers in World War II, Hampf writes, "Women's sexual agency became a symbol for gender deviance, as became clear in the stereotype of the 'mannish woman.' The perceived masculinization of women by the military posed the threat of feminization to the military as a whole" ("'Dykes' or 'Whores,'" 16). Avoiding the stigma of gender deviance is clearly not limited to women in the military; Belkin, *Bring Me Men*, documents various ways in which male service members managed their behavior to avoid the perception of being gay.

18 Francke, "Women in the Military," 139.

19 The military gender line is enforced across all aspects of institutional training. According to Francke, "Women recruits in the Marines received less training time than men, as did female pilots in the Navy and Air Force: additional combat training was reserved for men." In addition, "While male recruits' heads are ritually shaved in all the services to submerge their individual identities into the male collective, [the *Marines Recruit Training Manual* stipulates that] women are required to wear their hair 'in an attractive, feminine style' not longer than their uniform collars but not so short as to appear mannish" (Francke, "Women in the Military," 139).

20 The enforced mandate to adopt heteronormative standards of women's attractiveness held for military women across ranks. At one gathering of female veterans, a woman holding the rank of captain spoke about being sexually harassed and assaulted by lower-ranking men. When she attempted to sanction the men, her superiors blamed her both for appearing too attractive and for not asserting proper control over subordinates. She said, "My colonel said it was my fault—that I should have uglied it up" (interview with YR, April 10, 2011). Keilani's fourteen medals and commendations include a Navy Meritorious Unit Commendation awarded for exceptionally meritorious conduct in performance of outstanding services in Iraq combat zones (Military Awards of the U.S. Department of the Navy). Note that the

Marine Corps is a component of the U.S. Department of the Navy, while a separate branch works closely with the Navy for training, transportation, and logistical support. Therefore, awards and commendations are issued by the Navy.

21 This officially sanctioned gendered designation shows up in official documents as recently as 2006.

22 Keilani explained that the appellation "Wookiee monsters" referred to large furry alien creatures from the *Star Wars* films.

23 Scully and Marolla, "Convicted Rapists' Vocabulary of Motives," 542, cited in Nelson, *For Love of Country*, 85.

24 Enloe, *Does Khaki Become You?*; Enloe, *Bananas, Beaches and Bases*; Enloe, *Globalization and Militarism*; Francke, "Women in the Military"; Benedict, *The Lonely Soldier*; Oliver, *Women as Weapons of War*; Herbert, *Camouflage Isn't Only for Combat*.

25 Male veterans also mentioned this slogan several times, but they saw it as inspirational and aspirational. The slogan helped remind them to internalize lessons of self-motivation and responsibility.

26 Francke, "Women in the Military," 136.

27 Francke, "Women in the Military," 139.

28 Francke describes military court testimony from Army private Sarah Tolaro, who said that sexual harassment and molestation with impunity was so much a part of everyday life that many military women gave up on reporting it: "Private Tolaro [did not report] the men who had exposed themselves to her nor the drill sergeant who had told his male troops to hit on female recruits because 'women specifically came into the Army for that reason.' 'Every time I have brought up anything that I felt was important to me, I have been told, *Do not make waves*,' Tolaro testified. 'I have discovered through my time in the service that if I take it any higher than me, I am going to come back with *I'm sure you deserved it anyway*, so, you know, *just drop it*'" (Francke, "Women in the Military," 155).

29 Francke, "Women in the Military."

30 The burgeoning of public and private-sector jobs in the Homeland Security sector offers employment opportunities for growing numbers of military veterans. An amalgam of research and service subfields, the Homeland Security sector represents one of the few expanding areas of job growth funded by the U.S. government.

31 DiRamio, Ackerman, and Mitchell, "From Combat to Campus"; Ackerman, DiRamio, and Mitchell, "Transitions"; Armstrong et al., *Courage after Fire*.

32 DiRamio, Ackerman, and Mitchell, "From Combat to Campus," 95.

33 In the same three-year period, I never knew of a club member who was openly gay.

34 Growing numbers of advertisements in media and trade journals target veterans for corporate jobs, and more veterans' advocacy groups are working to place veterans in the private corporate sector (Green Jobs 4 Veterans, Wounded Warrior at Work, etc.).

35 Terry never criticized or expressed opposition to the U.S. wars in Iraq and Afghanistan during interviews or in the informal conversations at su veterans' events. It is possible that he had complex and contradictory feelings about U.S. policy and the wars, but his public stance was unqualified support for the U.S. military.

36 Noncommissioned officers do not start out with a commission, or formal appointment upon entering the military, as happens with graduates of military academies or college ROTC programs. They most often enlist at entry-level ranks and rise to higher ranks through field promotions.

37 This was particularly evident at one Veterans Club meeting, when a panel of SU graduate student veterans were invited to talk to club members about applying to graduate school. The panel was made up of veterans getting advanced degrees in journalism, engineering, molecular biology, and law. When the panelists introduced themselves by name, branch of service, and military occupation, one panelist commented that her job accompanying troops as a field reporter involved "real work" and "real danger," in contrast to the ceremonial junkets made by the officers. Other club members joined in the humorously deprecating jokes about officers, followed by an awkward silence when the other graduate student panelists introduced themselves as commissioned officers.

38 I was staying in Orchard Valley at the time of the killings and attended nightly *rosarios*, or recitations of the Catholic rosary, in front of a makeshift altar outside of the deceased family's apartment. The gunman's family had emigrated from Mexico and lived in an apartment complex occupied primarily by other Mexican immigrants. Members of the close-knit community kept vigil outside the family's apartment, taking turns speaking to the press and ferrying donated coffee and *carnitas* from local restaurants. In the aftermath of the shootings, before the mother's body was found, friends and family joined the police search for her. For five nights, family, friends, and neighbors stood outside the home and offered intentions, or prayers, for the mother's safety and for the departed souls of the veteran and his sister. When the mother's next-door neighbor joined the group to announce that the Orchard Valley police had officially called off the search, believing her to be dead, the mood of sadness turned to outrage. "The only ones to blame in this are the Orchard Valley Police and [the veteran's] Army sergeant—they wouldn't take away his guns," said the mother's niece in Spanish. "[The mother] was so afraid of him. [The veteran] said to her, 'You are not my mother any more—you are the enemy.' [The police] came out to the house a lot, but they never took his guns. They should have taken his guns."

39 Despite SU's reputation as a site of protests against the Vietnam War, there is no official chapter of IVAW on the SU campus.

40 During my research, over the course of twenty-four months I regularly attended SU Veterans Club meetings. I was not present at the meeting described above, but the account comes from extensive interviews with Erica and other members who were present, and from members' posted responses to the incident from the group's Facebook page. This account is corroborated by members' comments posted in response to a published media interview Erica gave to a local newspaper. I witnessed other veterans' meetings in which sentiment against the wars was characterized as political while sentiments supporting the military were naturalized and characterized as apolitical.

41 Gramsci, *Selections from the Prison Notebooks of Antonio Gramsci*; Hall, "Race, Articulation and Societies Structured in Dominance."

Chapter 5. Spectral Wars and the Myth of the Antimilitary Campus

1 Gramsci, *Selections from the Prison Notebooks*.

2 Grandstaff, "Visions of New Men."

3 Grandstaff, "Visions of New Men," 2.

4 Frydl (*The GI Bill*) and Altschuler and Blumin (*The GI Bill*) and numerous other scholars have documented the legacy of the Servicemen's Readjustment Act of 1944, or the GI Bill, and its indelible imprint on U.S. veterans' services today.

5 For perspectives on the increasing militarization of public institutions and spaces, see Loeb, *Generation at the Crossroads: Apathy and Action on the American Campus*; Shaw, "Twenty-First Century Militarism: A Historical-Sociological Framework," in *Militarism and International Relations: Political Economy, Security and Theory*; Lembcke, *The Spitting Image*; Enloe, *Globalization and Militarism: Feminists Make the Link*; González, *Militarizing Culture: Essays on the Warfare State*

6 For perspectives on contemporary war veterans in college, see Herrmann et al. (2005); Ackerman and DiRamio, "Creating a Veteran-Friendly Campus"; Altschuler and Blumin, *The GI Bill*; Williamson, "A New GI Bill."

7 For example, Lembcke, *The Spitting Image*; Cahill, "Fighting the Vietnam Syndrome"; Beukenhorst, "Whose Vietnam?"

8 Gramsci, *Selections from the Prison Notebooks*.

9 As bitter and divisive as this experience was for the people of the United States, it is crucial to note that, as in all wars, an incalculable cost was paid by the people in whose countries this war was fought. The people of Vietnam, Cambodia, and Laos—insurgents and U.S. allied forces as well as noncombatant civilians—suffered the devastating effects of war: massive destruction in the physical, emotional, and environmental realms.

10 Mendible, "Post Vietnam Syndrome," http://www.radicalpsychology.org/vol7-1/mendible.html (link is no longer active).

11 Rowe, *The Cultural Politics of the New American Studies*.

12 This political aversion impeded legislative approval for, if not actual, military interventions during the 1980s—principally in Nicaragua and El Salvador—but also in Grenada, Libya, Iran, and Panama, among other nations. Mendible, "Post Vietnam Syndrome"; Cahill, "Fighting the Vietnam Syndrome." Kimball, "The Enduring Paradigm of the 'Lost Cause,'" argues that this represents the U.S. version of the *Dolchstoss* "stab in the back" betrayal theory which held that insufficient support from German civilians resulted in the Weimar Republic's defeat in World War I, and that the U.S. version of this myth "blamed leftists, liberals, the press, the anti-war movement, civilian policymakers, Democratic Party presidents and the Congress of the United States—and particularly the 'dovish' representatives within it—for snatching defeat from the jaws of victory" (233).

13 Mendible, "Post Vietnam Syndrome."

14 Mendible, "Post Vietnam Syndrome."

15 Lembcke, *Spitting Image*. 1995; Cahill, "Fighting the Vietnam Syndrome"; and Sitikoff, "The Postwar Impact of Vietnam," all note the salience of the

apocryphal spurned Vietnam War veteran rooted in U.S. popular cultural memory.

16 This position is made explicit in Shepherd and Shepherd, "War and Dissent"; Shepherd and Shepherd, "War Attitudes and Ideological Orientations"; Stever, "The Veteran and the Neo-Progressive Campus"; Roth-Douquet and Shaeffer, AWOL: *The Unexcused Absence of America's Upper Classes from Military Service*; Herrmann et al., *Educating Veterans in the 21st Century*; Downs and Murtazashvili, *Arms and the University*.

17 Rowe, *The Cultural Politics of the New American* Studies, 54.

18 Among the most adamant about this position are Shepherd and Shepherd, "War and Dissent"; Shepherd and Shepherd, "War Attitudes and Ideological Orientations"; Stever, "The Veteran and the Neo-Progressive Campus"; Roth-Douquet and Shaeffer, AWOL: *The Unexcused Absence of America's Upper Classes from Military Service*; Herrmann et al., *Educating Veterans in the 21st Century*; Thomas, "Safe Zone for Veterans."

19 Burke, "Doing and Saying," wrote about perfecting myths as a corrective to the universalizing archetype. Lembcke (*The Spitting Image*), Carmichael (*Framing History*), and Kimball ("The Enduring Paradigm of the 'Lost Cause'"): have applied this concept to the principles of propaganda and the production of popular consent for U.S. wars, including the Cold War.

20 Barthes, *Mythologies*, 10.

21 Hegemony can be constructed through what Stuart Hall, "Gramsci's Relevance for the Study of Race and Ethnicity," calls articulation, wherein social relations, attitudes, and beliefs that may be contradictory combine to create ideological positions and practices that come to appear coherent rather than contradictory. The concept of articulation, often associated with Althusser ("Ideology and Ideological State Apparatus"), has been taken up and reworked by Hall ("Race, Articulation and Societies Structured in Dominance"; "Gramsci's Relevance for the Study of Race and Ethnicity") and Gillian Hart ("Changing Concepts of Articulation"; *Re-thinking the South African Crisis*) to mean newly created relations of linkages and affectivity between relatively autonomous social, cultural, and economic elements. These autonomous (and sometimes disparate) elements—such as discourses of militarism, social inclusion, civil rights, and veteran support—are structured as an ideological unity that in turn becomes a social force that both defines and produces social meanings and practices.

22 This invocation of hostility toward veterans almost always came from veterans' advocates; representatives of the VA, Vet Centers, VFW, or military support agencies. I never heard the veterans themselves say they felt targeted for abuse.

23 My emphasis. From Shane, "Student Vets Say Anti-military Attitudes Persist on Campus."

24 Loeb, *Generation at the Crossroads*; Lembcke, *Spitting Image*; Lembcke, *Hanoi Jane*; Cahill, "Fighting the Vietnam Syndrome"; and Beukenhorst, "Whose Vietnam?"

25 Armstrong, Best, and Domenici, *Courage after Fire*; Ackerman et al., "Transitions: Combat Veterans as College Students"; and Thomas, "Safe Zone for Veterans."

26 For example, Herrmann et al., *Educating Veterans in the 21st Century*; DiRamio, Ackerman, and Mitchell, "From Combat to Campus"; Stever, "The Veteran and the Neo-Progressive Campus"; and Thomas, "Safe Zone for Veterans" all cite personal experience in the military in their biographical introductions.

27 Herrmann, Raybeck, and Wilson, "College Is for Veterans, Too"; Herrmann et al., *Educating Veterans in the 21st Century*; Stever, "The Veteran and the Neo-Progressive Campus"; Shepherd and Shepherd, "War and Dissent"; Shepherd and Shepherd, "War Attitudes and Ideological Orientations."

28 As noted in DiRamio, Ackerman, and Mitchell, "From Combat to Campus"; Herrmann et al., *Educating Veterans in the 21st Century*; Persky and Oliver, "Veterans Coming Home to the Community College"; and Lewis, "Serving Returning Vets."

29 This strand of argument cautions professors that expressing disagreement with military or government policy might not only make veterans feel uncomfortable and alienate them in class, but that it might also expose colleges to potential lawsuits: Persky and Oliver ("Veterans Coming Home to the Community College") warn that alleged antimilitary bias by faculty might potentially become the basis for civil rights lawsuits by veterans against colleges. "From an institutional perspective, employee training may soon be a necessity. [Some faculty respondents] viewed veterans as the forgotten minority and explained that treating any other group of students the way veterans are treated would result in equal opportunity issues. . . . Colleges need to address anti-military bias as a potential liability issue" (117–118). For more claims of faculty bias against student veterans, see DiRamio, Ackerman, and Mitchell, "From Combat to Campus"; Herrmann, Raybeck, and Wilson, "College Is for Veterans, Too"; Lewis, "Serving Returning Vets."

30 My emphasis. Herrmann, Raybeck, and Wilson, "College Is for Veterans, Too," 2–3.

31 My research has found this not to be the case; many student veterans expressed great ambivalence about U.S. military missions and their actions in war. This perspective, however, is discussed very rarely, if at all, in campus veteran support literature. I suspect one reason behind this apparent foreclosure of the possibility of antiwar veterans of the Iraq and Afghanistan wars is that it provides a social corrective to widespread dissent against the Vietnam War carried out by drafted and enlisted GIs.

32 For example, the curriculum "Welcome Home: Creating a Campus Climate of Wellness for Returning Veterans," a program created in 2012 by the organization Swords to Plowshares and presented to community college faculty in California, advises college instructors against classroom discussion of the wars to avoid offending veterans. Admonitions to silence form part of the best-practice literature (see chapter 3) and are informed by the trope of the antiveteran college faculty and student body. For examples, see Stever, "The Veteran and the Neo-Progressive Campus"; Shepard and Shepard, "War and Dissent: The Political Values of the American Professoriate."

33 Herrmann, Raybeck, and Wilson, "College Is for Veterans, Too," 2–3.

34 Significantly, this is a quote from an article titled "College Is for Veterans, Too." The title implies that the negation of this plaintive assertion—that veterans are

structurally and culturally excluded in civilian college—is the norm on contemporary campuses.

35 Ackerman and DiRamio, "Creating a Veteran-Friendly Campus"; DiRamio et al., "From Combat to Campus: Voices of Student/Veterans"; Armstrong, Best, and Domenici, *Courage after Fire*.

36 The term "military friendly" (schools, employers, workplaces, etc.) was coined by Victory Media, a company founded by military veteran entrepreneurs. "Victory Media has led the industry as a ratings entity for over a decade, surveying thousands of institutions and assembling lists that capture best practices in recruitment and retention of military employees, students and franchisees. The Military Friendly® ratings program has been instrumental in the development of corporate and college military recruiting programs. Veterans benefit when companies and schools invest in engaging, educating and employing them. Our nation benefits. Victory Media takes its role in the growth of Military Friendly® as a personal guarantee to every person who wore the uniform. Our survey-driven Military Friendly® lists have been published every year since 2003." "About the Program," Military Friendly®—A division of Victory Media, http://militaryfriendly.com/about-us/, accessed Feb. 18, 2017.

37 From Lederman, "What Makes a College 'Military Friendly'?"; and Ackerman and DiRamio, "Creating a Veteran-Friendly Campus."

38 Ackerman and DiRamio, "Creating a Veteran-Friendly Campus," 1. The terms "military friendly" and "veteran friendly" are often used interchangeably. Shenk, "Veterans Returning to College," refers to the goal of creating a "military friendly campus," while Ackerman and DiRamio, "Creating a Veteran-Friendly Campus," describe strategies to create "veteran-friendly" campuses.

39 This protest was successful in abolishing that school's ROTC program until 2014.

40 The protesters' demands included replacement of ROTC scholarships with Harvard scholarships. The protest spokesperson shouted to the crowd, "If they [Harvard administrators] are so concerned about those ROTC scholarships, give them [ROTC students] Harvard Scholarships. Give the ROTC boys Harvard Scholarships!" Duehren and Talkoff, "Boots on the Ground." For a sociological study of the contested history of ostensible campus hostility toward Vietnam veterans, see Jerry Lembcke's *The Spitting Image*.

41 Ackerman and DiRamio, "Creating a Veteran-Friendly Campus," 1.

42 This Vietnam-era framing of veterans' needs is part of the conventional wisdom informing contemporary student affairs services. The organization Student Affairs Professionals in Higher Education or NAPSA, a leading association of student affairs professionals, promotes a webinar called "Approaches to Creating a Veteran-Friendly Campus" with the description, "Colleges did not respond well to the needs of military personnel who came to the campus following the Vietnam conflict. Using the lessons from that era, researchers and program planners have developed strategies for aiding student veterans and many campuses have in place initiatives designed to facilitate the transition students make when they leave campus for military service and when they return from service. Student affairs play a crucial leader-

ship role in preparing for, serving, and successfully graduating these students." www.napsa.org (link is no longer active).

43 Lokken et al., "A Strategic Approach to Creating Veteran-Friendly Campuses," 45.

44 Ford, Northrup, and Wiley recommend that campus staff "engage with military leaders, including retired personnel, to develop programs and services that meet the needs of active-duty students. . . . Along these lines, the chief student affairs officer could appoint a task force of military students and student life personnel to collaborate with local Veterans of Foreign Wars (VFW) to create an SVA [Student Veterans of America] chapter on campus. . . . It is helpful to note that veterans groups such as the VFW have been instrumental in the development and support of SVA chapters" ("Connections, Partnerships, Opportunities, and Programs," 67–68).

45 Ford, Northrup, and Wiley, "Connections, Partnerships, Opportunities, and Programs," 68.

46 Ford, Northrup, and Wiley, "Connections, Partnerships, Opportunities, and Programs," 68. The authors refer to "students who are in the military," implying that their recommendations are directed toward active-duty military members. However, these recommendations are clearly intended for postdischarge student veterans as well as the broader college community (evidenced by repeated recommendations for military collaboration with SVA, an organization that works primarily with postdischarge veterans, and the call for campus-wide military appreciation events).

47 These arguments were put forward in an unsigned article in the *Harvard Crimson* when the campus was debating the discontinuation of ROTC programs at Harvard University (see "No Military Training at Harvard," *Harvard Crimson*, December 2, 1968).

48 Jorge Mariscal argues this about the contemporary wars in "The Poverty Draft." Christian Appy makes similar arguments about Vietnam War military conscripts in *Working Class War*.

49 The speaker e-mailed me a copy of written text of this speech, in response to my request.

50 Indeed, in subsequent correspondence, the speaker wrote to me that she had received criticism after the event for praising members of the military: "I actually received some negative responses for not being anti-military in the speech and it was a bit disheartening that that was all some people walked away with after a vigil" (personal communication, March 15, 2012). My claim is not that antipathy toward the U.S. military does not exist on the SU campus; only that if it does exist, it is rarely expressed publicly.

51 By comparison, at a protest of the same incident in another city, the mood was explicitly negative toward the institutional U.S. military. One protester, an Iraq War veteran, was quoted in a press report saying, "[U.S. soldiers] are subjected to indoctrination and learn to dehumanize people. I remember I was in the military actually when 9/11 happened and I remember when the words 'Hajji' and 'towel head' started being introduced into our lexicon. . . . I think that the effects of these wars on the soldiers show you that they're wrong, that they're suffering and that

they become inhuman themselves and commit these inhuman acts" (*San Francisco Chronicle*, March 15, 2012).

52 I am assuming that the anonymous author was male, because there were only two female veterans in the class, neither with physical combat injuries.

53 This event forms part of what Binder and Wood call a "provocative style" of conservative organizing on college campuses—a national strategy sponsored by advocacy groups (such as Young America's Foundation and the Leadership Institute, among others) that promotes an aggressive style of conservative engagement intended to polarize and inflame tensions on campus by lampooning liberal ideologies with high-profile, public, headline-generating events (*Becoming Right*, 81–91, 169).

54 Stever, "The Veteran and the Neo-progressive Campus"; Herrmann, Raybeck, and Wilson, "College Is for Veterans, Too."

55 For a fuller discussion of how the politics of ressentiment and umbrage affect the contemporary U.S. political landscape, see Wendy Brown's *States of Injury*.

56 The movement to bring back ROTC to college campuses has been ongoing since the 1970s, but gained serious traction after the U.S. military policy of "Don't Ask, Don't Tell" was repealed, and with that, a major stated objection to ROTC presence on campus—that the U.S. military discriminated against gay and lesbian members— was rendered moot. Harvard University reinstated the program in 2011, as did Stanford in 2012. For more on this move to bring ROTC back to Ivy League campuses, see Downs and Murtazashvili, *Arms and the University*.

57 See Karni, "Hero's Unwelcome"; Roth, "Students Surprised, Worried by National Media Coverage on ROTC"; Jordan, "Heckled Vet Bucks Columbia Critics," published February 25, 2011, Military.com, http://newsmilitary.com (link no longer active).

58 The origin of this iconic yet apocryphal story is contested in scholarly historical accounts, notably in Jerry Lembcke's *Spitting Image*.

59 The public outrage about charges of intolerance and disrespect expressed by the military advocates left an indelible impression on the broader campus community and extended beyond the campus, and this outrage about Columbia students' and faculty's alleged mistreatment of veterans, though disavowed by Maschek, was leveraged to gain sympathy for the ROTC cause. This was made possible by the articulation of progressive discourses of inclusion and diversity with a claim of discrimination against the military. "Some of the most persuasive arguments for ROTC were based on applying the university's core values to the military itself: diversity of thought and non-discrimination. With the demise of DADT (the discriminatory Don't Ask, Don't Tell policy), the anti-ROTC position was now seen as close-minded and discriminatory in its own right. In other words, ROTC was now being accepted on the basis of the core value system of the university, while its opponents now wore the mantle of close-mindedness and discrimination" (Downs and Murtazashvili, *Arms and the University*, 224.)

60 Hall, "Gramsci's Relevance for the Study of Race and Ethnicity," 43. See also chapter 4 for more discussion on the process and function of articulation.

61 Thomas, "Safe Zone for Veterans," 6.

62 Thomas, "Safe Zone for Veterans," 7.

63 Thomas, "Safe Zone for Veterans," 7.

64 Brown, *States of Injury.*

65 Thomas, "Safe Zone for Veterans," 3. This assertion that student veterans on contemporary college campuses are at risk of discrimination or harassment rests on the
contention that contemporary college faculty members are more politically liberal
and thus more likely to oppose military action than members of the general public.
Through unsubstantiated assertions and ad hominem arguments, post-Vietnam
war era college faculty are characterized as both war-averse and hostile to military
veterans. While no substantiated link is established between an alleged liberal bias
in faculty and ostensible antimilitary attitudes and actions, it is argued that a lack of
awareness of veterans 'issues and a putative "post-Vietnam era academic tradition of
opposition to armed conflict" pose potential barriers to student veterans' success in
college (Thomas, "Safe Zone for Veterans," 3).

66 Thomas, "Safe Zone for Veterans," 3.

67 Thomas, "Safe Zone for Veterans," 3.

68 Thomas, "Safe Zone for Veterans," 6.

69 The assertion of threat parity with LGBT students does not depend on documented
facts: according to an FBI report of single-bias incidents of hate crimes, the number
of victims targeted because of sexual orientation came in as third highest, following
the number of victims targeted because of their race and religion. The FBI report,
released in November 2016, found that of the 7,121 reported victims of hate crimes
in 2015, 59.2 % percent of the victims were targeted because of the offender's bias
against a race, ethnicity, or national origin, and 19.7 percent were targeted because of
a bias against religious belief. This is followed by 19.4 percent of the victims targeted
because of sexual orientation or gender identity. The other hate crime bias categories, in descending order, were disability (1.2 percent) and gender (0.4 percent). FBI
Uniform Crime Report, Hate Crime Statistics, https://ucr.fbi.gov/hate-crime/2015,
accessed May 15, 2017. As of this writing, I have been unable to find any reported
hate crimes by civilians against veterans based on their military status.

70 Thomas, "Safe Zone for Veterans."

71 "Just as Safe Zone programs recognize the importance of including heterosexual allies in the creation of positive environments for LGBT students on campus (Bullard,
2004); the inclusion of non-veteran allies is a critical piece in the development of a
Veterans Ally program" (Thomas, "Safe Zone for Veterans," 7).

72 Image of VNA decal found in Thomas "Safe Zone for Veterans," 111. http://www.ed
.gov/documents/ . . . /vet-net-ally-seminar.doc, link no longer active.

73 Example from Radford University, VA, Radford University Safe Zone Facebook page,
https://www.facebook.com/SafeZoneRU.

74 Thomas, "Safe Zone for Veterans," 111.

75 California State University, Chico, "Mission Statement," Safe Zone Ally Program,
http://www.csuchico.edu/diversity/safezone/index.shtml.

76 Thomas, "Safe Zone for Veterans," 119.

77 The program rationale can be seen as a response to the following problem statement in the VNA pilot project: "As is the case with many groups with special needs

in the academy, faculty and staff may not be aware of the issues faced by this population or the services available on the campus to assist them in their personal and academic endeavors. Additionally, since the Vietnam era, faculty members are significantly more politically liberal and are more likely to oppose military action than the public at large (Shepard and Shepard 1994, 1996). Lack of awareness of veterans' issues and the Vietnam and Post-Vietnam era academic tradition of opposition to armed conflict may intersect to create barriers to the success of veterans who are pursuing higher education. Veterans may be marginalized or even harassed about their service by other students, staff, or faculty (Herrmann, Raybeck, and Wilson 2008; Stever 1997), Thomas "Safe Zone for Veterans," 3–4. This problem statement frames the rationale behind VNA as a lack of awareness of veterans' needs and faculty's antimilitary attitudes. Denial of academic freedom is not put forward as a problem that must be addressed by the VNA program.

78 The program description notes, "No weapons or ammunition were used in this demonstration" (Thomas, "Safe Zone for Veterans," 44).

79 My experience as an instructor in adult education classes convinced me that services such as designated staff, peer-support groups, and population-specific classes would be helpful not simply for student veterans, but for any nontraditional college students, such as first-generation college students or older returning students, who might be unfamiliar with college norms and practices, or who have been out of the educational milieu for an extended period of time.

80 Frantz, "Developing a Comprehensive State-wide Veterans Re-entry Education Program."

81 Redden, "Campuses as Vet-Friendly Zones."

82 Herrmann, Raybeck, and Wilson, "College Is for Veterans, Too," 13.

83 Redden, "Campuses as Vet-Friendly Zones."

84 Redden, "Campuses as Vet-Friendly Zones."

85 From VA Campus Toolkit: "From Combat to Classroom: Understanding Student-Veterans and Servicemembers": "This training guide, developed with collaboration between the George E. Wahlen Department of Veteran Affairs Medical Center, the Brain Injury Association of Utah and many state and community agencies and organizations, provides information about post-deployment issues, mental health and medical issues, tips for colleges and universities, and resources." http://www.mentalhealth.va.gov/studentveteran/gettinghelp.asp, accessed May 15, 2017.

86 The Blue Star Mothers of America (known colloquially as Blue Star Moms) is a national organization, conceived and founded during World War II by former Army assistant morale officer George H. Maines to support the U.S. military mission: "Mothers volunteered throughout the tough times of World War II. They worked in hospitals, train stations, packed care packages for soldiers and were a working part of homeland security during times our time of war. The organization waned in size over the years but has held together by mothers showing pride in both their children and country. In recent times we have began [sic] to grow in strength. Being attacked on our own soil has once again started mothers hanging flags in their windows at home proclaiming pride in the fact that we have

children protecting our freedom during at time of war." Our organization not only provides support for active duty service personnel, promotes patriotism, assists Veterans organizations, and is available to assist in homeland volunteer efforts to help our country remain strong." http://www.bluestarmothers.org/history, accessed May 15, 2017.

87 Though some might consider the entire list of questions an attempt to circumscribe and control communication between civilians and veterans, I have no problem recommending against asking veterans with whom one has no prior relationship about their experience of killing. I believe that it is voyeuristic and intrusive to ask this very personal question without a prior contextual relationship. Yet veterans told me that civilians and civilian students commonly and casually asked them, "Did you kill anyone?," "How many people did you kill?," and "What is it like to kill someone?" This indicates a strong cognitive and emotional disconnection between many civilians and the consequences of war. The ability to casually ask strangers about highly traumatic incidents shows that the questioners are unaware of the human cost of war-related violence, for both the victim and the perpetrator. I believe that this disconnection indicates the need for more, not less, serious discussion of wars and their human toll. However, this kind of discussion should not require that veterans discuss details of their combat experience in casual conversation with strangers.

88 From a handout developed by David M. Joseph, PhD, with information adapted from presentations given by Minnesota Army National Guard Chaplin Lieutenant Colonel John Morris. "Welcome Home: Creating a Campus Climate of Wellness for Returning Veterans," a program offered in 2012 by the organization Swords to Plowshares and presented to community college faculty in California.

Chapter 6. "Thank You for Your Service"

1 Because the surveys were anonymous, respondents are not identifiable by race or gender.

2 Suppressive fire (also known as covering fire) is a military term for firing weapons at or in the direction of enemy forces with the primary goal of protecting troops when they are within range of enemy weapons. Suppressive fire differs from lethal fire (i.e., shooting to kill) in that its primary objective is to get the enemy to keep their heads down and thus reduce their ability to move, shoot, or observe their surroundings. While soldiers (and civilians) may be injured or killed by suppressive fire, this is not its main purpose. "Covering Fire," *DoD Dictionary of Military and Associated Terms*, JP 3–02, http://www.dtic.mil/doctrine/dod_dictionary/data/c/3500.html.

3 Psychiatrist and trauma specialist Robert Jay Lifton, a leading clinician behind the development of the PTSD diagnosis, developed a group treatment model to help Vietnam War veterans talk about the psychological conflicts and contradictions they faced coming home from the battlefield. Lifton's book *Home from the War: Learning*

from Vietnam Veterans became the basis for establishing peer support groups to treat combat trauma at veteran centers. Gutmann and Lutz, *Breaking Ranks*; Cantrell and Dean, *Once a Warrior*; and Brison, "Trauma Narratives and the Re-making of the Self" also write about the importance of peer support in coming to terms with the contradictory experience of trauma.

4 While Bridget was critical of the contemporary U.S. wars, she was not openly affiliated with antiwar activism, and as the president of her community college veterans' club, Bridget was an outspoken advocate for student veterans on her campus. She spoke at public events and successfully organized for the creation of a student veterans' center on campus.

5 Some studies estimate that 75 percent of combat veterans play war-themed video games occasionally too often, which was consistent with my research (this was one of the questions I asked participants). There is debate among cognitive and social scientists on the role of violent video games in veterans' psychological health. Gackenbach et al., "Video Game Play as Nightmare Protection: A Replication and Extension," argue that playing war-themed video games has a psychologically protective function for veterans in that the numbing effects of violent video games inures soldiers to the traumatic psychological sequelae of killing, which, they argue, helps soldiers feel more psychologically healthy. Grossman and DeGaetano, in *Stop Teaching Our Kids to Kill*, agree that playing video games has a numbing effect on soldiers, but argue that this has deleterious rather than salutary consequences: that numbing people to the practice of killing will inhibit recognition of human suffering, which in turn can inhibit their healing from war trauma.

6 Performative utterances are speech acts that do not simply or passively describe a given reality, but that change the social reality they describe. Austin, *How to Do Things with Words*; Searle, "How Performatives Work."

7 Comaroff and Comaroff, in "Ethnography on an Awkward Scale," use the phrase "animating vernaculars" to discuss what they call the necessarily "awkward scale" of ethnography in the current neoliberal era; the phrase describes the social and anthropological salience of representational themes and textual objects surfacing in many locales simultaneously. It is important to explore the meanings of such textual or representational objects that are locally situated while mapping iterations of those representations across diverse spaces and localities.

8 Deresiewicz, "An Empty Regard."

9 Gardiner, "In the Shadow of Service," 74.

Conclusion

1 Holland et al., *Identity and Agency in Cultural Worlds*.

2 "Characteristics of Student Veterans," U.S. Department of Veterans Affairs, April 22, 2014, http://www.mentalhealth.va.gov/studentveteran/docs/ed_todaysStudentVets.html.

3 "Characteristics of Student Veterans."

4　boyd and Crawford, "Critical Questions for Big Data."

5　U.S. Department of Veterans Affairs, Benefits Administration Report, states that during FY 2015 there were 1,016,664 beneficiaries of GI Bill education benefits, including veterans, active military members, reservists, eligible dependents. Seventy-seven percent of those beneficiaries were enrolled in community colleges and undergraduate degree programs. Source: VA Benefits Administration Report, http://www.benefits.va.gov/REPORTS/abr/ABR-Education-FY15–12122016.pdf.

6　For Budweiser, Zillow, Plenty of Fish and True.com, and Iams respectively.

7　All three have continued their educations at prestigious research universities. Mack earned his masters' degree, and Brandon is expected to complete his PhD in May 2017, and Connor is on track to receive his doctorate.

8　This program's acronym—VITAL—offers yet another example of the performative power of naming practices as a method of instilling the ideology of military superiority, wherein a program of student support services discursively invokes a population that is decisively important, indispensable, crucially significant, and necessarily integral.

9　See VITAL website at: http://www.mentalhealth.va.gov/studentveteran/vital_education .asp#sthash.grdBbWO1.dpuf.

10　The Vet Center program is a community-based counseling component of the VA dedicated to combat veterans. Vet Centers are located and operate outside of the VA hospital system and are based on a peer treatment model developed by psychiatrist Robert Jay Lifton for work with traumatized Vietnam veterans. Some Vet Centers employ civilian staff, but the primary therapists are (trained and credentialed) former combat veterans.

Bibliography

Abu-Lughod, Lila. "Do Muslim Women Really Need Saving? Anthropological Reflections on Cultural Relativism and Its Others." *American Anthropologist* 104, no. 3 (September 2002): 783–90.

———. *Writing Women's Worlds: Bedouin Stories.* Berkeley: University of California Press, 2008.

Acker, Joan. "Hierarchies, Jobs, and Bodies: A Theory of Gendered Organizations." *Gender and Society* 4, no. 2 (1990): 139–58.

Ackerman, R., and D. DiRamio, eds. "Creating a Veteran-Friendly Campus: Strategies for Transition and Success." Special issue, *New Directions for Student Services*, no. 126 (Summer 2009).

Ackerman, R., D. DiRamio, and R. L. Garza Mitchell. "Transitions: Combat Veterans as College Students." *New Directions for Student Services*, no. 126 (Summer 2009).

Althusser, Louis. "Ideology and Ideological State Apparatus." In *Essays on Ideology.* London: Verso, 1984.

Altman, Howard. "Military Suicide Rates Surge." *Tampa Tribune*, October 10, 2010.

Altschuler, Glenn C., and Stuart M. Blumin. *The GI Bill: A New Deal for Veterans.* New York: Oxford University Press, 2009.

American Council on Education. *Serving Those Who Serve: Higher Education and America's Veterans* (Issue Brief). Washington, DC: Clark and Coyner, 2008. http://www.acenet .edu/news-room/Pages/Georgetown-Summit.aspx.

American Psychiatric Association. *Diagnostic and Statistical Manual of Mental Disorders*, 4th ed. Washington, DC: APA, 2000.

Anderson, Benedict. *Imagined Communities: Reflections on the Origin and Spread of Nationalism.* London: Verso, 1983.

Apple, Michael, and N. King. "What Do Schools Teach?" In *The Hidden Curriculum and Moral Education*, edited by Henry Giroux and David Purpel, 82–99. Berkeley, CA: McCutchan, 1983.

Appy, Christian G. *Working Class War.* Chapel Hill: University of North Carolina Press, 1993.

Armstrong, Keith, S. Best, and P. Domenici. *Courage after Fire: Coping Strategies for Troops Returning from Iraq and Afghanistan and Their Families.* Berkeley, CA: Ulysses, 2006.

Artexaga, Begonia. "Engendering Violence: Strip-Searching of Women in Northern Ireland." In *History in Person: Enduring Struggles, Contentious Practice, Intimate Identities.* Santa Fe, NM: School of American Research Press, 2001.

Asch, Beth J. *Attracting College-Bound Youth into the Military: Toward the Development of New Recruiting Policy Options.* Santa Monica, CA: Rand, 1999.

Asch, Beth J., Paul Heaton, and Bogdan Savych. *Recruiting Minorities: What Explains Recent Trends in the Army and Navy?* Santa Monica, CA: Rand, 2009.

Austin, J. L. *How to Do Things with Words: The William James Lectures at Harvard University in 1955.* London: Oxford University Press, 1962.

Axelrod, Alan. *America's Wars.* New York: John Wiley & Sons, 2002.

Bacevich, Andrew J. *The New American Militarism.* Oxford: Oxford University Press, 2005.

Bady, Aaron. "Roosevelt's Manliness and Civilization." Zunguzungu, January 20, 2010. https://zunguzungu.wordpress.com/2010/01/20/roosevelts-manliness-and-civilization/.

Bakhtin, M. "Discourse in the Novel." In *The Dialogic Imagination*, edited by Michael Holquist and Vadim Liapunov. Austin: University of Texas Press, 1981.

———. "Heteroglossia." In *The Bakhtin Reader*, edited by Pam Morris, 73–80. London: Arnold, 1994.

Barthes, Roland. *Mythologies.* Translated by Annette Lavers. Paris: Les Lettres nouvelles, 1957.

Bass, Margaret M., Maria M. Llabre, and Catherine A. Duchowny. "The Effect of Therapeutic Horseback Riding on Social Functioning in Children with Autism." *Journal of Autism and Developmental Disorders* 39, no. 9 (Sept. 2009): 1261–68.

Becker, A., and G. W. Schulz. "Cops Ready for War." Center for Investigative Reporting, December 21, 2011. www.cironline.org, http://www.thedailybeast.com/articles/2011/12/20/local-cops-ready-for-war-with-homeland-security-funded-military-weapons.html.

Bederman, Gail. *Manliness and Civilization: A Cultural History of Gender and Race in the United States, 1880–1917.* Chicago: University of Chicago Press, 1995.

Belkin, Aaron. *Bring Me Men: Military Masculinity and the Benign Facade of American Empire, 1898–2001.* Oxford: Oxford University Press, 2012.

Benda, William, Nancy H. McGibbon, and Kathryn L. Grant. (2004.) "Improvements in Muscle Symmetry in Children with Cerebral Palsy After Equine-Assisted Therapy (Hippotherapy)." *The Journal of Alternative and Complementary Medicine* 9, no. 6 (July 2004): 817–25. DOI:10.1089/107555303771952163.

Benedict, Helen. *The Lonely Soldier: The Private War of Women Serving in Iraq.* Boston: Beacon, 2009.

Bennett, Eric. "How Iowa Flattened Literature." *Chronicle of Higher Education*, February 10, 2014.

Bennett, Michael J. *When Dreams Came True: The GI Bill and the Making of Modern America.* Washington, DC: Brassey's International Defense, 1999.

Berdahl, Daphne. "Voices at the Wall: Discourses of Self, History and National Identity at the Vietnam Veterans Memorial." *History and Memory* 6, no. 2 (1994): 88–118.

Beukenhorst, H. B. "Whose Vietnam?—'Lessons Learned' and the Dynamics of Memory in American Foreign Policy after the Vietnam War." PhD diss., University of Amsterdam, 2012.

Billig, Michael. *Banal Nationalism*. London: Sage, 1995.

———. "Reflections on a Critical Engagement with *Banal Nationalism*—Reply to Skey." *Sociological Review* 57, no. 2 (2009): 347–52.

Binder, Amy J., and Kate Wood. *Becoming Right: How Campuses Shape Young Conservatives*. Princeton, NJ: Princeton University Press, 2014.

Blatt, Martin, and David R. Roediger, eds. *The Meaning of Slavery in the North*. New York: Garland, 1998.

Bogart, Brian. *Unwarranted Influence: Chronicling the Rise of US Government Dependence on Conflict*. London: Institute for Policy Research and Development, 2007.

Boudreau, Tyler E. *Packing Inferno: The Unmaking of a Marine*. Port Townsend, WA: Feral House, 2008.

Bouffard, Leana A. "The Military as a Bridging Environment in Criminal Careers: Differential Outcomes of the Military Experience." *Armed Forces and Society* 31 (2005): 273.

Boulton, Mark. "A Price on Freedom: The Problems and Promise of the Vietnam Era G.I. Bills." PhD diss., University of Tennessee, 2005.

Bourdieu, Pierre. *Distinction: A Social Critique of the Judgement of Taste*. Cambridge, MA: Harvard University Press, 1984.

———. *In Other Words: Essays towards a Reflexive Sociology*. Stanford, CA: Stanford University Press, 1987.

———. *The Logic of Practice*. Translated by Richard Nice. Stanford, CA: Stanford University Press, 1980.

———. *Outline of a Theory of Practice*. New York: Cambridge University Press, 1977.

———. *Practical Reason: On the Theory of Action*. Stanford, CA: Stanford University Press, 1998.

Bourdieu, Pierre, and J.-C. Passeron. *Reproduction in Education, Society and Culture*. London: Sage, 1990.

boyd, danah, and Kate Crawford. "Critical Questions for Big Data." *Information, Communication and Society* 15, no. 5 (2012): 662–79. DOI:10.1080/1369118X.2012.678878.

Brecht, B. *Brecht on Theater*. Translated by John Willett. New York: Hill and Wang, 1964.

Briggs, Bill. "Stray Anti-military Vibes Reverberate as Thousands of Veterans Head to College." MSNBC *News Report*, October 17, 2012. http://usnews.nbcnews.com/_news /2012/10/17/14469487-stray-anti-military-vibesreverberate-as-thousands-of-veterans -head-to-college?lite.

Brint, Steven. "Few Remaining Dreams: Community Colleges since 1985." *Annals of the American Academy of Political and Social Science* 586 (2003): 16.

Brison, Susan J. "Trauma Narratives and the Re-making of the Self." In *Acts of Memory: Cultural Recall in the Present*, edited by M. Bal, J. Crewe, and L. Spitzer, 39–54. Hanover, NH: University Press of New England, 1999.

Brokaw, Tom. *The Greatest Generation*. New York: Random House, 1998.

Brown, Wendy. *Edgework: Critical Essays on Knowledge and Politics*. Princeton, NJ: Princeton University Press, 2005.

———. *States of Injury*. Princeton, NJ: Princeton University Press, 1995.

Bryant, Richard R., V. A. Samaranayake, and Allen Wilhite. "The Effect of Military Service on the Subsequent Civilian Wage of the Post-Vietnam Veteran." *Quarterly Review of Economics and Finance* 33, no. 1 (1993): 15–31.

Bunting, Josiah, III. "Class Warfare." *American Scholar* 74, no. 1 (2005).

Burke, Kenneth. "Doing and Saying: Thoughts on Myth, Cult and Archetype." *Salmagundi* 7 (1971): 100–119.

Byman, Daniel. "Veterans and Colleges Have a Lot to Offer Each Other." *Chronicle of Higher Education* 54, no. 16 (2007): B5.

Cahill, Charlotte. "Fighting the Vietnam Syndrome: The Construction of a Conservative Veterans Politics, 1966–1984." PhD diss., Northwestern University, 2008. ProQuest (UMI 3336524).

Cantrell, Bridget C., and C. Dean. *Once a Warrior: Wired for Life*. Seattle: WordSmith, 2005.

Carmichael, Virginia. *Framing History: The Rosenberg Story and the Cold War*. Minneapolis: University of Minnesota Press, 1990.

Carroll, Ward. "Are Military Hate Groups on the Rise?" Military.com, September 12, 2012. http://www.military.com/daily-news/2012/09/12/hate-groups-and-the-military.html.

Cate, C. A. *Million Records Project: Research from Student Veterans of America*. Washington, DC: Student Veterans of America, 2014.

Chaiklin, Seth, and Jean Lave. *Understanding Practice: Perspectives on Activity and Context*. Cambridge: Cambridge University Press, 2002.

Clark, Susan G. and Sandra Coyner. "From Access To Accommodation: Serving America's War Veterans in Post-Secondary Education." Paper delivered at The Clute Institute International Academic Conferences Maui, Hawaii, 2013. http://www.cluteinstitute.com/proceedings.html.

Coben, Diana. "Metaphors for an Educative Politics." In *Gramsci and Education*, edited by Carmel Borg, Joseph A. Buttigieg, and Peter Mayo, 263–90. New York: Rowman and Littlefield, 2002.

———. *Radical Heroes: Gramsci, Freire and the Politics of Adult Education*. New York: Garland/Taylor and Francis, 1998.

Cock, Jacklyn. "Rethinking Militarism in Post-Apartheid South Africa." Crisis States Research Centre working papers series 1, 43. London: London School of Economics and Political Science, 2004. http://eprints.lse.ac.uk/28221/.

Cohen, A. P. *The Symbolic Construction of Community*. London: Tavistock, 1985.

Comaroff, Jean, and John Comaroff. "Ethnography on an Awkward Scale: Postcolonial Anthropology and the Violence of Abstraction." *Ethnography* 4, no. 2 (2003): 147–79.

Connell, R. W. *Masculinities*. Berkeley: University of California Press, 1995.

Cooley, Charles Horton. *Human Nature and the Social Order*, rev. ed. New York: Charles Scribner's Sons, 1922.

Crawford, N. C. "War-Related Death, Injury, and Displacement in Afghanistan and Pakistan 2001–2014." Costs of War, Watson Institute for International Studies, Brown University, May 22, 2015. http://watson.brown.edu.

Cunningham, Finian. "A Sign of Empire Pathology." *Global Research Bulletin*, January 29, 2010.

Davenport, C. "The Mission." *Washington Post*, August 8, 2004, W12.

Dean, E. T. "The Myth of the Troubled and Scorned Vietnam Veteran." *Journal of American Studies* 26, no. 1 (1992): 59–72.

de Certeau, M. *The Practice of Everyday Life*. Berkeley: University of California Press, 1984.

Demirović, Alex. "Foucault, Gramsci and Critical Theory—Remarks on Their Relationship." Cultural Political Economy Research Centre, Lancaster University. Accessed October 16, 2010. http://www.lancaster.ac.uk/cperc/docs/CR-Demirovic-Foucault.pdf.

Deresiewicz, William. "An Empty Regard." *New York Times Sunday Review*, August 20, 2011.

Derrida, J. *On Cosmopolitanism and Forgiveness*. London: Routledge, 2001.

DiRamio, David, R. Ackerman, and R. L. Mitchell. "From Combat to Campus: Voices of Student/Veterans." *NASPA Journal* 47, no. 1 (2008): 73–102.

Dowd, Nancy. *The Man Question: Male Subordination and Privilege*. New York: NYU Press, 2010.

Downs, Donald, and Ilia Murtazashvili. *Arms and the University: Military Presence and the Civic Education of Non-military Students*. Cambridge: Cambridge University Press, 2012.

Dreier, Ole. "Research in Social Practice." In *Psychotherapy in Everyday Life*. New York: Cambridge University Press, 2008.

DuBois, Barbara. "Passionate Scholarship: Notes on Values, Knowing and Method in Feminist Social Sciences." In *Theories of Women's Studies*, edited by Gloria Bowles and Renate Duelli Klein, 105–17. London: Routledge and Kegan Paul, 1983.

Duehren, Andrew M., and Emma K. Talkoff. "Boots on the Ground: ROTC at Harvard." *Harvard Crimson*, February 26, 2015.

Durkheim, Emile. *The Division of Labor in Society*. Translated by W. D. Halls. 1893. Reprint, New York: Free Press, 1997.

Dyson, A. H., and C. Genishi. *On the Case: Approaches to Language and Literacy Research*. New York: Teachers College Press, 2005.

Elbogen, Eric B., Sara Fuller, Sally C. Johnson, Stephanie Brooks, Patricia Kinneer, Patrick S. Calhoun, and Jean C. Beckham. "Improving Risk Assessment of Violence among Military Veterans: An Evidence-Based Approach for Clinical Decision-Making." *Clinical Psychology Review* 30 (2010): 595–607.

Engestrom, Yuri. "Learning by Expanding: Ten Years After." In *Lernen durch Expansion* [Learning by expanding]. Translated by Falk Seeger, 1–16. Reihe Internationale Studien zur Tatigkeitstheorie, vol. 5. Marburg: BdWi-Verlag, 1999.

———. "The Zone of Proximal Development as the Basic Category of Expansive Research." In *Learning by Expanding*. Helsinki: Orienta-Konsultit, 1987.

Enloe, C. *Bananas, Beaches and Bases*. Berkeley: University of California Press, 1990.

———. *The Curious Feminist*. Berkeley: University of California Press, 2004.

———. *Does Khaki Become You?* London: South End, 1983.

———. *Globalization and Militarism: Feminists Make the Link*. Lanham, MD: Rowman and Littlefield, 2007.

———. *Maneuvers: The International Politics of Militarizing Women's Lives*. Berkeley: University of California Press, 2000.

Erikson, Kai T. *Everything in Its Path: Destruction of Community in the Buffalo Creek Flood*. New York: Simon and Schuster, 1976.

Fain, Paul. "Follow the Money." *Inside Higher Education*, July 26, 2013.

Feder, Jodi. *Military Provisions under the No Child Left Behind Act*. Washington, DC: Congressional Research Service, January 29, 2009.

Feldman, Allen. "The Actuarial Gaze: From 9/11 to Abu Ghraib." *Cultural Studies* 19, no. 2 (2005).

———. *Formations of Violence: The Narrative of the Body and Political Terror in Northern Ireland*. Chicago: University of Chicago Press, 1997.

Feldman, Ilana. "Difficult Distinctions: Refugee Law, Humanitarian Practice, and Political Identification in Gaza." *Cultural Anthropology* 22, no. 1 (2007): 129–69.

Ford, Deborah, Pamela Northrup, and Lusharon Wiley. "Connections, Partnerships, Opportunities, and Programs to Enhance Success for Military Students." In *New Directions for Student Services*, no. 126 (June 2009): 61–69.

Foster, Don. "The Truth and Reconciliation Commission and Understanding Perpetrators." *South African Journal of Psychology* 30, no.1 (2000): 2–9.

Foucault, Michel. *The Archaeology of Knowledge and the Discourse on Language*. Translated by A. M. Sheridan-Smith. New York: Vintage, 1972.

———. *Discipline and Punish*. Translated by A. Sheridan. New York: Vintage, 1995.

———. *Power/Knowledge: Selected Interviews and Other Writings, 1972–1977*. New York: Pantheon, 1980.

Franke, Linda Bird. "Women in the Military." In *America's Military Today: Challenges for the Armed Forces in a Time of War*, by Tod Ensign. New York: New Press, 2006.

Franke, Volker C. "Duty, Honor, Country: The Social Identity of West Point Cadets." *Armed Forces and Society* 26 (2000): 175–202.

Franklin, H. Bruce. *Vietnam and Other American Fantasies*. Amherst: University of Massachusetts Press, 2001.

Frantz, Steven. "Developing a Comprehensive State-wide Veterans Re-entry Education Program." *Ijournal (Insight into Student Services)*, no. 28 (Spring 2010).

Freid, Marc. "Grieving for a Lost Home: Psychological Costs of Relocation." In *Urban Renewal: The Record and the Controversy*, edited by James Q. Wilson. Cambridge, MA: MIT Press, 1966.

Frydl, Kathleen. *The GI Bill*. Cambridge, MA: Cambridge University Press, 2009.

Gackenbach, Jayne, Mycah Darlington, Mary-Lynn Ferguseon, Arielle Boyes. "Video Game Play as Nightmare Protection: A Replication and Extension." *Dreaming*, 23, no. 2 (2013): 97–111. DOI:10.1037/a0032455.

Gardiner, M., and M. M. Bell. *Bakhtin and the Human Sciences: No Last Words*. Thousand Oaks, CA: Sage, 1998.

Gardiner, Steven. L. "In the Shadow of Service: Veteran Masculinity and Civil–Military Disjuncture in the United States." *North American Dialogues* 16, no. 2 (2013): 69–79.

———. "The Warrior Ethos: Discourse and Gender in the United States Army since 9/11." *Journal of War and Culture Studies* 5, no. 3 (2012): 371–83. DOI:10.1386/jwcs.5.3.371_1.

———. "Heroic Masochism: Masculine Privilege and the Uses of Pain." Library of Social Science Working Paper, 2014. https://s3.libraryofsocialscience.com/pdf/Gardiner-HeroicMasochism.pdf.

Gee, James P. "Identity as an Analytic Lens for Research in Education." *Review of Research in Education* 25 (2001): 99–125.

Gellner, E. *Nations and Nationalism.* Ithaca, NY: Cornell University Press, 1983.

Glantz, Aaron. "The Truth about Veteran Suicides." *Foreign Policy in Focus*, May 8, 2008.

———. *The War Comes Home: Washington's Battle against America's Veterans.* Berkeley: University of California Press, 2010.

Goffman, Erving. *Asylums: Essays on the Social Situation of Mental Patients and Other Inmates.* New York: Doubleday, 1961.

———. *Stigma: Notes on the Management of Spoiled Identity.* Englewood Cliffs, NJ: Prentice-Hall, 1963.

González, Roberto J. *Militarizing Culture: Essays on the Warfare State.* Walnut Creek, CA: Left Coast, 2010.

Graham, Stephen. "Countergeographies." In *Cities under Siege: The New Military Urbanism.* London: Verso, 2010.

Gramsci, Antonio. *Selections from the Prison Notebooks of Antonio Gramsci.* Edited and translated by Q. Hoare and G. N. Smith. 1971. Reprint, New York: International, 2005.

Grandstaff, Mark. "Visions of New Men: The Heroic Soldier Narrative in American Advertisements during World War II." *Advertising and Society Review* 5, no. 2 (2004).

Grimmett, Richard F. "Instances of Use of United States Armed Forced Abroad, 1798–2009." Congressional Research Service (Jan. 27, 2010). http://www.au.af.mil/au/awc/awcgate/crs/rl32170.pdf

Grossman, D. *On Killing: The Psychological Cost of Learning to Kill in War and Society.* New York: Back Bay Dissertations, 2009.

Grossman, D., and G. DeGaetano. *Stop Teaching Our Kids to Kill: A Call to Action against TV, Movie and Video Game Violence.* New York: Crown, 1999.

Grubb, Norton, Norena Badway, and Denise Bell. "Community Colleges and the Equity Agenda: The Potential of Noncredit Education." *Annals of the American Academy of Political and Social Science* 586 (2003): 218–40.

Guffey, Mary Ellen. *Essentials of Business Communication*, 8th ed. Independence, KY: South-Western/Cengage Learning, 2010.

Guttman, Matthew, and C. Lutz. *Breaking Ranks: Iraq Veterans Speak Out against the War.* Berkeley: University of California Press, 2010.

Hall, Edward T. *Beyond Culture.* New York: Anchor Books/Doubleday, 1976.

Hall, Stuart. "Gramsci's Relevance for the Study of Race and Ethnicity." *Journal of Communication Inquiry* 10, no. 2 (1986): 5–27.

———. "Race, Articulation and Societies Structured in Dominance." In *Sociological Theories: Race and Colonialism.* Paris: UNESCO, 1980.

―――. "The Toad in the Garden: Thatcherism among the Theorists." In *Marxism and the Interpretation of Culture*, edited by C. Nelson and L. Grossberg. Urbana: University of Illinois Press, 1988.

Hampf, M. Michaela. "'Dykes' or 'Whores': Sexuality and the Women's Army Corps in the United States during World War II." *Women's Studies International Forum* 27 (2004): 13–30.

Haraway, Donna. *Simians, Cyborgs and Women: The Reinvention of Nature*. London: Free Association, 1991.

Hardy, D., and D. Purcell. "Growing Hesitancy over a Military Test." *Philadelphia Inquirer*, August 6, 2008.

Hart, Gillian. "Changing Concepts of Articulation: Political Stakes in South Africa Today." *Review of African Political Economy*, no. 111 (2007): 85–101.

―――. *Re-thinking the South African Crisis: Nationalism, Populism, Hegemony*. Scottsville, South Africa: University of KwaZulu-Natal Press, 2013.

Harvey, David. *A Brief History of Neoliberalism*. Oxford: Oxford University Press, 2005.

Hastings, Matt. "The Runaway General." *Rolling Stone*, June 25, 2010.

Hautzinger, Sarah, and Jean Scandlyn. *Beyond Post-Traumatic Stress: Homefront Struggles with the Wars on Terror*. Walnut Creek, CA: Left Coast Press, 2013.

Hedges, Chris. *War Is a Force That Gives Us Meaning*. New York: Anchor, 2003.

Herbert, Melissa. *Camouflage Isn't Only for Combat: Gender, Sexuality and Women in the Military*. New York: New York University Press, 1998.

Herrmann, Douglas, Charles Hopkins, Roland B. Wilson, and Bert Allen. *Educating Veterans in the 21st Century*. Douglas Herrmann, 2013.

Herrmann, Douglas, D. Raybeck, and R. Wilson. "College Is for Veterans, Too." *Chronicle of Higher Education*, November 21, 2008, A99.

Hobsbawm, E., and T. Ranger. *The Invention of Tradition*. Cambridge: Cambridge University Press, 1983.

Hoge, Charles W., Carl A. Castro, Stephen C. Messer, Dennis McGurk, Dave I. Cotting, and Robert L. Koffman. "Combat Duty in Iraq and Afghanistan: Mental Health Problems and Barriers to Care." *New England Journal of Medicine* 351, no. 1 (2004).

Holland, D., and Jean Lave. *History in Person: Enduring Struggles, Contentious Practice, Intimate Identities*. Santa Fe, NM: School of American Research Press, 2001.

Holland, D., and Debra Skinner. "From Women's Suffering to Women's Politics." In *History in Person: Enduring Struggles, Contentious Practice, Intimate Identities*. Santa Fe, NM: School of American Research Press, 2001.

Holland, D., D. Skinner, W. Lachiotte Jr., and C. Cain. *Identity and Agency in Cultural Worlds*. Cambridge, MA: Harvard University Press, 2003.

Holloway, Kinsey. "Understanding Reentry of the Modern-Day Student-Veteran through Vietnam-Era Theory." *Colorado State University Journal of Student Affairs* 18 (2009): 11–17.

Holm, J. *Women in the Military: An Unfinished Revolution*. New York: Ballantine, 1992.

Horses & Humans Research Foundation. "Facts: Veterans Rehabilitation and Equine Assisted Activities/Therapies" http://www.horsesandhumans.org/Veterans_Fact_Sheet_HHRF.pdf.

Hopkins, Charles, Douglas Herrmann, Roland B. Wilson, Bert Allen, and Lynn Malley, eds. *Improving College Education for Veterans.* Booksurge, 2010.

Humes, Edward. *Over Here: How the GI Bill Transformed the American Dream.* Orlando, FL: Harcourt, 2006.

Ignatiev, Noel. *How the Irish Became White.* New York: Routledge, 1995.

Irish, H. Allen. "A 'Peace Corps with Guns': Can the Military Be a Tool of Development?" In *The Interagency and Counterinsurgency Warfare: Stability, Security, Transition, and Reconstruction Roles,* edited by Joseph R. Cerami and Jay W. Boggs. Carlisle, PA: Strategic Studies Institute, U.S. Army War College, 2007.

Jaffee, Alexandra. "The Limits of Detachment: A Non-ethnography of the Military." *National Association for the Practice of Anthropology Bulletin* 16, no. 1 (1995): 36–47.

Janowitz, Morris. "The Social Demography of the All-Volunteer Armed Force." *Annals of the American Academy of Political and Social Science* 406, no. 1 (1973): 86–93.

Janowitz, Morris, and Charles Moskos. "Racial Composition in the All-Volunteer Force." *Armed Forces and Society* 1, no. 1 (November 1974).

Jelinek, Pauline. "Report Estimates Half of Vets on GI Bill Graduate." Associated Press, March 24, 2014.

Jordan, Bryant. "Heckled Vet Bucks Columbia Critics." Military.com, February 25, 2011.

Jorgensen, Joseph G., and Eric R. Wolf. "A Special Supplement: Anthropology on the Warpath in Thailand." *New York Review of Books,* November 19, 1970.

Jungk, Robert. *Brighter Than a Thousand Suns: A Personal History of the Atomic Scientists.* San Diego, CA: Harcourt Brace Jovanovich, 1958.

Kane, T. "The Best and the Brightest." *American Legion,* June 2007.

Karni, Annie. "Hero's Unwelcome." *New York Post,* February 20, 2011.

Katznelson, Ira. *When Affirmative Action Was White: An Untold Story of Racial Inequality in Twentieth-Century America.* New York: Norton, 2005.

Kimball, Jeffrey. "The Enduring Paradigm of the 'Lost Cause': Defeat in Vietnam, the Stab-in-the-Back Legend, and the Construction of a Myth." In *Defeat and Memory: Cultural Histories of Military Defeat in the Modern Era,* edited by Jenny Macleod, 233–50. Basingstoke, UK: Palgrave Macmillan, 2008.

Kirk, Gwin, and M. Okazawa-Rey. *Women's Lives: Multicultural Perspectives,* 5th ed. New York: McGraw-Hill, 2010.

Kirkwood, Lauren. "More Veterans Taking Advantage of Post-9/11 GI Bill." McClatchy News Service, March 14, 2014. http://www.mcclatchydc.com/.

Klein, Gerald, Margaret Salter, Gary Riccio, and Randall Sullivan. *Enhancing Warrior Ethos in Soldier Training: The Teamwork Development Course.* Wexford Group International, Infantry Forces Research Unit. Arlington, VA: U.S. Army Research Institute for the Behavioral and Social Sciences, 2006.

Klein, Joe. "The New Greatest Generation: How Young War Veterans Are Redefining Leadership at Home." *Time,* August 29, 2011, 26–34.

Kleykamp, Meredith A. "College, Jobs, or the Military? Enlistment during a Time of War." *Social Science Quarterly* 87, no. 2 (2006).

———."Military Service and Minority Opportunity." PhD diss., Princeton University, 2007.

Kraines, S. J. "The Veteran and Postwar Education." *Journal of Higher Education* 16, no. 6 (June 1945): 290–98. http://www.jstor.org/stable/1976944.

Koca, Tuba Tulay and Hilmi Ataseven. "What is Hippotherapy? The Indication and Effectiveness of Hippotherapy." *Northern Clinics of Istanbul* 2, no. 3 (2015): 247–52. DOI: 10.14744/nci.2016.71601.

Kraska, Peter B. *Militarizing the American Criminal Justice System: The Changing Roles of the Armed Forces and the Police.* Boston: Northeastern University Press, 2001.

Kupo, V. L. "Creating a Veteran-Friendly Campus." Media Review. *Journal of Student Affairs Research and Practice* 47, no. 3 (2010): 400–403. DOI:10.2202/1949–6605.6166.

Lagotte, Brian W. "Gunning for School Space: Student Activists, the Military, and Education Policy." In *Be the Change: Teacher, Activist, Global Citizen*, edited by R. Verma. New York: Peter Lang, 2010.

———. "Selling the Services: Military Recruiting and Education Policy." In *Children's Human Rights and Public Schooling in the United States*, edited by J. Hall. Rotterdam, Netherlands: Sense, 2013.

———."Turf Wars: School Administrators and Military Recruiting." *Educational Policy*, November 2012, 1–31.

Lagotte, Brian W., and M. W. Apple. "Neoliberalism, Militarization, and Education Reform." In *Critical Issues in Peace and Education*, edited by P. Trifonas and B. Wright. London: Routledge, 2010.

Lande, Brian. "Breathing Like a Soldier: Culture Incarnate." *Sociological Review* 5, suppl. 1 (2007): 95–108.

Lave, Jean. "The Practice of Learning." In *Understanding Practice: Perspectives on Activity and Context*, edited by Seth Chaiklin and Jean Lave. Cambridge: Cambridge University Press, 2002.

Lave, Jean, and E. Wenger. *Situated Learning: Legitimate Peripheral Participation.* Cambridge: Cambridge University Press, 1991.

Lederman, D. (2008). "Preparing for an Influx." *Inside Higher Education*, June 6, 2008. http://www.insidehighered.com:80/news/2008/06/06/vets.

———. "What Makes a College 'Military Friendly'?" *Inside Higher Education*, February 22, 2008.

Lembcke, J. *Hanoi Jane: War, Sex, and Fantasies of Betrayal.* Amherst, MA: The University of Massachusetts Press. 2010.

———. *The Spitting Image: Myth, Memory and the Legacy of Vietnam.* New York: New York University Press, 1998.

Lepper, M. R., D. Greene, and R. E. Nisbett. "Undermining Children's Intrinsic Interest with Extrinsic Reward: A Test of the 'Overjustification' Hypothesis." *Journal of Personality and Social Psychology* 28 (1973): 129–37.

Lewis, C., and E. B. Moje. "Sociocultural Perspectives Meet Critical Theory: Producing Knowledge through Multiple Frameworks." *International Journal of Learning* 10 (2004).

Lewis, W. S. "Serving Returning Vets." *Student Affairs Leader* 36, no. 12 (2008): 4–5.

Lifton, Robert Jay. *Home from the War: Vietnam Veterans—Neither Victims nor Executioners.* New York: Simon and Schuster, 1973.

Lighthall, Alison. "Ten Things You Should Know About Today's Student Veteran." *Thought & Action, NEA Higher Education Journal* (Fall 2012). https://www.ndsu.edu/fileadmin/valor/docs/10-things-student-veterans.pdf.

Lipka, Sara. "Student Veterans: A National Survey Exploring Psychological Symptoms and Suicide Risk." Washington, DC: National Center of Veterans Studies, 2011.

Litz, Brett T., Nathan Stein, Eileen Delaney, Leslie Lebowitz, William P. Nash, Shira Maguen. "Moral Injury and Moral Repair in War Veterans: A Preliminary Model and Intervention Strategy." *Clinical Psychology Review* 29 (2009): 695–706.

Loeb, Paul R. *Generation at the Crossroads: Apathy and Action on the American Campus.* New Brunswick, NJ: Rutgers University Press, 1994.

Lokken, Jayne M., Donald S. Pfeffer, James McAuley, and Christopher Strong. "A Strategic Approach to Creating Veteran-Friendly Campuses." *New Directions for Student Services*, no. 126 (June 2009): 45–54.

Lutz, Amy (2008). "Who Joins the Military?: A Look at Race, Class and Immigration Status." *Journal of Political and Military Sociology* 36 (2) 167–88.

Lutz, Catherine. "Empire Is in the Details." *American Ethnologist* 33 (2006): 593–611.

———. "Living Room Terrorists." *Women's Review of Books* 21, no. 5 (2004): 17–18.

———. "Making War at Home in the United States: Militarization and the Current Crisis." *American Anthropologist* 104, no. 3 (Sept. 2002): 723–35.

Lykes, M. Brinton. "Activist Participatory Research among the Maya of Guatemala: Constructing Meanings from Situated Knowledge." *Journal of Social Issues* 53, no. 4 (1997): 725–46.

Madriaga, Manuel. "The Star-Spangled Banner, US Military Veterans and the Category of Whiteness." Paper presented at Flying the Flag: Critical Perspectives on Symbolism and Identity, Cultural Complexity in the New Norway, University of Oslo, November 24–25, 2005.

Maguen, Shira, and Brett Litz. "Moral Injury in Veterans of War." *PTSD Research Quarterly* 23, no. 1 (2012). http://www.ptsd.va.gov/.

MacCallum, Mike. "Diversisty in Transition." *IJournal Insight into student services*, No. 28 (Spring 2010). http://.ijournal.us.

Maniaty, Tony. "From Vietnam to Iraq: Negative Trends in Television War Reporting." *Pacific Journalism Review* 14, no. 2 (2008): 89–101.

Mann, Michael. *Incoherent Empire.* London: Verso, 2003.

———. "The Roots and Contradictions of Modern Militarism." *New Left Review* I/162 (March–April 1987).

Mariscal, Jorge. "Chicano and Chicana Experiences of the War." In *Next Stop Vietnam: California and the Nation Transformed*, edited by Marcia Eymann and Charles Wollenberg. Berkeley: University of California Press, 2004.

———. "The Poverty Draft: Do Military Recruiters Disproportionately Target Communities of Color and the Poor?" *Sojourner's Magazine*, June 2007.

Marlantes, K. *What It Is Like to Go to War.* New York: Atlantic Monthly Press, 2011.

Marx, Karl, and Frederick Engels. "The German Ideology." In *The Marx-Engels Reader*, 2nd ed., edited by R. Tucker. 1846. Reprint, New York: Norton, 1978.

Mazzucato, Mariana. *The Entrepreneurial State.* London: Demos. 2011.

Mendible, Myra. "Post Vietnam Syndrome: National Identity, War, and the Politics of Humiliation." *Radical Psychology* 7 (2008).

Merryfinch, Lesley. "Militarization/Civilization." In *Loaded Questions: Women in the Military*, edited by W. Chapkis, 9–13. Washington, DC: Transnational Institute, 1981.

Mettler, Suzanne. *Soldiers to Citizens: The GI Bill and the Making of the Greatest Generation.* New York: Oxford University Press, 2000.

Moje, Elizabeth Birr, and Cynthia Lewis. "Examining Opportunities to Learn Literacy: The Role of Critical Sociocultural Literacy Research." In *Reframing Sociocultural Literacy Research: Identity, Agency, and Power*, edited by Cynthia Lewis, Patricia Enciso, and Elizabeth Birr Moje. Malwah, NJ: Lawrence Erlbaum, 2007.

Moore, Ellen. "Art, Politics and Education: Ideological Becoming of Solidarity Activists." Unpublished manuscript, 2009.

Morson, Gary S. "The Process of Ideological Becoming." In *Bakhtinian Perspectives on Language, Literacy, and Learning*, edited by Arnetha F. Ball and Sarah Warshauer Freedman. Cambridge: Cambridge University Press, 2004.

Moskos, C. C. "The Military." *Annual Review of Sociology* 2 (1976): 55–77.

Moskos, C. C., and Frank R. Wood. *The Military: More Yhan Just a Job?* McLean, VA: Pergamon-Brassey's International Defense, 1988.

Moskos, C. C., and John Sibley Butler. *All That We Can Be: Black Leadership and Racial Integration the Army Way.* New York: Basic Books, 1997.

Moskos, C. C., John Allen Williams, and David R. Segal. *The Postmodern Military: Armed Forces after the Cold War.* New York: Oxford University Press, 2000.

Mosse, G. L. *Fallen Soldiers: Nationalism and Sexuality: Middle Class Morality and Sexual Norms in Modern Europe.* Madison: University of Wisconsin Press, 1990.

———. *The Image of Man: The Creation of Modern Masculinity.* New York: Oxford University Press, 1996.

Nader, Laura. "Controlling Processes: Tracing the Dynamic Components of Power." Sidney Mintz Lecture. *Current Anthropology* 38, no. 5 (December 1997): 711–37.

Nagel, Joann. "Masculinity and Nationalism: Gender and Sexuality in the Making of Nations." *Ethnic and Racial Studies* 21, no. 2 (1998).

National Priorities Project "Military Recruitment 2010." https://www.nationalpriorities.org/analysis/2011/military-recruitment-2010/.

Nelson, T. S. *For Love of Country: Confronting Rape and Sexual Harassment in the U.S. Military.* Binghamton, NY: Haworth, 2002.

Nietzsche, F. *On the Genealogy of Morality.* 1887. Reprint, New York: Cambridge University Press, 2006.

Nieva, Veronica F., Susan Berkowitz, and Wayne Hintze. *Career Decision-Making: Youth Futures in Context.* Westat Institute Report no. AO89363, 1999.

Noble, David F. *America by Design: Science, Technology and the Rise of Corporate Capitalism.* New York: Knopf, 1977.

———. *Forces of Production: A Social History of Industrial Automation.* New York: Knopf, 1984.

O'Brien, Tim. *The Things They Carried.* Boston: Mariner, 2009.

Oliver, Kelly. *Women as Weapons of War: Iraq, Sex and the Media*. New York: Columbia University Press, 2007.

Olshansky, Norman, and Linda Lysakowsky. *You and Your Nonprofit: Practical Advice and Tips from the CharityChannel Professional Community*. Rancho Santa Margarita, CA: CharityChannel Press, 2011.

Pérez, Gina M. *Citizen, Student, Soldier: Latino/a Youth, JROTC, and the American Dream*. New York: New York University Press, 2015.

Persky, K. R., and D. E. Oliver. "Veterans Coming Home to the Community College: Linking Research to Practice." *Community College Journal of Research and Practice* 35 (2011): 111–20.

Petrovic, Kara. "Anti-Military Sentiments on an Elite American College Campus." VFW *Magazine*, September 2005.

Pew Research Center. The Military-Civilian Gap: War and Sacrifice in the Post-9/11 Era. Washington: Pew Research Center, 2011. http://www.pewsocialtrends.org/2011/10/05/war-and-sacrifice-in-the-post-911-era/.

Pratt, M. L. "Arts of the Contact Zone." *Profession*, 1991, 33–40.

Price, David H. *Anthropological Intelligence: The Deployment and Neglect of Anthropology in the Second World War*. Durham, NC: Duke University Press, 2008.

———. "Cloak and Trowel: Should Archaeologists Double as Spies?" *Archaeology*, September 2003, 30–35.

———. *Weaponizing Anthropology: Social Science in the Service of the Militarized State*. Oakland, CA: AK Press, 2011.

Ravitch, Diane. *The Troubled Crusade: American Education 1945–1980*. New York: Basic Books, 1983.

Redden, Elizabeth. "Campuses as Vet-Friendly Zones." *Inside Higher Education*, June 5, 2009.

Reeves, R. "The New American Segregation: The Military." Truthdig, May 31, 2011. http://www.truthdig.com/report/item/the_new_american_segregation_the_military_20110531.

Robbins, M. S. *Against the Vietnam War: Writings by Activists*. Syracuse, NY: Syracuse University Press, 1999.

Roediger, David. *The Wages of Whiteness: Race and the Making of the American Working Class*. London: Verso, 1991.

Rose, Nikolas. *Powers of Freedom: Reframing Political Thought*. Cambridge: Cambridge University Press, 1999.

Roth-Douquet, Kathy and F. Schaeffer AWOL: *The Unexcused Absence of America's Upper Classes from Military Service—and How It Hurts Our Country*. New York: HarperCollins, 2006.

Roth, Sammy. "Students Surprised, Worried by National Media Coverage on ROTC." *Columbia Daily Spectator*, February 22, 2011.

Rowe, John Carlos. *The Cultural Politics of the New American Studies*. Open Humanities Press. Hosted by Michigan Publishing, a division of the University of Michigan Library, 2012. DOI: http://dx.doi.org/10.3998/ohp.10945585.0001.001

Rowe, S., J. V. Wertsch, and T. Y. Kosyaeva. "Linking Little Narratives to Big Ones: Narrative and Public Memory in History." *Culture and Psychology* 8 (2002): 96.

Sander, Libby. "Out of Uniform: At Half a Million and Counting, Veterans Cash In on Post-9/11 GI Bill." *Chronicle of Higher Education*, March 11, 2012.

Sasson-Levy, O. "Constructing Identities at the Margins: Masculinity and Citizenship in the Israeli Army." *Sociological Quarterly* 43, no. 3 (2002): 357–83.

Schwartz, B. "The Creation and Destruction of Value." *American Psychologist* 45 (1990): 7–15.

Scully, Diana, and Joesph Marolla. "Convicted Rapists' Vocabulary of Motives: Excuses and Justifications." *Social Problems* 31 (1984): 530–44.

Searle, John R. "How Performatives Work." *Linguistics and Philosophy* 12, no. 5 (1989): 535–58.

Segal, David R., and Mady Wechsler Segal. "America's Military Population." *Population Bulletin* 59, no. 4 (2004).

Shane, Leo, III. "Student Vets Say Anti-military Attitudes Persist on Campus." *Stars and Stripes*, January 7, 2013.

Shaw, Martin. *Post-Military Society: Militarism, Demilitarism and War at the End of the Twentieth Century*. Cambridge: Polity Press, 1991.

———. "Twenty-First Century Militarism: A Historical-Sociological Framework." In *Militarism and International Relations: Political Economy, Security and Theory*, edited by A. Stavrianakis and J. Selby. London: Routledge, 2012.

Shay, Jonathan. *Odysseus in America: Combat Trauma and the Trials of Homecoming*. New York: Scribner, 2003.

Shenk, Ed J. "Veterans Returning to College." *Ijournal (Insight into Student Services)*, no. 28 (Spring 2010).

Shepherd, Gordon, and Gary Shepherd. "War and Dissent: The Political Values of the American Professoriate." *Journal of Higher Education* 65, no. 5 (Sept.–Oct. 1994): 585–614.

———. "War Attitudes and Ideological Orientations of Honors Directors in American Higher Education." *Journal of Higher Education* 67, no. 3 (May–June 1996): 298–321.

Sheppler, Susan. A. "Conflicted Childhoods: Fighting Over Child Soldiers in Sierra Leone." PhD diss., University of California, Berkeley, 2005.

Sherman, Nancy. *The Untold War: Inside the Hearts, Minds, and Souls of Our Soldiers*. New York: Norton, 2011.

Sherry, Michael S. *In the Shadow of War: The United States since the 1930s*. New Haven: Yale University Press, 1995.

Silva, Jennifer M. "A New Generation of Women? How Female ROTC Cadets Negotiate the Tension between Masculine Military Culture and Traditional Femininity." *Social Forces* 87, no. 2 (December 2008): 937–60.

Sitikoff, H. "The Postwar Impact of Vietnam." In *The Oxford Companion to American Military History*, edited by John Whiteclay Chambers II. New York: Oxford University Press, 1999.

Skinner, B. F. *Science and Human Behavior*. Oxford: Macmillan, 1953.

Slotkin, Richard. *Gunfighter Nation: The Myth of the Frontier in Twentieth-Century America*. Norman: University of Oklahoma Press, 1992.

Smith, Rupert. *The Utility of Force: The Art of War in the Modern World*. London: Penguin, 2005.

Sparke, Matthew. "Critical Geographies of the Global South." *Global South* 1, no. 1 (2007): 117–26.

———. "Political Geography: Political Geographies of Globalization (1)—Dominance." *Progress in Human Geography* 28, no. 6 (2004): 777–94.

Stavrianakis, Anna and J. Selby. *Militarism and International Relations: Political Economy, Security, Theory.* London: Routledge. 2013.

Stever, James A. "The Veteran and the Neo-progressive Campus." *Academic Questions* 10, no. 1 (1997): 41–52.

Sturken, M. "The Wall, the Screen, and the Image: The Vietnam Veterans Memorial." *Representations*, no. 35 (Summer 1991): 118–42.

Sue, D. W. "Whiteness and Ethnocentric Monoculturalism: Making the 'Invisible' Visible." *American Psychologist* 59, no. 8 (November 2004): 761–69.

Thomas, Marshall W. "Safe Zone for Veterans: Developing the Vet Net Ally Program to Increase Faculty and Staff Awareness and Sensitivity to the Needs of Military Veterans in Higher Education." PhD diss., California State University, Long Beach, 2010. ProQuest (UMI 3425191).

Thompson, Edward P. "Exterminism: The Final Stage of Civilisation." In *Exterminism and Cold War*, edited by New Left Review, 1–34. London: New Left Books, 1982.

Tick, E. *War and the Soul: Healing Our Nation's Veterans from Post-Traumatic Stress Disorder.* Wheaton, IL: Quest, 2005.

Tönnies, Ferdinand. *Community and Society.* Translated by Charles P. Loomis. 1887. Reprint, Mineola, NY: Dover, 2002.

United States Army Recruiting Command. *U.S. Army Recruiter Handbook,* USAREC Manual No. 3–01. Fort Knox, Kentucky: U.S. Army. November, 22, 2011.

United States Army Training and Doctrine Command, (TRADOC) Army Regulations AR 350–1 Section 3–24. "Initial Military Training and Warrior Transition Course." Revised Dec. 18, 2009. http://www.apd.army.mil/pdffiles/r350_1.pdf.

U.S. Department of Defense. *DoD Dictionary of Military and Associated Terms.* Joint Publication 1–02. November 15, 2012.

Varenne, Hervé, and Ray McDermott. *Successful Failure: The School America Builds.* Boulder, CO: Westview, 1999.

Vojdik, Valorie K. "The Invisibility of Gender in War." *Duke Journal of Gender Law and Policy* 9 (Summer 2003): 261–70. http://scholarship.law.duke.edu/djglp/vol9/iss2/6.

Williams, Kayla, and Michael Staub. *Love My Rifle More Than You: Young and Female in the U.S. Army.* New York: Norton, 2006.

Williamson, V. "A New GI Bill: Rewarding Our Troops, Rebuilding Our Military." Report by the Iraq and Afghanistan Veterans of America, January 2008.

Willis, Paul. *Learning to Labour: How Working Class Kids Get Working Class Jobs.* Hampshire: Gower, 1977.

Wilson, Michael C., Susan Berkowitz, and Jerome D. Lehnus. "The Meanings of Propensity: Perspectives from In-Depth Interviews." In *Youth Attitude Tracking Study 1999: Propensity and Advertising Report.* Arlington, VA: Defense Manpower Data Center, 1999.

Wright, W. "Review: Profane Culture." *American Journal of Sociology* 85, no. 5 (March 1980): 1312–16.

Zambo, R., and D. Zambo. "The Impact of Professional Development in Mathematics on Teachers' Individual and Collective Efficacy: The Stigma of Underperforming." *Teacher Education Quarterly* 35, no. 1 (2008): 159–68.

Index

Note: page numbers in *italics* refer to illustrations.

Harvard University, 230n56

Harvey, David, 127

hate crimes, statistics on, 231n69

hazing, 33–34

health clinics, mobile, 219n31

Hedges, Chris, 78

hegemony theory, 128, 226n21

Herbert, Melissa, 103

heroic masochism, 83

heroic narratives and mythos, 128–29, 132, 147, 174, 175. *See also* valorization, military; victim-hero tension

hierarchy, dominance, and subordination: basic training and, 30, 31–33, 35; transition to college and respect for authority, 61–63; uniforms as markers, 36–37

Hispanic enlistment rates, 66, 216n21

Holland, Dorothy, 192

Homeland Security Department, U.S., 4

Homeland Security sector, 107–8, 223n30

hostile-campus trope. *See* antimilitary campus narrative

hot nationalism, 165

housing costs, 214n5

humiliation and shaming, 30, 38, 100

hypervigilance, 69

identification, politics of, 86

identity trimming, 29–30

individualism, 38–39, 58–60

Initial Military Training (IMT). *See* basic training

Inside Higher Education, 156–57

intimacy, 100–101

Iraq Veterans against the War (IVAW), 119, 120, 123, 192

Iraq War. *See* Global War on Terrorism (GWOT) and militarization; war

isolation: in basic training, 30; from public glorification, 175–76. *See also* social distance and isolation from other students

Jaffee, Alexandra, 209n79, 214n6

"kicker," 56, 215n13

Kimball, Jeffrey, 225n12, 226n19

kinesthetic learning style, 52–56

Klein, Joe, 11–12

Kleykamp, Meredith A., 66, 216n21

Kraines, S. H., 77

Kraska, Peter, 9, 78–79

Lande, Brian, 31

Latino/a enlistment rates 66, 216n21

Lave, Jean, 212n14

law enforcement careers, 107–8

lawsuits, concern about, 227n29

learning styles, kinesthetic vs. abstract, 52–56

Lembcke, J., 134, 226n19

LGBT Safe Zone program, 148–54, 152, 157. *See also* sexual orientation

Lifton, Robert Jay, 233n3, 235n10

Loeb, Paul R, 134

Lokken, Jayne, M., 138

Lutz, Amy, 205n23, 208n62

Lutz, Catherine, 14

Maines, George H., 232n86

Mann, Michael, 8

Mariscal, Jorge, 138, 216n21

Marolla, Joseph, 104

Maschek, Anthony, 145–47

masculinity and masculinization: antimilitary campus trope and, 147; basic training and, 27, 39; Belkin on, 211n10; frontier mythology and, 81–82; heroic masochism, 83; interpersonal intimacy and, 100–101; male veterans as support service providers and, 81–85; militarism and, 13; military superiority ideology and, 78; negation or annihilation of the feminine, 99–100; perception as gay, avoiding, 222n17; social bonding and, 99–101

Matott, Drew, 125

Mazzucato, Mariana, 201n3, 201n5

medical benefits system, 213n1

men. *See* masculinity and masculinization

Mendible, Myra, 130

mentorship, peer, 90–91, 109–11, 112–14

Merryfinch, Lesley, 8

militarism: banal, 11; campus manifestations and rituals of, 163, 163–64; masculinization and, 13; paradox of civilian–military distance with, 79; scholarly notions of, 8–11; as social practice, 10. *See also* common sense, militarized; "military-friendly campus" narrative; military superiority ideology

Student Veterans of America (SVA), 229n44, 229n46

success of veterans in higher education, 7–8, 202n11, 217n3

suicide, 12, 206n43, 207n57, 217n13

superiority. *See* military superiority ideology

support programs on campus: "best practices" reinforcing military culture, 85; civilian-military divide and, 78–79; civilian support groups, military identification in, 85–86; diversity of needs and, 192; funding shifts and, 220n34; masculinism in, 81–85; military superiority ideology and, 78–81, 92–93, 96; peer mentorship, 90–91; reentry class for veterans, 91–95; service providers, 95–96; services at the campus sites, 86–89. *See also* "military-friendly campus" narrative; self-help

suppressive fire, 170, 233n2

survey from veterans' class, 141–44, 166–70

Swords and Plowshares, 227n32

symbolism and banal militarism, 11

"thank you for your service" as phrase, 183–88

theoretical comprehension vs. practical competence, 56–57

Things They Carried, The (O'Brien), 178–79

Thompson, Edward P., 8–9

tinnitus, 72, 216n27

Tolaro, Sarah, 223n28

total institutions, 25–26, 28, 101, 213n30

transfer students: California tiered universal-access system, 220n36; campus veteran services and, 88; successful transition and, 91

Transition Assistance Program (TAP), 43–44, 213n1–214n2

transition to college: being early vs. on time, 48, 214nn7–8; class contradictions, 65–67; collective practice vs. individualistic culture, 58–60; divergent logics, traditions, and missions, 46; explicit vs. covert formality and hierarchy, 61–63; habituation to external command vs. self-regulation, 64–65; high school experience vs. college, 49–50; kinesthetic vs. abstract learning styles, 52–56; military-civilian transition, 43–45; "mission accomplishment" mentality, 47–49; outbursts in class, 215n15; practical competence vs.

theoretical comprehension, 56–57; relations of formality and informality, 63–64; silence and erasures, 46, 73–76; social bonds and, 98–99; social distance and isolation, 62, 67, 73–74; traumatic response in the classroom (Cody case study), 67–73; veteran's clubs and, 111; work habits and discipline, 49–52. *See also* "military-friendly campus" narrative; support programs on campus

trauma, sexual. *See* sexual harassment and sexual assault

traumatic response and post-traumatic stress disorder (PTSD): alienation and isolation from, 59; as barrier to academic success, 7–8; Cody case study, 67–73; contradictory thoughts and feelings, coming to terms with, 172; hypervigilance, 69; insomnia, 71; public trope of, 12; symptoms of, 68; trauma, 12, 206n54; Vet Centers and VA mental health treatment programs, 197, 235n10; veteran's clubs support and, 111, 114–15

"Tribute to the Troops" video, 219n30

unfriendly college campuses. *See* antimilitary campus narrative

uniform, civilian cult of, 184

uniforms, military, 36–37, 213n27

upward social mobility narratives, 7, 110

valorization, military: common sense and, 10–11; discursive power of silence and praise, 183; heroic narratives and mythos, 128–29, 132, 147, 174, 175; "hostile" stereotype alongside, 3; as intervention strategy, 128, 147–48, 153–55; militarism and, 10; military-friendly campuses and, 156–58; public glorification as isolating, 175–76; veteran's clubs and, 119–20; Veterans Day celebrations and, 158–61; victim-hero tension, 148, 156. *See also* common sense, militarized

VA medical care, 213n1

VA mental health treatment programs, 197, 235n10

Vet Centers, 197, 235n10

veteran exceptionalism, 6, 203n15

Veteran Ranch Days, 81, 82